We The People's
GUIDE TO
Divorce

*A Do-It-Yourself Guide
To Reaching an Agreement with
Your Spouse and Getting a
Hassle-Free Divorce*

Ira and Linda Distenfield

WILEY

John Wiley & Sons, Inc.

Published by John Wiley & Sons, Inc., Hoboken, New Jersey.
Published simultaneously in Canada.

For general information on our other products and services please contact our Customer Care
Department within the United States at (800) 762-2974, outside the United States at (317) 572-3993
or fax (317) 572-4002.

Wiley also publishes its books in a variety of electronic formats. Some content that appears in print
may not be available in electronic books. For more information about Wiley products, visit our web
site at *www.Wiley.com.*

Library of Congress Cataloging-in-Publication Data:
ISBN-13 978-0-471-73045-3
ISBN-10 0-471-73045-9

Printed in the United States of America

10 9 8 7 6 5 4 3 2 1

CONTENTS

FOREWORD

Access to information is essential to life. Access to the legal system often supports a *successful* life. As Attorney General of California, I am a great admirer of We The People and the progress this enterprise has made to significantly improve access to the legal system for all Americans. We The People has led the way by being dedicated to arming people with the information to understand difficult legal situations and the role that certain legal documents can play in their lives.

My ability to access quality information has allowed me to make good decisions throughout my personal and professional life. That's the whole point of information: It permits you to solve problems and be a smart and confident decision maker. Information educates, trains, prepares, and opens new doors. It imparts knowledge; and it can also console, warn, and advise. I like to think of access to information as a basic necessity alongside food and water, and therefore it should be easy, inexpensive, and inviting. Unfortunately, it's not always that way. When it comes to the legal system, the gap between those privileged to access and use the law to their advantage and those who cannot is real for many Americans. And for the more than 1 million Americans who file for divorce each year, facing the courts can be an overwhelming task.

As Attorney General, I have witnessed the law's positive impact on people's lives, but I've also watched the legal system grow more complex and expensive every day. For too many Americans, the legal system is an 800-pound gorilla that sits on the other side of the table. One can have all the technology that money can buy and yet still feel completely cut off from the legal system, which is a necessary part to getting a divorce . . . or an annulment or legal separation, and even determining paternity.

Every day, millions of Americans need to complete and file basic legal documents with the courts. (You are three times more likely to find yourself in a court of law than in a hospital.) Many of these documents don't require an attorney or a fancy degree to complete. I understand the need for competent independent counsel when necessary, but I also support the right to manage one's own legal affairs. Ira and Linda Distenfield founded We The People with a simple mission: to serve people who need to make uncontested legal transactions but who don't know how to approach the legal system and who have neither the resources nor the desire to hire a lawyer. What I like best is seeing people served regardless of wealth or privilege.

This book helps you navigate the complex and daunting procedures for filing for divorce while providing do-it-yourself assistance for clerical preparation and court filing. Whether you can afford legal representation or not, this book equips you with knowledge and skills required by the courts for understanding and completing your own divorce filing, including how to reach certain agreements with your spouse to minimize the pain and costs related to divorce.

Twenty years ago few people had personal computers; no one had heard of the Internet; no one had e-mail or a way to carry a library of information on a computer chip that you keep in a handheld device the size of your wallet. Fast-moving technology has given us ever more access to more information, has changed our expectations, and has changed our way of thinking. The impact that widespread information has had on Americans is evident: Americans feel better equipped and comfortable making pivotal life decisions, such as entering the housing market, changing careers, or starting a small business. Why? Information empowers people to change their lives for the better and make hard decisions. It is the ultimate equalizer.

My experiences have taught me about responsibility, leadership, and the value of being an independent thinker. I prepare relentlessly and always encourage others to do the same through studying, reading, and learning independently. My advice for anyone contemplating divorce or going through a divorce is to gather as much information as you can before, during, and after the process. Only then can you be assured that you're doing your absolute best to plan for and safeguard your future. You must also keep the best interests of your children in mind.

Success is not measured by status or wealth, but by how we deal with the challenges we face, by how we overcome those challenges through the decisions we make, and by the steps we take to move forward in our lives. This book allows you not only to access and gain information, but to use its information to make sense of a difficult situation and take control of your life. You are entitled to the law's help in restarting your personal life as much as anyone else. Be prepared for whatever course you take—with or without a lawyer by your side—and you'll welcome the rewards that await you in your future.

Bill Lockyer
California Attorney General

ABOUT THE AUTHORS

Ira Distenfield is the Cofounder, Chairman of the Board, and Chief Executive Officer of *We The People Forms And Service Centers USA, Inc.,* a company he started with his wife in 1993. *We The People* is presently the largest independent paralegal company in the nation with offices in more than 150 cities and 31 states. Before his involvement with *We The People,* Mr. Distenfield was a Senior Vice President with Gruntal & Co., Inc., and a First Vice President with Smith Barney. He is a former President of the Port of Los Angeles, which, under his leadership, became the largest revenue producing port in the United States. He is an active member in his community and was named among the Outstanding Young Men of America by the U.S. Chamber of Commerce. He presently serves on the Santa Barbara County Sheriff's Council and is a member of the Santa Barbara County Parole Board.

Linda Distenfield is the Cofounder, President, and Chief Operating Officer of *We The People Forms And Service Centers USA, Inc.* Before her involvement with *We The People,* Mrs. Distenfield served as Santa Barbara County's first full-time Film Commissioner. She also served as the Scheduling Director to the Honorable Tom Bradley, former Mayor of Los Angeles and gubernatorial candidate for the State of California. Mrs. Distenfield is active in several Santa Barbara organizations, and is a founding member of the Santa Barbara Firefighters Alliance.

The Distenfields live in Santa Barbara, California, but travel extensively throughout the country as they expand their company and support the franchise's growth. They enjoy seven children and three grandchildren.

ACKNOWLEDGMENTS

We owe our success to the thousands of customers we have helped through the years regain control of their lives or simply access the information they need to move forward and plan smartly. They continue to inspire, teach, and challenge us. Without them, this book would not have been possible.

Thanks to our supervising attorneys for their guidance and support of We The People, and especially Jason Searns, Esq., and Debbie Hrbek, Esq., who graciously reviewed the manuscript and offered their own expertise. Thanks to Derek Thiele, Esq., for his contributions to the manuscript. Also to Bonnie Solow and Kristin Loberg for their direction and help through the writing and publishing process.

Finally, we'd like to dedicate this book to the millions of people out there who seek sound knowledge and have the courage to take charge of their own legal affairs—with or without the support of attorneys and professionals—and use what they learn to enhance their lives.

Introduction

I f you're not a lawyer and don't have access to one through family, friends, colleagues, or coworkers, facing a legal dilemma is a challenge—and mightily intimidating. Many transactions in life require legal documents, from a blissful marriage to an ugly divorce, from the birth of your children to the death of your parents. In fact, most all transactions in life that we experience at some point involve legal documents. "What's a legal document?" you ask. Legal documents are nothing more than papers that state a contractual relationship (example: marriage) or grant a right (example: trademark). Some are filed in a court, while others are kept between two agreeing people. All legal documents provide information of an official nature, and they are as prevalent as the air you breathe and the water you drink.

Life Is a Series of Transactions

The most significant transitions in life are punctuated by legal documents; you can think of life as a series of transactions, for which you leave a paper trail of official and unofficial records: birth (certificate), education (degrees), work (employment permit or contract), marriage (certificate), major purchases (titles, deeds), minor purchases (receipts), travels (passport), maybe divorce (agreement), retirement (investment portfolios), and death (certificate). Dozens more also come to mind. If you gathered up all the legal documents that you have amassed since birth, your collection would impress you. And you'd wonder how you managed to accumulate so many important pieces of information (about you!) without really thinking about it along the way.

Some transactions are easier to make than others. Some require sticking to specific laws and the approval of courts or government agencies. Examples include agreements, guardianships, child custodies, prenuptials, small claims, incorporations, trademarks, copyrights, and evictions. But even the more common transactions of everyday life often involve legal documents. When you buy a house, secure a loan, finance a car, obtain your baby's birth certificate, purchase insurance, rent an apartment, hire a general contractor for home improvements, renew your driver's license, get a new credit card, or even accept the risk of parking your car in the mall lot, you deal with special legal documents without even realizing it.

Why Some Transactions Are Easy, Others Are Not

The difference between the seemingly mindless transactions and the complicated ones is clear: Someone else does most of the work in executing the simple transactions, and those transactions frequently don't involve the courts or a remote agency. For example, the document you sign when you lease a car is a legal document—a contract—that is between you and the car dealer, which will be upheld in a court of law (if you don't live by the contract's rules, such as making those monthly payments). You don't think so much about this contract as being a legal document, though, because the car dealer does all the work (and sometimes manages to squeeze more money from you in the form of "document prep and dealer fees"). Such a contract does not involve attorneys or filing with the courts, either, so the process is much less intimidating. You fill in the blanks, sign or initial your name on dozens of lines, and eventually drive off in a new car.

But for other, bigger transactions in life, such as filing for divorce or getting a legal annulment, it's hard to find someone to do the work for you at a low cost. The process seems more complicated, more remote, involving more people, more filing, more knowledge in areas you don't know, and sometimes engages the courts or other entities to complete. Moreover, these complex transactions typically necessitate specific sets of documents you don't find in your corner market (or that are not handed to you without asking), and they incur certain fees that are unavoidable. Where do you find these documents? How do you fill them out and pay for these transactions? Who can tell you what to expect?

Help! I Don't Know How to Do This

In an information age, you start by educating yourself about your particular need and research ways of getting what you want for the least amount of money (and you ponder hiring that prominent, expensive attorney if you can't figure out how to do it on your own). Trouble is, because these transactions do entail unavoidable fees, attorneys jump at the chance to maximize profits based on those fees—and based on making you believe that you can't execute those transactions on your own. Truth is, you can. And you don't need a special degree or legal background to do so.

Welcome to We The People. We are a company that specializes in legal document preparation without the high costs related to lawyers. We are the first and only nationwide legal document preparation service in the country. Over the past decade, we have successfully served more than 500,000 consumers, including 20,000 bankruptcies in the last year alone. With 150 offices nationwide and growing every month, we have researched the requirements of most local jurisdictions, down to the color of paper and exact wording preferred.

By the time a publisher approached us to put our valuable information into a book, we were the nation's number one experts in the ins and outs of legal document preparation. And as founders of We The People, we felt exceedingly well equipped to share our knowledge and experience. We've empowered hundreds of thousands of people over the past 10 years and we hope to empower millions more by sharing with you all the information that we've gathered. As you'll soon find out in the next few pages, *knowledge is power.*

This book is part of a series of We The People books that give you the information you need to complete the trickier transactions in life that make most people cringe. They make people cringe because people don't know the how-tos of these complicated transactions, and the guidance they need is not so obvious in the real world. So you are not alone if you are reading this book and searching for help.

Divorce: A Commonly Shared Reality

Filing for divorce doesn't make you a bad person, nor does it ruin your chance of having a happy and productive life. To the contrary, filing for divorce might give you the right beginnings for ultimately achieving all that you've dreamed for your future. Going through a divorce is an emotionally troubling experience for most, but how you go about your divorce can make a big difference in how you recover and move forward in your life. Hopefully, the lessons you learn about yourself through this process help you in your future, whether you choose to remarry or not.

A Glance at the Stats*

Percentage of population that is married: 59% (down from 62% in 1990, 72% in 1970)

Percentage of population that has never married: 24%

Percentage of population that is divorced: 10% (up from 8% in 1990, 6% in 1980)

Percentage of population that is widowed: 7%

Median age at first marriage: Males: 26.9   Females: 25.3

Median age at first divorce: Males: 30.5   Females: 29

Median age at second marriage: Males: 34   Females: 32

Median age at second divorce: Males: 39.3   Females: 37

Median duration of first marriages that end in divorce: Males: 7.8 years   Females: 7.9 years

Median duration of second marriages that end in divorce:
    Males: 7.3 years   Females: 6.8 years

Median number of years people wait to remarry after their first divorce:
    Males: 3.3 years   Females: 3.1 years

Percentage of married people who reach their 5th, 10th, and 15th anniversaries:
    5th: 82%   10th: 65%   15th: 52%

Percentage of married people who reach their 25th, 35th, and 50th anniversaries:
    25th: 33%   35th: 20%   50th: 5%

Number of unmarried couples living together: 5.5 million

Drop in standard of living of females after divorce, as of 2000: 45%

Percentage of households that are family households: 68.8%

Percentage of households with their own children under 18: 33%

Percentage of all households run by single moms: 9.2%

Percentage of all households run by single dads: 1.9%

Number of single parents: Males: 2.04 million   Females: 9.68 million

*These statistics are based on the last census, taken in 2000. In particular, the U.S. Census Bureau released a report in 2002 titled "Numbers, Timing, and Duration of Marriages and Divorces: Fall 1996," by Rose M. Kreider and Jason M. Fields (Current Population Reports, pp 70–80, U.S. Census Bureau, Washington, D.C.). Other good sources of data include the U.S. National Center for Health Statistics (www.cdc.gov/nchs) and Americans for Divorce Reform (www.divorcereform.org). You can find the U.S. Census Bureau at www.census.gov.

If you know you're dealing with a transaction like divorce that must involve the courts, you might feel like you are on one side of the table and the legal community (that is, your local family court) is on the other—untouchable and impossible to penetrate without money and an expensive attorney. It doesn't have to be this way. Filing for divorce is much like any business transaction: You complete the proper forms and follow the court's procedures from beginning to end, at which point the court grants you a divorce and you are free from your spouse.

Facing a divorce is scary on two fronts: It's a transaction that involves court filings (thus fees and following a specific protocol), and it's usually a deeply emotional experience. You're not driving off in a new car or getting ready to marry your soul mate. To the contrary, you're surrendering to a series of personal challenges in your family life that call for divorce. If you have children, your struggles are amplified by their needs and emotions.

If you've scanned the selection of self-help legal software and books at your local book-seller or online and you still feel overwhelmed by the task of initializing your divorce and doing it right, you've come to the right place.

In This Book

This book explains the process of filing for divorce in simple, practical language. As unique as your particular situation might be, we have heard a version of your story from someone who walked into one of our offices, and we know how to treat each and every case success-fully. We know how daunting the task of filing for divorce can be. And we know the relief cus-tomers feel once we guide them through the paperwork and proper filings. We see it every day with smiles, gifts, notes of thanks, and grand sighs of relief from our customers. We hope this book becomes your friend, a lifeline similar to the way our offices become lifelines to the people courageous enough to walk in and ask for help.

Throughout the book, we answer questions you have about the kinds of dilemmas you are facing: What are my other options besides divorce? What do I have to do to avoid a litigated custody battle? Can my spouse and I reach an agreement that a judge will approve?

In addition to the nuts-and-bolts knowledge we impart about divorce procedures throughout this country, we also give you a resource for making other, similar transactions, such as separating (formally or informally), getting temporary orders from a court while you and your spouse work on your divorce agreement, seeking an annulment, or asking the court to determine paternity and order custody, visitation, and support. Although divorce laws vary across the United States and every divorce court will have its own set of rules and guidelines, this book can get you through a divorce in any state. Using the information in this book, you'll know how to navigate your local courthouse and get your paperwork done successfully. We are your guiding light through this dif-ficult, sometimes painful process. If you log on to our web site at www.wethepeopleforms.com and access our divorce page, you'll find useful links to your local family law courts that handle divorces. On many of these links you'll be able to download forms directly from your court.

We encourage you to go to www.wethepeopleforms.com or www.wiley.com/go/ wethepeopleforms to access useful and up-to-date information. You'll find links to your local family courthouse and from there, you'll be able to download forms.

The Story Behind *We The People*

Before we begin, let us explain how We The People came to be. We are Ira and Linda Distenfield, the founders of We The People, who came from different experiences that, conjoined, made for a perfect union in our new venture. It all began in the early 1990s. As senior vice president of a major New York Stock Exchange member firm and president of the Los Angeles Port Authority, Ira frequently hired attorneys to handle his affairs. But something always struck him as odd. Why was he charged the same hourly rate for document preparation—primarily a clerical function—as for high-level legal advice?

Considering a career change, Ira began to research the paralegal field. He uncovered some surprising facts: The legal industry is a $100 billion business. At least half of a typical attorney's practice involves the processing of simple legal documents, often performed by non-attorneys. And if consumers hired independent paralegals rather than attorneys, their legal bills could be cut by as much as 90 percent.

While the marketplace offered an array of alternatives to attorneys, such as do-it-yourself legal software and court-run Internet web sites, Ira saw an unfilled niche. We believed that legal forms were designed to confuse, created for lawyers—"the club"—and not the average consumer. Even though people can pick up legal forms at a drive-through courthouse kiosk or download them from the Web, they still need help filling them out.

We knew we needed marketing, organizational, and legal expertise to succeed in our venture. As far as marketing, Ira capitalized on his 25 years as a stockbroker and experience traveling around the world encouraging countries to export their goods via Los Angeles Harbor, as president of the L.A. Port Authority. Linda took advantage of her administrative skills honed during her tenure as scheduling director for former Los Angeles mayor Tom Bradley. Together we attended paralegal school for a year to learn how to process legal documents, and we hired an attorney to supervise our work.

In 1994, we opened our first We The People office in Santa Barbara, California. We knew this kind of service made sense in our lives, but we wondered if it would make sense for others. Was there a market for this type of service? Within three months, we got our answer.

Gifts started appearing at our door. "You got me through this bankruptcy for $199, and my lawyer wanted $3,000. Here, we bought a little box of candy for you," read a typical note. In Ira's 25 years of business experience, he had never witnessed such a personal gesture.

Our tiny one-room office in an executive suite filled a huge consumer need. For prices as much as 90 percent less than lawyer fees, customers who didn't require the advice of an attorney got help with more than 80 kinds of legal documents, such as divorce, bankruptcy, incorporation, living trusts, and wills. Customers provided information in simple workbooks. That information was then typed into the appropriate forms.

The Future of *We The People*

Ten years later, customer enthusiasm has fueled the launch of 173 offices in 32 states. In 2003, our company handled approximately 20,000 bankruptcies, 13,000 wills, and 38,000 divorces—more than any single law firm in the United States. We The People's multi-million-dollar revenues continue to rise as more stores open and meet the needs of more people. Under the guidance of former New York City mayor Rudolph Giuliani's consulting firm, Giuliani

Partners, we have opened 28 stores throughout the five boroughs of the City of New York this year and expand into additional markets nationwide. As testament to our careful research of the rules of each local jurisdiction, We The People has helped more than half a million people to successfully complete their legal matters. What makes us exceptional: We The People staffers not only have become experts in the preparation of documents, but we know what many local courts require. Our company's expanding markets continue to afford us greater power in getting more information for fulfilling our customers' needs. An attorney can have only so much information. A robust company operating in more than half of the United States, however, can supply a wealth of information, from the broadest of help to the most localized.

No Lawyers Means You Save Money

More and more people are seeking alternatives to the high cost of attorneys. According to an American Bar Association study in 1996, each year half of all low- and moderate-income households need legal help but must forgo it—in part because they can't afford a lawyer. As attorney fees rise to an average of $200 per hour, the number of people forced to navigate the system on their own has also climbed. In fact, fees have risen to such a point that even some lawyers privately say that, should they need it, they might be priced out of the legal market!

Whether it's buying in bulk at Costco or trolling the Internet for the best deal on a printer, consumers are driven now more than ever to get the most for their money. Legal services are not immune.

According to the U.S. Bureau of Labor Statistics, the legal forms business is the largest growth industry in the nation, second only to home health care.

The simple truth is that lawyers are not necessary for many legal services. The head of one nonprofit that provides legal help for low-income folks has estimated that only about 5 percent of its typical clients actually require a full-range, high-cost lawyer. As a result, a growing number of Americans are choosing to represent themselves in legal matters. In California, for instance, more than 50 percent of bankruptcies and 60 percent of divorces are now filed without an attorney. Our entry into the self-help legal industry has made a major impact on people's ability to access the legal system, and as we continue to open more stores nationwide, those statistics might change.

You have three choices for getting legal documents completed:

1. Type them yourself.
2. Go to a reputable legal document assistant (such as We The People).
3. Go to a lawyer.

This book is useful for any of these options. Even if you decide to hire a lawyer to help you through your divorce (assuming you find a good one), you still need to educate yourself about the process and be as knowledgeable and prepared as possible. The more you know, the better your outcome, and the more successful you will be. Good information and competent advice are the two key ingredients for completing all legal documents.

While some do-it-yourself legal resources provide general information, few provide guidance that can assist you in whichever court you must file. By reading this book, you set yourself up for completing your entire divorce transaction, from reaching agreements with your

In its March 1991 issue, the American Bar Association *Journal* reported a study in which it was estimated that consumers can save more than $1.3 billion annually by representing themselves in just four routine legal transactions: uncontested divorces, wills, bankruptcies, and incorporations. When you represent yourself in a legal matter, it's referred to as doing it *pro se* (for yourself).

spouse to using the court's guidelines for figuring out spousal support, child support, and visitation arrangements. You'll know how to approach your local court with confidence and a strong foundation. Should you need further assistance, one of our offices can also assist you in understanding the specific requirements of your local family court (see appendix B for a listing of We The People stores by state), and we can help you type your paperwork if you choose to use our services.

None of this book's contents can substitute for the person-to-person contact you can get when you walk into one of our offices, but this book is an excellent companion for those who don't have access to one of our locations or who prefer to complete the process as independently as possible. Backed by We The People's expertise, this book reflects years of experience and stands at the top of the self-help legal document market. No organization can claim that it has assisted 500,000 people over the past decade in filling out and filing basic legal documents.

Your Future

When you're considering a divorce, legal separation, or annulment, or filing a paternity case, the first questions that rush through your mind are: How long does a divorce take and what kind of paperwork do I have to file if I don't hire an attorney? What are the steps I have to take? How much is it going to cost? How long will it take? What is expected of me?

Terminating a relationship you once thought was forever requires following certain procedures. You had to file paperwork when you got married, and the same holds true for getting a divorce. When you separate yourself from a person, whether through formal separation, a divorce, or an annulment, you must treat the breakup as a business deal: You have certain financial needs that must be reconciled at the breakup, and so does your partner. Perhaps you don't know whether your marital troubles will result in divorce, for which this book can help you separate on certain terms that allow each of you the breathing room for making that ultimate decision. Now that paternity cases outnumber divorce cases in many courts, we've dedicated a section (in chapter 2) to how to pursue paternity cases and get you what you deserve from the other parent of your child or children. We also provide tips for dealing with the financial fallout that accompanies divorce, such as parting with assets, modifying your lifestyle, and preparing to run a household without the contribution of your spouse.

Divorce is not a transaction to take lightly. It has far-reaching effects on your life that are both financial and emotional. By now, you've already begun a financial and emotional journey that likely makes you uncomfortable and uneasy. Just considering separation and/or divorce is a serious matter. But it doesn't have to be so terrifying as to paralyze you and prevent you from making good choices. That's what this book is about.

Finally, having a greater sense of control over your situation by doing most of the work yourself is an empowering experience. With this book, and the knowledge you gain from it, you will succeed in a difficult transaction and move forward in your life.

So let's begin.

"I Want a Divorce!"

S eldom do people want to utter these words, but they've become frequently spoken and heard in today's world where 50 percent of marriages fail. There is no use philosophizing over the whys of this reality but to say that divorce is real for many Americans regardless of race, wealth, social circle, and religion. It's unfortunate that marriage is an easier contract to make than to break, but the best way to a clean and uncomplicated divorce entails reaching certain agreements with your spouse and setting a plan for your family's legal breakup. And that can also entail leaving the lawyers out and working hard at doing all the negotiating yourself.

Divorce is a state-governed transaction. Every state has different laws regarding how one can get a divorce and what options are available for pursuing divorce. You are bound by your state's divorce laws and must abide by them for your divorce to be final. By having the right information and the right attitude, you can settle your own divorce without many hassles—and without leaving you bankrupt.

The decision about whether to file for divorce can be a difficult one. Knowing what is involved and how to prepare for your divorce are the subjects of chapters 2 and 3. We start, however, by introducing you to the basic laws that apply to divorce settlements throughout the country. This chapter also lays the necessary groundwork for understanding divorce and minimizing costly mistakes throughout the process. Always remember that the more knowledge you can obtain, the better positioned your family will be to emerge from your divorce quickly and less painfully.

Knowledge Is Power

We will repeat this truth throughout this book: *Knowledge is power!* Repeat this statement out loud to yourself and feel the confidence it gives you. Facing a divorce might make you feel crippled, but do your best to keep things in perspective. Use the information in this book to empower yourself and make good decisions for your future. Keep this statement in the back of your mind as you move through these chapters. It will fuel you with the energy you need to conquer your fears related to ending your marriage, do what you need to get done, and move on.

Fundamentals of Family Law

Family law is almost as old as humans. As soon as people started roaming the earth and inter-mingling, rules had to emerge to help manage the dynamics of family life. Before formal governments existed, when people lived together in tribes, cultures developed their own customs or adopted rules from their deities. In Western culture, particularly after the Norman Conquest in 1066, the church initially took the responsibility of regulating marriage and divorce. But as the entities of church and state separated over time, civil courts and legislatures began enforcing more control over family law. And eventually, the regulation of family law grew more and more complicated. A woman, for example, cannot divorce her husband today by simply leaving her husband's moccasins outside on the doorstep, as a Pueblo woman could once do.

As with many legal matters, the advancement of our culture has led to more complex rules and more hurdles to clear. Periodic legislative reforms have tried to simplify the rules, but for the most part, we are stuck with a complicated system that we must navigate carefully. Part of the reason divorce is so much harder to execute than marriage is that society would rather support a marriage—the union of two people for the sake of a family—than sanction a divorce. No matter how far we've come in our modernized world that attempts to separate church from state, or moral ethics and values from the law, certain meshes still exist.

Family law is also known as *matrimonial law* or the *law of domestic relations. Family law* is a general term that does not just involve separation and divorce but also includes the requirements of marriage and adopting a child. Any relationship shared between a couple, between two parents, or between a parent and child falls under family law. Family law can also extend to refer to the various actions regarding violence between family, friends, or acquaintances.

The actions that come under the body of family law include the following:

- Dissolution of marriage (divorce)
- Legal separation
- Nullity of marriage
- Summary dissolution of marriage (a simpler form of divorce for those who qualify)
- Establishing parentage (also called *paternity*)
- Petition for custody and support of minor children
- Custody and visitation
- Child support
- Spousal support
- Domestic violence restraining orders
- Civil harassment

Because more couples have children outside of wedlock today than a hundred years ago, paternity plays an important role in the family courts today. The issues that revolve around paternity are nearly identical to the issues that revolve around divorce. We'll explore the topic of paternity in chapter 2.

Child Custody Laws

The court's view of children has changed vastly over the past two centuries, flipping between a system that once favored fathers having custody to mothers having custody. Now, the right

Family law covers inherently emotional issues. It deals with marriage, separation, divorce, adoption, and spousal obligations, as well as parental obligations. As society evolves and changes its attitude or values, family law typically reflects those changes. For example, now that more women work outside the home, the courts must take that into consideration when deciding on alimony or who will serve as the primary caretaker of children. A woman is more likely to pay alimony to her husband now than she was 30 years ago. Women are less likely, however, to get sole custody of their children, since the courts view both parents as having an equal right to share custody.

to have custody of children is generally shared unless the specific circumstances of a couple dictate some other arrangement. Children are no longer considered property as they were throughout much of history. In fact, some states prefer to use the phrase *parental responsibility* over *custody*. We'll explore the different types of custody arrangements in chapter 4. There is a difference, for example, between legal and physical custody. Shared *legal* custody—whereby both parents share decision-making responsibilities for the children—is common nowadays, but shared *physical* custody—whereby both parents split their time evenly with the children—is often still impracticable except in the most amicable of situations.

Before the Industrial Revolution, children were essential participants in the family unit as workers on the family farm. When a couple divorced, the father typically got the children so they could continue working on the farm. But once men moved into factory jobs and mothers began to take more responsibility for the daily caring of their children, the legal system began to favor mothers as the primary caretaker. And by the mid-1800s, mothers were typically granted full custody of their children in a divorce. Family law judges used a standard that was known as the *tender years doctrine.* Under this standard, a child of tender years—under the age of eight—was automatically awarded to its mother. The only way to prevent this was to prove that the mother was unfit to raise the child. The *best interests of the child* standard has eliminated the tender years doctrine. Mothers are no longer automatically awarded custody of young children, but some states still make use of the tender years doctrine, without calling it such.

Not until the 1960s, with the civil rights movement and the migration of women from the home to the workplace, did family law experience another shift. States began to view each parent as equally fit for raising the children. States also began to favor shared or joint custody rights. Men have also become more aggressive in asserting their legal rights to custody. There are three times more men who have full custody of their children today than there were 30 years ago. From 1970 to 2003, the proportion of single-mother family groups grew to 26 percent from 12 percent and that of single-father family groups grew to 6 percent from 1 percent.

Courts now assume that mothers and fathers share an equal responsibility for meeting their children's needs, both financially and emotionally. In almost all states, both parents are presumed to have an equal right to custody, as well as an equal responsibility to support their children. Neither parent automatically has a superior legal right to custody. Moreover, one parent may not have to show the other to be unfit in order to obtain custody. If a judge must decide how custody arrangements will work, the court will consider the children's best interests, including the children's relationship with each other and with their parents; the

In many states, such as Colorado, the term *custody* has been replaced with *parental responsibility.*

children's adjustment to home, school, and community; the mental and physical health of all children and their parents; and, in certain circumstances, the wishes of the child or children.

Most Divorces Avoid the Courtroom Battle

When you seek a divorce, you hope to avoid the proverbial divorce court that gets dramatized on television. You will be bound by the family laws of your state and have to comply with the legal system, but you do not necessarily end up in an actual courtroom before a judge, with you on one side and your spouse on the other. (And rarely do divorce cases get decided by a jury.) A divorcing couple who can work out their divorce amicably can usually avoid the costly trip to court. In fact, only about 5 percent of divorces end up in court; 95 percent of divorces happen outside the courtroom. Even in complicated or messy divorces you can find a way to avoid the litigated divorce that will do nothing but cost you more money, anguish, time, and frustration. Couples with children should avoid litigated divorces. This book will show you how to resolve all of your divorce issues, including the most troubling or combative. If you do have to appear in court, it will be brief, and it will not entail arguing over major issues so that a judge can decide what will happen in your future.

What Is Marriage Anyway?

Marriage is more than a romantic gesture. It's more than a union of two people under one roof who share assets, offspring, and a last name. Marriage is a public, legal commitment and not merely a private exchange of sentimental wishes. Marriage is also a legal contract that encompasses a legal, financial, and social relationship. It requires a license from your state, which gets filed in a government office, usually the county clerk's office. Marriage does not entail as many qualifications as divorce. Any adult (defined by each state) can obtain a marriage license with the proper signatures and proof of blood work (if even required by that state), participate in a ceremony with any witness, and be considered married. Reversing this process, however, is not so easy. And the longer you are married, the harder it gets to break that contract. A married person assumes certain responsibilities that often get glossed over during an elaborate service and forgotten during troubled times or when contemplating divorce. Some of those obligations include the following:

- Supporting your spouse financially—through good times and bad
- Giving some—if not all—of your assets to your spouse at your death
- Allowing your spouse a right to certain retirement, pension, Social Security, or other benefits
- Caring for your spouse and making decisions for him or her if he or she cannot, such as when your spouse is on life support
- Assuming responsibility for shared debt
- Sharing all acquired assets and income acquired during the marriage, no matter who is responsible for bringing that income in or acquiring that asset

All the property (assets) that you and your spouse acquire during your marriage is presumed to be *marital property,* regardless of whose name is on the asset. (A common misperception is that you can keep things from your spouse by keeping his or her name off it. This is not true.)

Most states define marriage as a civil contract between a man and a woman to become husband and wife. When a man and a woman marry, their relationship acquires a legal status. According to the United States Supreme Court in an 1888 case, "The relation once formed, the law steps in and holds the parties to various obligations and liabilities." It is because of these obligations and liabilities that divorce can be difficult. The rights and obligations of married persons are not the same as those of single persons. Married people share rights that single people do not have with anyone else. For example, married people may have rights to their partner's property and future income, they may be responsible for each other's debts, and they are subject to different tax rates than single persons. State and federal laws determine the scope of the married person's new rights and duties.

If a marriage produces children, you assume even greater obligations. Beyond the custody, visitation, and support you must figure out in your divorce, you have obligations as a parent that have nothing to do with your divorce. These include providing for your children with food, clothing, shelter, and necessary medical care. Your children must receive a minimal education, typically through high school, in either a private, a public, or a home-school setting. You can choose where you want to live and how you want to raise your children, but the courts will intervene if the choices you make for your children result in jeopardizing their lives or threatening their livelihood. The laws exist to protect both you as a parent with rights and your children with their own set of rights—regardless of a divorce. If one parent is not meeting these legal obligations, the court will see to it that the other spouse gets custody of the children. Parental obligations remain until children reach legal adulthood, which can be 18 in some states and 21 in others.

On a moral note, your job as a parent is to see your children mature into thoughtful, productive adults. Because so many divorces occur during children's maturing years, it's especially important that you tune in to your children's needs and concerns more than anyone else's, including your own. We will touch upon issues related to children throughout this book, and talk about custody and visitation specifically in chapter 4. The important thing to keep in mind is that getting a divorce when you have children is not about making a good decision for yourself—it's about making good decisions for you *and* your children. Divorcing parents who neglect the needs of their children spend a lifetime trying to resolve perpetual problems.

In most people's eyes, marriage is a private bond between two people, but it is also an important social, legal, and as some would say, financial institution. Because of the assumed obligations of marriage, ending a marriage requires terminating these obligations in a manner that is fair for both people involved.

Three states now offer so-called covenant marriages, which are optional forms of marriage that make divorce more difficult to obtain. They are designed to combat the divorce rate. In general, covenant marriage laws lay ground rules that limit reasons for divorce to spousal or child abuse, imprisonment for a felony, and infidelity. And before most divorces can be filed, couples are usually required to seek counseling during a mandatory waiting period that can, in some cases, last up to two years. The states that allow covenant marriages include Arkansas, Arizona, and Louisiana. Twenty-five other states have proposed such laws, and the idea of covenant marriages is gaining popularity across the country.

WE THE PEOPLE'S GUIDE TO DIVORCE

14

Despite the divorce reforms of the 1970s that gave us no-fault options, some states have attempted to reverse the process of making divorces easy by taking away the no-fault option and permitting fault divorces only. This makes divorce more difficult, costly, and complicated. The result? Fewer divorces. States have also proposed longer waiting periods for obtaining a divorce in an attempt to prevent divorces. Because the concepts of marriage and divorce have become a much-debated issue at the state (and federal) level in recent years, no one can be certain what will happen in the future. Strategies to save marriages and prevent divorces may not seem like concerns of the government, but until they become private matters managed outside of the law, people are bound by the laws and, unfortunately, the morals and values that are inherently part of those laws. At some point, it may become just as hard to get married as it is to get divorced. But only time and history can make that determination.

Later in this book, we'll give you some information about situations that bring the legality of your marriage into question, such as common-law marriage rules or a case in which one spouse was a noncitizen before the marriage or a couple got married in another country. For now, this book assumes that you are legally married and have chosen to legally divorce. Refer to chapter 7 for a discussion of atypical scenarios. That chapter will also explain how prenuptials and postnuptials work.

What Is Divorce?

Every 13 seconds, a divorce is finalized in the United States. By definition, divorce is a legislatively created and judicially administered process that legally terminates a marriage. Divorce is also known as *dissolution of marriage*. Traditionally, divorce was fault based, meaning one of the spouses had to be at fault for the divorce. One spouse was labeled as innocent or injured and was able to obtain a divorce from the at fault spouse. This system didn't work because so many marriages that fail have nothing to do with one spouse doing something wrong. Not all divorces are the result of adultery, abuse, desertion, or some other concrete reason. Back when the fault system was in place, one spouse had to allege wrongdoing by the other—a very adversarial system that obviously was not flexible enough to include more frequent and realistic reasons for divorce, such as irreconcilable differences, incompatibility, or just an undefined breakdown of the marriage. In the 1970s, the no-fault system emerged. Today, we still have a little more than a dozen states that allow fault divorce, while in the others you have a choice between the two. No-fault divorces typically cost less and cause much less anguish for both parties involved.

In the court's eyes, divorce is the breakup of a partnership, particularly a business partnership. Just like a business's breakup or dissolution, there are assets to be divided, financial details to work out, and items or people to be shared, such as children. No matter how at odds you may be with your spouse, divorce is a deeply emotional and personally challenging transition to make in life. The courts treat divorces as case numbers, and so long as you maintain a positive outlook, a fair perspective, and a good support system (that does not include the courts or a lawyer if you have one), you'll be okay.

The decision to file for a divorce is just the first of many decisions to be made during the process. Common initial questions include these:

- Do I need an attorney? What if things get combative?
- Do I need to be separated before I get divorced?

- How long will it take?
- Should I worry about the fate of my children?

These are all good, relevant questions. By the end of this chapter, you'll have their answers.

Do I Need an Attorney?

For uncontested divorces, you typically do not need an attorney. If you and your spouse can come to an agreement about your divorce and the decisions you need to make about your assets, debts, children (if any), and continued family support (spousal and child's), you may not need the involvement of lawyers. You will, however, need to complete legal documents that set out the terms of your divorce and become accepted by the courts. Some courts offer help in filling out the proper forms and knowing how to complete the documents that your particular court wants. Most are straightforward and self-explanatory, but we'll give you tips for getting through the documents carefully. We'll also provide you with some sample documents from various states so you can see what they look like. It's not rocket science—but you do need to get your paperwork done right and know exactly what you should ask for in your divorce. It can be hard to make major changes or fix something in your final divorce decree if you forgot to ask about an entitlement you may have had before the judgment was rendered. Later chapters in this book will explore all that you may or may not be entitled to have at your divorce, which will help you understand your local family court's procedures and your rights.

If you think you need help filling out and completing your paperwork, you can always visit a We The People store (see appendix B for a list of stores across the country). We can also help you navigate the particulars of your local family court. Remember that the court's job is to review your documents and suggest the proper adjustments for finalizing your divorce. The courts—not attorneys—are responsible for certifying your divorce.

What Do You Mean by "Uncontested"?

Lots of people think that *uncontested* means simply that both parties want a divorce. That's not what the word *uncontested* means. In fact, a divorce is uncontested only if both parties agree to the divorce *and* all the issues involved in a divorce, such as who gets custody of any children, whether and how any spousal support will be paid, who buys whom out of the house, what will happen to the marital debts and assets, and so on. If you agree to get divorced but you and your spouse are still fighting over the kids or the house, it's not an uncontested divorce—it's a contested divorce. Contested divorces don't always reach the courtroom in a drawn-out legal battle. You can take your contested issues through mediation and arrive at an agreement that turns your contested divorce into an uncontested one. Generally, if you and your spouse have an uncontested divorce, you can proceed without an attorney. But you do need to educate yourself about your rights and understand what you may be entitled to in a divorce. That's why you need this book, as it will give you the information you should know so you can proceed confidently. And if you do decide to hire an attorney to help, you'll have a head start and know how to maximize the use of your attorney.

Between your efforts and any outside help you get, such as that of a mediator (to work out tough issues) and a legal document preparer, you can do this yourself and avoid the high cost of attorneys, who tend to complicate matters.

Resolving the issues of your children, your money, and your assets may require the help of a neutral third party, such as a mediator, but that does not always entail attorneys and/or a judge. It may require a little more time and effort to work out difficult issues, but once you do, what remains is simply asking the court to grant you a divorce. This all happens with paperwork, so you may never need to actually appear in court. Many courts now make it relatively easy for people to handle the whole process without a lawyer. The more you can cooperate with your spouse, the quicker you can reach an agreement and get your divorce finalized.

Despite what most people think, lawyers do not always make processes easier or quicker. Lawyers—particularly divorce lawyers—may make your situation worse. Remember: Lawyers are trained to argue, and they make a living by fighting for what *they* think is best. In other words, they have built-in financial incentives to make cases difficult, long, time consuming, and combative. It's nearly impossible to have one lawyer play a neutral role for both spouses' interests. Even amicable divorces with attorneys involve each spouse having his or her own attorney. But because each attorney fights for one spouse's best interests, clashes can emerge that never would have had the couple avoided attorneys entirely.

Once lawyers are in the equation, there's no telling where your divorce case will go. You may find it harder to control your divorce and you may also find that the extra cost, frustration, and mounting arguments are not worth it.

Some circumstances command that you seek an attorney. Examples of such circumstances are the following:

- You have very large assets to divide.
- You have a very large estate (a total of what you own and owe).
- Your spouse has an attorney (you had planned on representing yourself, but you find that your spouse has hired a savvy attorney who is ready to fight for everything you stand to lose, such as assets, custody of your children, and necessary alimony).
- There is a real problem with abuse (spousal, child, sexual, or substance). A lawyer can help you arrange for your protection, as well as protection for your children, if any.
- Your spouse is extremely uncooperative or is behaving dishonestly or vindictively.
- You believe your spouse may be hiding substantial assets that you may be entitled to.

When you take the uncontested route to divorce, you forgo *discovery,* or the process whereby the court requires both parties to disclose all of their assets to one another. You

Family law attorneys come with a price. Hourly rates vary. An experienced family attorney can charge $150 an hour or more than $300 an hour. Costs can skyrocket out of control—along with your emotions—and before you know it, your divorce costs you more than you can afford and you owe tens of thousands of dollars once it's over. The average cost of a divorce today is $15,000 in legal fees alone *for each spouse* (or $30,000 total). Divorce is second only to the death of a spouse on the psychic pain meter, according to the experts who rate such things, and has been known to trigger panic attacks and major depressive episodes.

cannot ask for a share in something that you didn't know existed. (However, we'll see that uncontested divorces routinely involve so-called disclosure statements, which are documents exchanged between both parties that list all assets and debts.)

You may have the best intentions of representing yourself in your divorce, but should your spouse be so unwilling to cooperate with you that he or she hires a lawyer, you need to seek an attorney who can fight for your best interests. This is especially true if you have children or are facing complicated financial issues. It is your legal right to ask the judge for an adjournment (a postponement) so you, too, can look for an attorney. If you cannot afford a lawyer, call your local legal aid office. If you qualify financially, a lawyer will, at a minimum, discuss the legal aspects of your case with you and may continue to answer questions on an ongoing basis during your proceedings. If the legal aid attorney's caseload permits, he or she may take your case, usually at little or no cost. You can also inquire about a pro bono program, which is a program run by your local county bar association that has a list of private attorneys who are willing to take on cases recommended by legal aid. These services are also available at little or no cost. If you don't qualify for legal services or pro bono help, ask friends and family members for referrals to trustworthy and reliable attorneys.

Always keep your children in mind, because attorneys can indirectly make the impact of the divorce harder on them. Your children may need their own attorney to represent their interests, and as the arguments among vying attorneys commence, the ones who suffer most are the children. Children are profoundly affected by divorce, both in self-esteem and in their sense of safety and comfort. Adding bitterness and strangers (that is, attorneys) to an already bad situation has no benefits. It does lasting damage. You must also think about your post-divorce life and how your children will continue to be part of both your and your spouse's lives forever—no matter how much you dislike your spouse. The more chaotic and unpleasant you make your divorce, the harder it will be for your family to move beyond the divorce and feel confident about the future. After all, wouldn't *you* rather negotiate over such vital matters as how your children will be raised, what happens to the family home, and how your property will be divided than let attorneys do the haggling for you? You know your interests better than anybody, and chances are, you know your spouse's interests, too.

> Lawyers do not make divorce any easier or quicker. To the contrary, attorneys can create more problems than they help resolve. The more people you have participating in your divorce, the longer it will take, and the more money you will spend. The risk of a messy, angry, and emotional divorce is greater once lawyers enter the scene.

> Divorcing couples sometimes lose sight of how the divorce will affect the entire family for a long time. The emotions generated by divorce can boil out of control during the acute phase of the divorce, which ultimately creates many scars that remain—and remain more so with children. So even though the divorce may be over for the parent and that parent may move on in life, the impact of the divorce on the children may not dissipate so quickly. This is why it's in your best interests to work hard at having a cooperative and lawyer-free divorce. We know that divorce is an emotional journey that may bring you more bad days than good days, but you'll get through it eventually and regain your sense of well-being. If you stay calm and cooperative throughout your divorce, you'll remain in control of it and not become subject to court rulings against your wishes.

What You Need to Figure Out

Unlike when you got married, you have to figure out several things before you can divorce. In our stores, we tell customers they have three items—A, D, K—to work out: assets, debts, and kids. Marriage does not require a commitment to have children, a decision about future marital assets, or a formula for dealing with future marital debt. Divorce, however, requires that you set plans for and make decisions about the following:

- How you will divide marital property (the property you acquired while you were married) as well as debt (what you jointly owe). As with marital assets, marital debt generally includes all debt acquired during the marriage, regardless of whose name is on the debt.

- Whether or not one spouse will pay alimony (or *maintenance*) to the other, and if so, how much and for how long.

- How your children, if any, will be shared, including financial and caring responsibilities.

These may seem like easy decisions to make, but once the conversation gets going, you may find yourself at odds with your spouse, and before long you cannot come to any agreement. Having a difficult time resolving these issues, however, does not mean you will land in court and have an all-out battle with lawyers and a judge. With a little more time, patience, and perhaps some mediation (which we'll discuss), you can figure it out for the best of all parties involved—including the children.

Types of Divorce

There is only one way down the aisle, but there many avenues to divorce. The goal of this book is to guide couples through divorces that minimize the role of the courts and lawyers. Even a messy divorce can avoid the drama of a court scene. Consider it the option of last resort. The following are your choices when it comes to divorce:

- *In agreement (uncontested):* If you and your spouse can come to terms with the important decisions and draw up an agreement, you can file a no-fault divorce and proceed quickly. You can even hire a legal document preparer to help you complete your paperwork professionally. This is the best way to get a divorce. It's the *healthiest* way to get a divorce, saving you pain and anguish.

- *Not in agreement (contested):* If you and your spouse are having difficulties reaching an agreement on the major issues, there are other options to consider before going in front of a judge. Mediation is the best and most popular option, which we'll discuss in chapter 3. Even though you may have disagreements at the start of your divorce, this does not mean you cannot ultimately have an uncontested divorce. Once you work through your differences, you can arrive at an agreement and proceed as if it were uncontested.

- *Go to court before a judge:* If the court must step in and make decisions for you and your spouse because you cannot reach an agreement, you will lose control. Courts do not like to make decisions for warring couples, especially when it comes to parents fighting over their children. A court will strongly encourage parents to make decisions for their kids and even go as far as sending the parents to more mediation programs before ruling. If you cannot reach an agreement through cooperation, mediation, and even the use of attorneys, you will have to go to court and have a family law judge make decisions for you and your family. Television and movies may make divorce court look straightforward and painless, but it's not. It can be the most heart-wrenching, expensive, and time-consuming process to endure. Children are particularly vulnerable.

In most cases, complicated and disputed divorces do not have to reach the courts. But there are situations that are characterized by a combination of the aforementioned scenarios. You and your spouse may experience a combination of agreeing on most issues, contesting some, and needing a judge to have the final say in a few important matters.

Cooperative Divorce Law with Attorneys (or Collaborative Divorce)

Another type of divorce that is gaining popularity is called the *collaborative divorce*. This type of divorce seems too good to be true because it counters most attorneys' natural instincts. In a collaborative divorce, the attorneys for both spouses agree to assist the couple in resolving conflicts or legal issues (as opposed to arguing and disagreeing with one another). Whereas the classic divorce lawyers reflect an adversarial process, collaborative divorce lawyers reflect a supportive process that is mutually beneficial.

The collaborative process started in the Twin Cities area of Minnesota in 1990 with a group of four family law attorneys. The goal is to arrive at a divorce using cooperative strategies rather than adversarial techniques and court proceedings. Since its inception, this type of divorce has spread throughout the United States and Canada. It requires, however, that both attorneys be trained in collaborative law, which is a relatively new field. Because collaborative law still involves attorneys representing the interests of their respective clients, it's not the same as mediation, which entails a neutral third party who does not take sides.

Under the collaborative law process, both spouses attend informal discussions and conferences with their attorneys. Hostility is kept out of the room and instead an atmosphere of honesty, cooperation, integrity, and professionalism is (supposed to be) present. Both spouses must provide all important and relevant documents, as well as any information related to the issues in question. If experts are needed, both parties agree to the experts. Couples work together and reach a shared resolution that keeps the future well-being of the family the number one priority.

Using a team approach has its advantages. Collaborative divorce law is less time consuming and adversarial, and more cost-effective than the alternate divorce lawyer route. This process limits the fear of going to court and encourages a win-win situation for both spouses. The attorneys involved also share the payment, so there is no disparity, especially if one spouse has fewer funds than the other.

If the collaborative process fails and a settlement cannot be reached, the collaborative lawyers withdraw from the case and both parties must retain trial attorneys to pursue the matter in court. This also means that the divorce process must start all over again.

Is Collaborative Law Right for Us? Not every case can employ the collaborative divorce process. First, you must find two attorneys who specialize in this kind of law and are willing to take on your case. If you live in California, Minnesota, Ohio, Oregon, or Texas, you may find it easier to locate such an attorney. But if you live elsewhere, your options may be limited. Second, if the process reaches an impasse, you and your spouse will be back at square one and you risk your divorce landing in court, where you may experience nasty litigation.

For the majority of divorcing couples, collaborative law is not a good option if you can work your issues out without any lawyers and extra expenses (because collaborative law is not free). Both collaborative law and choosing to go about settling your divorce on your own require a strong commitment on both sides to be honest and open in exchanging information. If you live where collaborative law is available, you may want to reserve this as an option for if and when you cannot come to an agreement with your spouse, you've tried mediation, and you think it's best that each of you hires an attorney. Any option that further prevents you from divorce litigation in court is a good idea.

Mediation

Not all couples can reach an agreement without outside help. Mediation is a process by which you work with a neutral third party to settle major issues and prepare your divorce agreement. This process is voluntary and nonbinding. Depending on how you look at mediation, it can make your divorce process quicker or longer. The more you need to resort to mediation, the longer it will take to reach an agreement; however, mediation is designed to help couples avoid pursuing legal battles with expensive attorneys and lengthy court proceedings. Mediation is an excellent way to resolve your contested issues.

The difference between the cost of an attorney-represented divorce and a mediated divorce can be staggering. An ordinary divorce agreement that might drag on for months and cost each spouse at least $15,000 (in legal costs alone) can sometimes be worked out with a mediator in three sessions, often for as little as $750. Unlike attorneys, however, mediators do not make the decisions for you. Moreover, just as every situation is different, every mediator has a different approach to mediation. It is the mediator's responsibility to structure the sessions so that you can successfully negotiate a divorce agreement with your spouse. A good mediator will encourage you to put the past behind you and focus on the facts at the present moment.

Mediation will be discussed in chapter 3.

A Glance at the Process

The exact process you'll experience in your divorce will depend on two things: (1) what kind of divorce you have (uncontested, contested, or litigated in court) and (2) how your state deals with divorce laws. For most couples who aim to avoid a litigated divorce and reach an agreement together in a no-fault and uncontested case, the following sequence of events is typical:

→ One or both of you *decide to separate and/or divorce.*

→ *Check with residency and separation laws* in your state and local jurisdiction.

→ *Go to your local court* that handles divorces (see links to courthouses in appendix A or go to www.wethepeopleforms.com for those links) and *request all the forms* you need to start your divorce proceeding. *Inquire about additional forms and/or documents* you must provide.

→ You (petitioner) *fill out the paperwork* and the *divorce petition,* also called a *complaint* in some states. Note: A petition is not necessarily just one piece of paper. When you file, most likely you will have to file a set of papers together with your petition. The court will provide all of this paperwork for you to fill out. Ask how many copies to provide, one set of which must go to your spouse.

→ *File the first set of papers* (including your petition) and pay the related *filing fee* to the court (again, refer to your local court's rules to meet specific requirements).

→ After you file the papers, your spouse needs to get copies of all the papers. You *serve the other spouse* copies of the paperwork with a deadline to respond—usually 20 to 60 days. Or if the divorce is amicable and mutually understood, the other spouse can *sign a waiver of service* and avoid getting formally served. (See chapter 5 for details on serving spouses.)

→ You and your spouse work together to *structure a divorce agreement,* or *marital settlement agreement,* that covers all the major and minor issues (example: money, children, assets, and debts).

→ If the spouse (respondent) who was served the divorce papers does not respond formally through the court within a set time period, he or she is said to *be in default* (this will go forward as an uncontested matter), which allows the divorce to move toward the judgment phase.

→ The filing spouse files a form declaring the other spouse to be in default and then files other final paperwork required by the court.

→ A judge signs your papers, *granting your divorce.*

→ *Divorce is final.* Copies of the divorce papers are delivered to both parties from the court.

Before the family judge certifies your divorce, a final hearing may or may not be scheduled, and depending on your particular state, the spouse who originally filed may have to make a brief appearance in court. As mentioned, each state has its own specific way of granting divorces. In addition to your state's specific laws and guidelines, your divorce is also subject to many other variables, such as local norms and customs, as well as the cultural, economic, and social values practiced by a particular family law judge. Family law judges may exercise a wide spectrum of power—from signing off on your marital agreement quickly to rearranging your spousal or child support figures and visitation rights. The laws and guidelines that govern divorce are flexible, so while you are hammering out your issues with your spouse and attempting to arrive at a fair and balanced agreement, don't forget that your decisions will ultimately be reviewed by a judge.

The exact paperwork, additional documents, time frames, and sequence of events will differ from state to state. In Maryland, for example, to receive an *absolute* divorce (which means that the divorce is permanent, permits remarriage, and terminates property claims), a hearing is set for even default cases. At this hearing, which both parties must attend, a corroborative witness must testify to the facts of the case, including how long the couple has been separated.

If the spouse who is served the papers does, in fact, respond to the court, the divorce is said to be contested. He or she is contesting the terms of the divorce initially filed with the court, which may include property, child custody, child support, alimony, and assumption of marital debts. But this can also mean that the spouse who responds simply wants to have a voice in the divorce proceeding, and he or she chooses to respond for purposes of placing his or her name in the case. When a spouse contests a divorce, it can go forward only by agreement (between the spouses) or by doing legal battle in court. Agreements can be reached in one of four ways: (1) between the husband and wife, (2) between the husband and wife with the help of a mediator, (3) between the husband and wife with attorney representation, and (4) by going to court with or without attorneys. If you end up in court, the judge will make

You can find a lot about how the family courts in your state deal with divorce, separation, paternity, and annulments by accessing their web sites. You may also be able to download forms and start your divorce proceeding right away. We've compiled a list of links that will take you to these web sites, and you'll find them on our site at www.wethepeopleforms. com, as well as in chapter 5 and in appendix A.

decisions *for you* (hence, the incentive to make decisions before you battle it out in court). As we said, this is a rare occurrence.

Remember: These events describe a *default* divorce, which is possible only in uncontested and no-fault divorces.

Of course, there are many situations that do not relate to default divorces. For example, what if one spouse wants a divorce but the other doesn't? What if one spouse has committed a heinous act and refuses to cooperate from the beginning? What if you cannot locate your spouse because he or she has left you? What if you don't even know if your original marriage was legal? These are unusual situations (some of which do qualify as default divorces), which we'll discuss in chapter 7. We will also go into the details of litigating a divorce in chapter 5.

Can We Make This Quick and Easy?

To answer this question, you have to ask yourself how fast you can settle your assets, debts, and kids with your spouse (in other words, only you can answer this question). The quicker you and your spouse can come to an agreement on the major issues, the sooner you will be divorced. However, you may have to comply with state laws regarding residency and separation. If you use mediation, or come to rely on attorneys and court proceedings, your divorce takes longer and longer to settle.

Even though you may have an uncontested divorce, the spouse who gets served with divorce papers may want to file a response to the court just so he or she has a voice in the case. In fact, this is a wise decision to make, as it shows the court that the responding spouse is playing an active part in the divorce proceeding and wants to be kept in the case.

Residency Requirements

All states require that one spouse be a resident of the state before filing for a divorce in that state. (Only one spouse has to qualify.) Only three states—Alaska, South Dakota, and Washington—have no statutory requirement for resident status.

If you and your spouse are living apart and in different states, you may want to file first so you know that your case will be handled close to you. This reduces traveling expenses and ensures that all divorce-related proceedings, which include future dealings beyond your official divorce, are handled in your local court. All states recognize a divorce, whether or not the divorce took place in one particular state.

When you file for divorce, you are filing a civil lawsuit against your spouse. The filing spouse automatically becomes the plaintiff (or petitioner) and the other spouse becomes the defendant (or respondent). If you are the plaintiff, you pay the initial court costs, and if your case ends up in court, your side goes first. This may not seem fair if you and your spouse are agreeing on your divorce, so what you can do is have each of you pay your own legal and court costs, and include the division of these expenses in your divorce agreement (or marital settlement). A provision in the agreement can allow for reimbursements so all costs are shared.

Residency Requirements by State

Alabama	6 months*	Montana	90 days
Alaska	No statutory provision	Nebraska	12 months
Arizona	90 days	Nevada	6 weeks
Arkansas	60 days	New Hampshire	12 months
California	6 months	New Jersey	12 months‡
Colorado	90 days	New Mexico	6 months
Connecticut	12 months	New York	12 months
Delaware	6 months	North Carolina	6 months
District of Columbia	6 months	North Dakota	6 months
Florida	6 months	Ohio	6 months
Georgia	6 months	Oklahoma	6 months
Hawaii	6 months	Oregon	6 months
Idaho	6 weeks	Pennsylvania	6 months
Illinois	90 days	Rhode Island	12 months
Indiana	6 months	South Carolina	12 months§
Iowa	12 months	South Dakota	No statutory provision
Kansas	60 days	Tennessee	6 months
Kentucky	6 months	Texas	6 months
Louisiana	6 months	Utah	90 days
Maine	6 months	Vermont	6 months
Maryland	12 months	Virginia	6 months
Massachusetts	12 months†	Washington	No statutory provision
Michigan	6 months	West Virginia	12 months¶
Minnesota	6 months	Wisconsin	6 months
Mississippi	6 months	Wyoming	60 days
Missouri	90 days		

*The months can also be translated to days. In other words, "6 months" can also mean "180 days," and you may be restricted to waiting out the length of time in actual days—not months.

†There is no residency requirement if the grounds for divorce happened inside the state of Massachusetts. If it happened outside the state, you must wait one year.

‡Required for all grounds but adultery.

§If both spouses are residents of South Carolina, the residency requirement is reduced to 3 months.

¶If the marriage occurred in West Virginia, there is no residency requirement as long as one spouse is a state resident. If the marriage took place in another state, one spouse must have lived in West Virginia for a year before filing.

If your spouse lives and files for divorce in another state, any decisions made by that court regarding the division of assets, alimony, custody, and child support, however, may not be valid unless you consent to that court's authority (you agree to abide by that court's jurisdiction). You consent by appearing at a court date or signing an affidavit of service (a formal document), which acknowledges receipt of the filed legal documents. You may also automatically consent by abiding by the ruling of the court, such as paying for court-ordered child support. This does not mean you should disobey a court order because you don't want to give consent (or you disagree with the order). If a court has the authority to rule, you have to obey court orders. You can waive objections to jurisdiction (for example, by signing off), but there is no guarantee that a court will refuse authority just because you'd prefer to be in your own home state.

Although different courts in different states will vary on this situation, the general rule is that a court can grant a divorce but not deal with the issues of assets and debts if it has no authority over that person. If the parent in the state where the divorce is filed physically has the children residing with him or her, the court in some states will usually deal with custody issues and possibly support.

If you receive documents from a foreign country, you should consult an attorney to advise you of whether your state court or the foreign court governs the issues. This depends on many factors, such as which particular country is involved, where the two people lived and for how long, and, of course, whether children are involved.

Your particular county may also set residency requirements that allow couples to file for divorce only when one has lived in that particular county for a specific period of time. For example, to file for divorce in Los Angeles, one spouse has to have lived in Los Angeles County for at least three months before filing for divorce. So even though you lived in San Francisco for years, if you try to file for divorce in Los Angeles, you will have to wait three months. If you have moved to California recently, you must wait six months, and when you do file, you must do so in a county where you have lived for a certain period of time (depending on that county's requirements).

Where you got married has nothing to do with where you can file for divorce. You do not need to file for divorce in the state where you got married.

Separation Requirements

Some states impose a separation requirement, which means you must be separated from your spouse (not living together) for a definite period of time. This is especially true in no-fault divorces. The exact time period varies from state to state, from as little as three months to as long as three years (technically, however, you could establish residency in another state with a lower separation requirement to obtain a quicker divorce). The purpose of separation requirements is to ensure that divorce is necessary. It can allow for a cooling-off period before an actual divorce, or it can allow for a much-needed time-out that prepares the couple to reconcile and rebuild a stronger marriage. The requirements intend to help promote reconciliation between spouses and prevent hasty divorces.

In chapter 2, we'll define the different kinds of separation that are possible alongside the various grounds for divorce. There are formal and informal ways to go about separating. In some states, the date you and your spouse decide you don't want to be husband and wife

According to the United Nations, there are 8.2 legal marriages performed and registered in the United States per 1,000 population in any given year. And there are 4.19 final divorce decrees granted under civil law per 1,000 population. The country of Chile boasts the lowest divorce rate (0.42 per 1,000), but divorce was legalized only in November of 2004. The country of Mauritius claims to have the highest marriage rate (9.2 per 1,000) and a surprisingly low divorce rate (1.00 per 1,000).

TIME OUT! *I Don't Understand What You Mean By . . .*

Plaintiff   The person (the spouse) who initially files the divorce papers with the court. Also called the *petitioner.*

Defendant   The person (the spouse) who is served divorce papers once the other spouse has filed. Also called the *respondent.*

Divorce petition   Your formal request to the court for a divorce. In your petition, which is also called a *complaint,* you establish the facts, present the issues of your divorce, and indicate what, if anything, you ask the court to order from your spouse, such as spousal support, child support, or custody of your children. This is one of the first papers you'll file to begin your case.

Answer   The formal response to the court once divorce papers have been served. In contested divorces, the spouse who is served divorce papers must respond to the court within a set time period, usually 20 to 60 days.

Property   Everything you own, both real (such as a home) and personal (such as your car). Also called *assets.* Assets you acquire during your marriage are called *marital assets.*

Debt   Something owed, an obligation to pay.

Alimony   Payment of support (not child support) from one spouse to another so that the spouse receiving the payment can maintain the lifestyle that he or she was accustomed to during the marriage. Also called *spousal support* or *maintenance.*

Custody   The legal right and responsibility awarded by the court for the care of a child.

anymore is the day you become separated, even if one spouse does not move out of the house. Should you decide to separate legally, which is a possibility in some states, you may have to file a petition with the court and work out details very similar to getting a divorce. See chapter 2 for a full explanation of the separation procedure.

Property Laws and Your Divorce

Besides the divorce laws of your states, how your state views property will affect your divorce, particularly in how your assets get divided.

If you live in a community-property state, marital assets should be divided evenly between you and your spouse. Community-property states include Arizona, California, Idaho, Louisiana, Nevada, New Mexico, Texas, Washington, and Wisconsin. (In Alaska, you can now sign an agreement that

If you've been married a very short time, have acquired little or no assets and debts, and have no young children, you may be able to get a simpler divorce in your state. Many states offer a shortened (or accelerated) divorce process for such couples. Ask your court if any such rules can apply to your situation.

A Statistical Look at Divorce*

Median age of divorce: Men: 35.6   Women: 33.2

Combined age of the world's oldest couple to get a divorce: 188

Median duration of a marriage: 7.2 years

Largest divorce settlement in United States: $43 million (awarded in 1998)

Percentage of first marriages that end in divorce: 50

Percentage of remarriages that end in divorce: 60

Percentage of women who are stalked by a current or former spouse, cohabitating partner, or date at some time in their life: 5

Percentage of men who are stalked by a current or former spouse, cohabitating partner, or date at some time in their life: 0.6

Estimated average cost of divorce: $15,000

Estimated average length of divorce proceedings: 1 year

---

*Sources: National Center for Health Statistics; *Guinness Book of World Records*

designates some or all of your property as community property.) In Mississippi, the lone title state, you keep only the property that is in your name, and the court divides the rest. In the remaining states, you divide the property according to what's "fair." Couples must figure out how to evenly divide their property, and if they cannot come to an agreement, a judge will decide how to split up the assets in a fair manner.

Remember: State laws set the framework for your divorce, but they are always open to interpretation. About 95 percent of divorces are settled out of court, which leaves plenty of room for negotiation. Just because you live in a community-property state does not necessarily mean that you are limited in your negotiations. As we'll see in upcoming chapters, the entire process of divorce is about agreeing, negotiating, and making certain concessions—and maybe a few sacrifices.

Community property is a form of asset ownership between a husband and wife. Under this form of ownership, all assets acquired prior to marriage and assets that one spouse receives either by gift or inheritance during the marriage are separate property. All other assets acquired during the marriage are community property. Each spouse owns one-half interest in the assets. Example: A married couple buys a home together; the husband is the breadwinner and pays the mortgage, while the woman is a stay-at-home mom. If they live in a community-property state, the wife still owns one-half of that home—regardless of her husband's responsibility for paying the bills. The community-property states are Arizona, California, Idaho, Louisiana, Nevada, New Mexico, Texas, Washington, and Wisconsin. Alaska has an optional community-property system.

JAMES'S STORY

"**Divorce was never** on my life's list of things to do. The decision to get a divorce was hard, but neither one of us was happy in the marriage. We got married too young and had been going in different directions for years. I think the hardest part of the process was telling people—our families, especially. No one expected us to ever divorce. But it was time for us to pursue separate lives.

My wife and I kept our divorce secret until we had it all worked out. We were both incredibly worried about the financial burdens related to divorce because we had accumulated tons of debt from graduate school and couldn't afford to spend a lot of money on lawyers. The house and our four-year-old daughter were our biggest concerns. We sat down and talked about how to proceed in the divorce as cheaply and in as uncomplicated a way as possible. It was one of the hardest things we've ever had to do, but we needed a game plan. We needed to know what kind of decisions we had to make, how to make them, and how to fill out all the paperwork that the courts would accept. I had a friend who had gotten divorced the previous year, and it ruined him financially. He ended up moving out of state and changing careers just to make ends meet. I didn't want that to happen to us. I wanted to save our friendship, our daughter from unnecessary pain, and our checkbooks.

We hit a lot of roadblocks, and at one point we didn't know if we'd be able to get through the divorce without hiring attorneys. Once I learned how to navigate through the paperwork and get to know my local family law court, I began to feel a bit better about the whole process. Then we found a mediator to help us sort through the tough issues (like dealing with those debts and dividing assets), and we eventually came to an agreement. There were days, however, when I was not in the mood to deal with it all. But I must admit, being in charge of our own divorce had an overwhelming sense of relief to it. We signed a Marital Settlement Agreement and a Parenting Plan, in which we set forth exactly how we'd divide our assets and share custody of our daughter.

About seven months after we filed, we were divorced. I had moved out and got my own apartment, not too far away. I intend to be as much of a parent in my daughter's life as I was when married. We are much happier now. I learned a lot about myself—and my ex-wife—as we went through the motions of a divorce. And in retrospect, I think that if we had given up and hired our own attorneys, we would not have come out of the divorce feeling as confident about our futures."

Conclusion

The preceding sample story could be similar to your own experience, but we don't want to sugarcoat it. Divorce is not a pleasant transaction in life, but if you stop and think rationally, compassionately, and methodically through your divorce, you and your family will be better off. You will have good days and bad days. You will feel like negotiating one day, but not the next. Divorce is an emotional roller coaster. It's okay to feel overwhelmed, frustrated, depressed, anxious, angry, sad, ashamed, and stressed. Just about every emotion possible will move through you at some point.

Making a sworn enemy of your spouse and approaching your divorce in an angry and vengeful manner will do no good and perhaps cause a lot of unintended harm. Studies are just emerging that clearly demonstrate how damaging an acrimonious and brutish divorce can be on a family. Spouses who fight constantly before divorce, through divorce, and even after divorce do lasting damage to their children that impacts their children's lives forever and influences the choices they make in their futures—long into adulthood.

In reality, the era of the nasty split and the bitter divorce may be over. The divorce rate peaked in the 1970s and 1980s, and leveled off in the 1990s. Some gen Xers today can recall the restraining orders, midnight screaming matches, and public displays of malice at graduations, birthdays, and celebrations that marred their childhoods. They know what they spare their own children by getting divorced in as friendly a manner as possible.

Because divorce has become a lifestyle for 50 percent of families, society has embraced a new way to view divorce and its inner workings among blended families. The law has also made some adjustments by allowing alternatives to formal litigation. Courts want to see the stability and healthy environment of the family survive divorce, which may explain why jurisdictions in 40 states require new divorces to undergo a four-hour education course on coparenting.

It's not uncommon now to find families—ex-spouses and new spouses and/or girlfriends/boyfriends—getting together over the holidays or on important days throughout the year for the sake of the children. And with mediation now available or required in 37 states, more couples than ever are splitting up without much rancor. Such displays of gallantry were rare before 1969, when California governor Ronald Reagan signed the nation's first law permitting no-fault divorce. No-fault divorce prevents couples from having to declare war and has since become the norm rather than the exception.

CHAPTER 2

Grounds (Reasons) for Divorce

Divorcing your spouse is not as simple as your ABCs and 123s. You cannot simply fill in a bunch of blanks and submit a stack of forms to the court. As we said in chapter 1, divorce is a lot more complex than marriage. The emotions that accompany divorce do not help, either, as they tend to be mixed and unexpected. You may feel as if you've lost control of your life, that you have failed, and that this experience will mark you as a bad or tainted person. This is not so. You are human and have every right to feel awful and lost, disappointed, and totally distraught about your divorce. Mourning the loss of your marriage—whether or not it was your decision to get divorced—is natural and constitutes a very personal journey. The grief can be overwhelming and change the way you view yourself and your place in the world. But you're not a bad person and this will not ruin your life. Marriages don't end suddenly, so you've probably been miserable for quite some time. If the situation at home is a terrible one—and you've tried all your resources—the quicker you terminate your current situation, the better. And once you get past this difficult decision, you'll move forward and embrace your future. Just by picking up and reading this book you're arming yourself with the necessary information for making the right decisions. Keep your confidence level high and you'll beat down a lot of unwanted feelings.

The divorce process may seem long and tedious, as if the state wants to drag you through the mud first by requiring lots of paperwork and commitments about child support, debts, spousal support, and the like, but the goal is to sever your previously made commitment to another person in a formal and legal manner that serves the best interests of all parties—including the silent parties such as your children. You have many options when it comes to contemplating divorce, as well as many options once you decide to divorce and start the procedure. Some of these options can have the effect of saving your marriage, while others pave the pathway to an actual divorce. This chapter explains some of your options, so you can pick the best route for you and your family to take. (Or by executing these options, your experience will dictate how you'll want to proceed farther down the road, whether you

> As we discussed in chapter 1, *knowledge is power.* Just by having this book you are well on your way to getting through a difficult process. Keep in mind that the more information you collect and the more skills you learn, the better suited you will be to take control of your affairs and minimize the pain and frustration involved.

move back in or permanently remain out.) We will also look at the topic of paternity, a legal process that gives children the legal rights to their father outside of marriage.

Because divorce is a serious, life-changing decision to make, we hope that you can make good choices every step of the way. There are many decisions to make in your divorce proceeding. Each one will impact you, your future, and your family.

Whose Fault Is It?

Each state has its own laws determining when and under what circumstances a divorce can be sought and granted. In some states both sides can agree to obtain a divorce with only a brief waiting period. Other states, however, have laws that claim to permit a divorce only if there are grounds (reasons), meaning that the divorce is one spouse's fault.

Fault divorces used to be the norm throughout the country and provided a financial windfall to the spouse making the allegations. Most states now offer some form of no-fault divorce, which prevents spouses from having to find true fault in the breakup of the marriage. If a state does not technically offer no-fault divorces, such as New York, this means a couple must separate for a specified period of time before they can file for divorce. They may have to formally separate by getting the court to order a legal separation. (More on separation later in this chapter.)

All divorces need a reason, but there is a difference between the reasons defined under no-fault and those under fault. Under no-fault, the spouse who initially files the paperwork does not have to prove that the other spouse did anything wrong, such as having committed adultery or having been physically abusive. When you file for a no-fault divorce, you simply admit that your marriage did not work out—that one or both of you no longer want to be married. This in itself is a reason to get a divorce, and terms used by the courts to say this include *irreconcilable differences, incompatibility,* and *irremediable breakdown of the marriage.* Some states may offer other reasons, such as *incurable insanity,* which appears on the California divorce petition. But incurable insanity grounds must be proven in court.

A number of states offer *only* no-fault divorce (you cannot file a fault divorce in those states even if one spouse was clearly at fault for the divorce). So if you live in one of these states, your initial petition may list one of the following:

1. The marriage is irretrievably broken

Or

2. One of the parties is mentally incapacitated.

How does one get divorced in a state that does not technically offer no-fault divorces? New York is an example of such a state that does not have a petition with "irreconcilable differences" as an option to indicate as the reason for divorce. New York has six grounds for divorce. Four of the grounds are one spouse's cruel and inhuman treatment, abandonment for one or more years, imprisonment for three or more years, and adultery. The other grounds are one year of living apart under a separation judgment granted by a court or one year of living apart under a separation agreement signed by both spouses. These last two grounds are what allow New Yorkers to obtain no-fault divorces, in which neither spouse is judged to be at fault. The spouse seeking the divorce, however, must comply with all the provisions of the agreement or judgment.

These are the options one has in Florida. Again, any mental incapacity will have to be proven in court for it to grant a divorce on this ground. Notice that in no-fault states there is no option for adultery; however, adultery may have a bearing on the equitable distribution of the marital assets if the adulterous spouse has expended marital funds on the adulterous affair.

A no-fault divorce has many implications: There is no defense to a no-fault divorce petition, so a spouse cannot threaten to fight a divorce; there is no derogatory testimony; and marital misconduct cannot be used to achieve a division of property favorable to the one spouse.

Fault Divorce

Fault divorces are less common today, since most marriages' endings cannot be blamed on one person. In a fault divorce, one party blames the other for the failure of the marriage by citing wrongdoing. Although fault used to have a big role in alimony decisions, it's no longer useful to declare fault for the purpose of getting your spouse to support you after the divorce. Fault is considered, however, in more than half of the states. This means that if one spouse successfully finds fault in the other for divorce, the court will divide the couple's assets, settle the debts, and work out the details of the divorce settlement in light of this fault. The no-fault spouse is likely to receive a better settlement and perhaps be favored over the at-fault spouse for custody of children. (Conversely, in a no-fault divorce or dissolution of marriage, the actions of the respective spouses in the breakdown of the marriage do not affect property distribution or spousal support rights. The division of property will be based on fair and equitable distribution.)

> The catch with no-fault divorces is the time period required by the court to obtain one. You have to separate—live apart—for a specified period of time that can be months or years, depending on your state. This catch, unfortunately, can motivate a spouse to file under the fault system and falsely allege that the other spouse did something wrong. To get a quick divorce—or try to receive a greater share of the marital property or more alimony—falsely accusing your spouse of wrongdoing is not a good idea.

Grounds for Divorce. To file for a fault divorce, specific wrongdoing must be cited. The following are typical grounds for a fault divorce:

- Physical or mental cruelty (this is the most frequently used ground for fault divorce, and may include homosexual conduct)
- Adultery or sodomy
- Desertion
- Alcohol or drug abuse
- Insanity
- Fraud
- Infecting the other spouse with a venereal disease
- Confinement in prison or conviction of a felony
- Impotence (physical inability to engage in sexual intercourse, if it was not disclosed before marriage)

All of these reasons must be proven in court.

Double Grounds for Divorce. If both spouses are at fault (example: both spouses deserted one another and had affairs),

> In New Hampshire, you can file for a fault divorce if your spouse joined the Shakers.

the court will grant a divorce to the spouse who is least at fault, under a doctrine called *comparative rectitude*. This means the court will compare the wrongdoing and decide which side gets favored in the divorce. The doctrine of comparative rectitude solved the problem the courts faced long ago when divorce could not be granted at all under such circumstances.

Filing a Fault Divorce. The spouse who files the initial divorce petition is usually the one who finds the other at fault. When the other spouse receives notice of the filing, he or she responds to the accusation by filing an *answer* (or *response*). Fault divorces are not so easy. Depending on the accusations alleged and the animosity between the couple, a fault divorce can take a long time to resolve—even though the waiting period of separation is less strict than in a no-fault divorce. This may require the assistance of an attorney.

Types of Divorce by State

The first two columns in Figure 2.1 set out whether a state allows a fault divorce or a no-fault divorce. (Note: If a state does not technically offer a no-fault divorce, couples who have nothing to blame but incompatibility for the breakdown of their marriage may have to formally separate for a specific period of time before they can ask the court to grant a divorce.) The last column in Figure 2.1 shows whether a separation is required before a no-fault divorce will be granted, and how long the separation must be.

Preventing a Divorce from Happening Once Filed

Most divorcing couples agree to divorce before filing, but sometimes one spouse files without the other knowing, and it comes as a surprise. This can happen, for example, if a couple decides to separate and one thinks that they will get back together, but the other does not. In no-fault divorces, one spouse cannot stop the court from granting a divorce. So long as the requirements for divorce are met, there is no stopping the court from granting the petitioner's request for divorce.

The situation is different, however, in fault divorces. If the at-fault spouse can prove that he or she was falsely accused of wrongdoing, the court cannot grant the divorce. Defending oneself in an at-fault divorce can get tricky. One must provide a reasonable defense. Here's an example: A wife and husband grow apart and the wife knows that the husband is having an affair. Her actions actually provoke him to seek attention and love elsewhere. This continues for years. She then decides to file for divorce on grounds of adultery. Her husband could defend himself by saying that she condoned his actions. Defenses of at-fault divorces are rare and do not make the process any quicker. After all, why would a person want to prevent a divorce when his or her spouse made serious allegations of wrongdoing? The courts will likely grant the divorce in the end because the courts do not want to be in the business of forcing people to remain married to one another when at least one person does not want to be. Unless the petitioner (the spouse who originally files for divorce) withdraws the petition, the divorce will proceed.

Separation

The act of separating from your spouse can be just as emotional and life altering as an actual divorce. Separating has legal and financial consequences as well—especially if you get legally separated, which entails getting court orders. If you have children, the physical

STATE	FAULT GROUNDS	NO-FAULT GROUNDS	LENGTH OF SEPARATION REQUIRED
Alabama	X	X	2 years
Alaska	X	X	None
Arizona		X	None
Arkansas	X		18 months
California		X	None
Colorado		X	None
Connecticut	X	X	18 months[1]
Delaware	X	X	None
District of Columbia			6 months
Florida		X	None
Georgia	X	X	None
Hawaii		X	2 years
Idaho	X	X	5 years
Illinois	X	X[2]	2 years
Indiana		X	None
Iowa		X	None
Kansas		X	None
Kentucky		X	None
Louisiana		X	180 days
Maine	X	X	None
Maryland	X		1 year
Massachusetts	X	X	None
Michigan		X	None
Minnesota		X	180 days
Mississippi	X	X	None
Missouri		X	None
Montana		X	None
Nebraska		X	None
Nevada		X	1 year
New Hampshire	X	X	None
New Jersey	X		18 months
New Mexico	X	X	None
New York	X		1 year
North Carolina	X		1 year
North Dakota	X	X	None
Ohio	X	X[3]	1 year
Oklahoma	X	X	None
Oregon		X	None
Pennsylvania	X	X	2 years
Rhode Island	X	X	3 years
South Carolina	X		1 year
South Dakota	X	X	None
Tennessee	X	X	2 years[4]
Texas	X	X	3 years
Utah	X	X	3 years
Vermont	X		6 months
Virginia	X		1 year[5]
Washington		X	None
West Virginia	X	X	1 year
Wisconsin		X	None
Wyoming		X	None

[1] In Connecticut, a couple who divorces after separating must allege incompatibility.
[2] The couple must allege irretrievable breakdown and separation for no-fault; if both parties consent, only six months is required.
[3] Divorce may be denied if one party contests ground of incompatibility.
[4] Divorce after separation is allowed only if there are no children.
[5] May be reduced to six months if there are no children.

Figure 2.1 Separation Requirements for No-Fault Divorce by State

separation will profoundly affect them and perhaps confuse them until they get used to the arrangement. People decide to separate for different reasons. You may want to determine whether separating allows you to see your marriage clearly and gives you the space you need to either get back together or proceed to a divorce; you may want a divorce and know that this is the first step in the process; you may be so estranged from your spouse that you cannot live in the same house anymore; or you may want your spouse to make serious changes, and moving out will convey a strong message. People have lots of other reasons for separating. Each couple's unique situation will determine what's best, but all couples should think seriously before making a move, as separating can have both good and bad outcomes. The distance that accompanies a separation can force a divorce as much as it can encourage a reunion. Keep in mind that separation does not break the ties that bind a marriage in the sense that you become semimarried. While you are separated, you remain legally married, and certain benefits such as health insurance, inheritance, pension rights, and Social Security remain intact during your separation.

Separation has different definitions in different states. In some states, it's sufficient to say you no longer want to be husband and wife to be considered separated, even if you remain living in the same house. In other states, one spouse must physically move out to be considered separated. Such a move can also affect property rights and shared assets and debts. Basically, there are two ways to separate: informally and formally.

Informal Separation

Most couples opt to separate informally for a while so they can reassess their marriage and its problems, and try to resolve some issues before contemplating divorce. This also affords each spouse the opportunity to see what it's like to live in separate places again and gain a different perspective on one another. If living together makes it impossible to deal with your problems, you might find an informal separation helpful toward understanding your relationship at this challenging time and pulling through it. Also, if you and your spouse are seeking counseling (discussed later), separating while you work through your differences with the help of a counselor may be beneficial. As we mentioned, however, each couple's situation will vary. You may still have to negotiate spousal and child support issues if you are informally separated, for example.

Trial Separation. In a trial (test run) separation, you and your spouse decide to spend some time apart—in effect, taking a time-out from your marriage before reconvening and deciding what to do. During a trial separation, you and your spouse continue to share assets and debts. You don't have to do any legal paperwork to declare your separation. This trial period can be short (days to weeks) or long (weeks to months). Despite the word *trial,* the courts are not involved. It's a *test* for you and your spouse, to see how a separation changes your outlook and thoughts on your marriage.

Living Apart. A trial separation can lead to living apart for a longer period than initially expected. If one spouse moves out and you remain separated for months but keep the separation informal, it's possible that you risk your marital rights changing in the eyes of the law. For example, if you do not plan to reconcile and you live apart for a long time, your state may view the assets and debts you and your spouse accumulate during your separation as separate—belonging to the spouse who acquired the asset or accumulated the debt. In most states, however, the separation does not change the property ownership of new assets and debts so long as the separation remains informal.

The Pitfalls of Informal Separations

Because informal separations don't have the added hassle of drafting an agreement or submitting papers to the court, informal separations are very common. But you have to be careful about separating informally if you have a lot to protect, such as children, a standard of living, large assets, and your sanity. Your spouse may appear obliging, cooperative, and even accommodating of your wishes at the start, but once separated may become distant, unsupportive, and a stranger. Good relationships can spoil quickly, soured by the unexpected ramifications of separating. A court cannot enforce an informal agreement as much as it can a formal agreement—particularly when there is nothing written down. If you and your spouse don't need each other financially, have no children, do not share all of your accounts, do not share a lot of debt, and do not share a great deal of assets, separating informally is not so risky. But you must also have great confidence in your spouse and feel good about pursuing this path.

Discuss your separation openly and honestly with your spouse. Understand why each of you has chosen to separate and where each of you thinks your relationship will end up. Consider setting a date on the calendar when you plan to reconvene and discuss the separation experience and how it has changed the two of you, for good and bad. Have goals for your separation. Think about counseling. Keep the conversation moving and talk about whether you think it's advantageous to see one another frequently or communicate regularly over the phone. If you and your spouse are at odds and cannot converse in any reasonable manner, you may want to schedule a counseling session or suggest a cooling off period that allows both of you to settle your emotions and prepare for dealing with your relationship cordially.

Informal separations should not start with "Let's separate" and end with "I'm moving out today." A breakdown in communication is among the leading causes of breakdowns in marriages (money is another leading cause), and if your marital communication disorder worsens during separation, you'll have little luck reuniting. What's more, if one spouse leaves abruptly and refuses to participate in any mutually beneficial negotiations, the other spouse may have grounds for a fault divorce on the basis of desertion or abandonment. If, on the other hand, you start talking before one person moves out, you lower your risk of losing more during an eventual divorce.

Use your separation to reevaluate your marriage and work hard at resolving your issues through sincere communication. Set some rules for your separation, and try to write them down alongside your goals. Date and sign this agreement and commit to revisiting it together at a later date. That way, if your separation does take a turn for the worse, you do have a document that records your intentions and your original agreement. Be sure to include as many financial matters as you can in this agreement. You may have future conflicts that will arise during your separation, and figuring out how to deal with them now could be in the best interests of both of you.

You may want to assume that your spouse will mismanage your finances during your separation and make room for that potential hazard in your agreement. Because creditors and the law in your state may recognize you as still married with shared assets and debts (even those accumulated during separation), you need to protect yourself. Otherwise, your credit score and your overall financial health can suffer greatly—the last thing you need if you do become single again and in need of good credit. Creditors may haul you into small claims court to

Money issues loom large in people's lives, and more so in the lives of couples under the cloud of separation or divorce. The more money you share in terms of assets, debts, bank accounts, lines of credit, benefits, retirement accounts, investments, and so on, the more complicated your separation and divorce become. Speak openly and candidly about your money issues the moment you decide to separate or contemplate divorce. The sooner you can come to an agreement about your shared money and debts, the better off you'll be and the more secure you'll feel. In your formal or informal agreement, don't be afraid to spell everything out and set specific terms for current and future financial obligations. If you intend to separate for an indefinite period of time, hoping for a breather that avoids confrontation, the more meticulous and unmistakable you make your terms as well as predict future situations in your agreement, the more rewarding your time apart will be for the future of your relationship.

recoup monies squandered by your spouse on your shared credit card. What's worse, if your spouse files for bankruptcy, you may automatically become a party to his or her bankruptcy filing and find your shared marital possessions getting sold or your home getting foreclosed upon. It's not unusual for people to resort to desperate measures during very difficult times. This is another reason to stay talkative and forthcoming about problems during your separation. Be flexible and willing to compromise, too. Not all of your negotiations will be a walk in the park. Neither spouse will get everything he or she wants. Neither spouse will walk away from the table feeling 100 percent good about everything. Always keep in mind that if you cannot come to an agreement, the court will do it for you, and you are less likely to get what you want. The closer you can come to an agreement with your spouse, the more likely you can stay in control of your divorce and get what you want in the end.

This is the time to protect your financial well-being as much as possible. Take time to think through all that you share—assets and debts—and have an explicit and unequivocal plan for dealing with these things during your separation. At the least, both of you should agree to not use either one's name on any new financial accounts; if one spouse must obtain the signature of the other spouse, the other spouse must be notified and agree to the signing. All financial documents should be brought to both spouses' attention during the separation, especially if they affect the lives of each person. If your separation or imminent divorce is contentious and you fear that your spouse will act in a malicious manner, such as removing shared funds from a bank account, abusing a shared credit card and racking up enormous debt, or destroying or stealing either your personal property or shared assets, you have to make quick and proactive decisions. Consider opening your own savings and checking

Filing papers with a court helps you memorialize your date of separation. In other words, it identifies the date of your separation. This can be important later on if your spouse decides to abuse joint credit in both of your names and the creditors start coming after you. Although creditors can still approach you so long as you remain legally married, having proof that you've filed papers with the court can help your argument against those creditors. Having that date written down in a formal manner may help you in other ways, too. For example, if your spouse commits a crime while you are separated, you further distance yourself from that crime by having those papers already filed with the court.

accounts at another bank and deposit half of what you shared with your spouse in those accounts. Close your joint accounts. And find safe places (outside of your home) to store personal assets or certain valuables that you fear your spouse may try to take, damage, or sell.

We'll revisit these money issues in chapter 3 when we talk about how to prepare for financial independence after divorce.

Formal/Legal Separation (Getting Court Orders)

Not all states require a formal separation before you file for divorce; you may be able to start divorce proceedings right away. If you do not anticipate that your separation will be short term and that you will eventually get divorced, a formal separation makes your arrangement more serious and in some states more binding. Two different types of formal separations apply: permanent and legal. They can follow an informal separation or happen as soon as you decide to separate.

Permanent Separation. If you and your spouse permanently separate, you act as though you are divorced, but by legal standards you are not. Permanent separation is often chosen by couples who cannot contemplate a divorce for religious or financial reasons. For example, a woman who is disabled and on her husband's health policy cannot risk losing her health insurance in a divorce, so they permanently separate and live separate lives in separate residences. In most states, all assets received and most debts incurred after permanent separation are the separate property or responsibility of the spouse incurring them. However, debts that happen after separation and before divorce are usually joint debts if they result from certain necessities, such as to provide for the children or maintain the marital home.

As with any separation, be sensible and compose an agreement with your spouse—especially if you plan to separate permanently. This agreement should lay out the same groundwork that a divorce agreement would with regard to spousal and child support, the division of assets and debts, and child custody and visitation. Keep in mind that your separation remains just that—a separation so you do not become divorced and your agreement does not automatically make your separation a legal one. Legal separations, described later, are the most formal types of separation. If the court must intervene in a permanent separation agreement, this often leads to legal separation. The court's role is always to protect your agreement. It does not want to make important decisions for you and your spouse—but it will if you cannot reach an agreement.

Legal Separation. This is the most formal type of separation possible. It's one step short of divorce, and in some states you can obtain a legal separation only as a prelude to divorce. You must draft an agreement that spells out the division of property and debts, spousal and child support, custody, and visitation, and the court certifies this agreement. The court does not, however, grant you a divorce, so you remain married in a technical, legal sense. Any spousal and child support ordered by the court is called *separate maintenance.* The spouse who helps support the other spouse and/or the children can claim an income tax deduction, but this requires a legal separation signed by the court. (The spouse who receives the support must claim it as income.) Both spouses cannot claim the children as deductions on their tax returns, so discuss this issue with your tax advisor. Generally, the parent who spends the most on the children during the tax year gets the deduction. Parents can also agree to a plan for taking those deductions in the future; for example, the two parents can alternate one year after the other who gets to take the deduction.

Divorce and separation are two different camps. If you truly plan to leave your spouse, start a new life on your own, and begin to date again, separation may not be the best option. Whether you separate formally or informally, you remain married in the eyes of the courts. This can present legal and financial consequences if you, for example, begin a new relationship and do not intend to get divorced right away. You may leave yourself vulnerable to more losses in a divorce proceeding if your spouse files under grounds of adultery. However, people do have reasons for getting a legal separation, which is just like a divorce except that you cannot remarry until you undergo the divorce process and obtain a divorce decree. You may find it more cost-effective to avoid the legal separation and start divorce proceedings as soon as you can—assuming you meet your state's separation requirements, if any. Getting legally separated and then divorced doubles your costs.

Because legal separations sometimes do come before divorce, having an agreement already in place makes the divorce process easier. Some, if not all, of your agreement can convert to your divorce agreement (if you file for divorce later on). Also, if one spouse fails to act in accordance with the agreement, the court can more easily intervene and enforce it than had you informally separated without any agreement.

Not all states recognize legal separations, but if you do not intend to get back together soon and you anticipate divorce somewhere down the road, having an agreement in place, whether it becomes legal or not, protects you and your spouse. Even if your separation is friendly and you hope to avoid divorce, making your arrangement formal by writing out the situation with regard to support, children, assets, and debts is essential for the well-being of your relationship and its future—no matter where it goes. *Keep these written agreements clear and simple.*

Separation Agreements: What to Address

- ☑ Your children's financial support (whether one spouse pays child support, how much, when, and the method of payment).
- ☑ Both spouses' financial support (alimony, if needed).
- ☑ Where your children will live.
- ☑ How both parents will take responsibility for the children's care, as decisions will continually need to be made for their benefit.
- ☑ When your children will visit the other parent and how the exchange will happen. Set a visitation schedule.
- ☑ How shared debts will be paid and how future debts incurred during separation will be handled.
- ☑ How the joint bank accounts and credit cards will be managed.
- ☑ Who gets to remain in the home and retain or use large assets, such as cars.
- ☑ How large shared assets—including the home—will be managed during the separation, especially if the home is expensive to keep up and pay down its mortgage.
- ☑ How liquid assets will be managed during the separation, especially if they become needed to help pay bills and for general living expenses.

Foremost on the minds of spouses during this troubling time are money issues that the agreement can address so both parties remain financially secure and stable. This does not mean one or both spouses do not have to sacrifice their former standard of living (as one usually moves out of the home and into another, smaller place of residence), but they at least will know that they can enjoy similar standards of living and not have to worry about ending up on the street or without any health insurance.

Women who are stay-at-home moms may feel tremendous stress over a separation, wondering whether they can even afford to separate. They may not have credit in their name or even access to credit if they've been linked to their spouse for a long time and lack a solid credit history (being an authorized user on a credit card does not help you build your own credit history). In chapter 3, we'll give you tips for recovering your financial health once you become independent at divorce (or separation). It may, for example, be smart to take out a separate credit card in your own name while you await the outcome of your separation and/or divorce, or have the credit reporting bureaus establish a credit file in your own name that is separate from that of your spouse. Moreover, if you and your spouse share joint accounts (to which debts are tied), you will have to discuss how you plan on paying for those debts and using those lines of credit in the future.

This, again, is why carefully written and comprehensive agreements are a good idea. Remember: Keep all written agreements clear and simple. You can also consider having any child support payments taken directly from your spouse's payroll check through the help of your local child support agency.

TIME OUT! *I Don't Understand What You Mean By . . .*

Liquid asset   Any asset that can be quickly and easily converted to cash. Paper money and coins are the most liquid form of cash. Other examples of liquid assets include bank accounts, stocks, Treasury bills, certificates of deposit, and money market accounts.

Pendente lite   Latin for "pending litigation." You may see this term in reference to alimony in your divorce agreement or separate maintenance in your separation agreement. Both *alimony pendente lite* and *separate maintenance* refer to spousal support. When spousal support payments get figured out for the purpose of a separation agreement, the court can use this figure later on during a divorce proceeding. Thus, the spousal support determined at separation is pending the litigation that happens at a later date during the actual divorce.

Maintenance   Another word for spousal support or alimony. Maintenance is often used in reference to separation agreements.

Creditor   The person to whom money is owed. During a separation and/or divorce, you and your spouse should have a clear understanding of how you will deal with the debts you owe and the creditors to which those debts are tied.

Grounds   The legal reasons for a divorce.

A *liquid asset* is anything that can be converted to cash quickly, including cash itself. Examples of liquid assets are money market accounts, stocks, savings and checking accounts, cash advances on credit cards, certificates of deposit, overdrafts, small bank personal loans, or any system that allows you to write checks against a promise to pay at a later date or against an investment. If spousal support is limited or nonexistent, one spouse may have to resort to using liquid assets for daily living expenses or for supporting the children. The agreement should allow either spouse to use any liquid assets for necessities, but the terms for using such assets should be clear and concise because these do remain shared assets so long as both spouses have access to them.

Commencing a Separation

Initiating a separation is quite easy: You and your spouse decide that you need to separate, and one person (usually) offers to move out. For informal separations, you do not need to notify anyone or file any papers with the court. If you formally separate, however, you may need to file papers for separation with your local family court, and once you and your spouse have reached a written agreement on the terms of your separation, that agreement and other papers will get filed with the same court. (Remember: Not all states offer legal separations, but no laws prevent a couple from informally separating and drafting an agreement signed by both spouses anyhow. Keep the agreement in a safe place. Consider giving a copy of it to a close friend or family member.)

Usually, the spouse who first suggests separating is the person to move out. But if children are involved, their care and needs must be considered and have priority. The primary caregiver typically remains in the home with the children. Separation can affect the children more than the parents. It's unwise to uproot children from the family home and move them out with one parent. Maintain their routines as much as possible throughout the separation, because their lives will inevitably be disrupted.

The courts do not play a major role in separations unless you cannot reach an agreement with your spouse (or you seek a formal separation). In that case, the court will decide what's best for your family, and a family law judge will issue a court-ordered separation agreement after conducting a hearing.

Before you sign any agreement, read everything over carefully. Question any terms or phrases that you don't understand. Be sure you agree to every provision in the agreement and do not be afraid to raise any concerns. This is your opportunity to make sure you can live with what's set out in your agreement. Because many legal separation agreements do become divorce agreements, do not assume that you can easily change your agreement's terms and provisions at a later date. However, you can include a provision in your agreement that states you do not want the terms of your separation agreement to automatically bind you in any divorce agreement.

Getting Back Together

For some, separating is the precursor to starting all over again and reviving your marriage. Separating forces both couples to take inventory of their lives and either learn to appreciate one another in a whole new way or adapt to singlehood again and decide not to go back to married life. No one can tell what the best time frame is for separating or how long it will take for you and your spouse to reach that point where the next decision should be made.

Separating is initially jarring because it entails a change of lifestyle. One spouse has to find a new living arrangement that may not be as nice as the family home, with the children, and under the care of another adult. The other spouse must take on more responsibility now that he or she has the children and a home to maintain. Couples may not realize—until they separate—just how much each party was contributing to the family's "moving parts," or what it takes to run a family. You might find yourself suddenly respecting and appreciating your spouse more than you ever did and wanting to repair your marriage and do what you can to make it work.

Reconciliation is another difficult step that many couples take when they decide they want to stick it out and avoid the legal breakup of their marriage. Counseling often strengthens reconciliation. Couples who come back together with a renewed sense of hope and excitement for their marriage may not take the time to reflect on the problems in their marriage that led them to separate. Instead, they enjoy this second honeymoon phase and avoid the real issues. If you bury your problems under the carpet, they are bound to resurface. However, having a counselor by your side to guide you back to the right place in your marriage and help you confront some of your deeply problematic issues will further guarantee that your reunion is long-lasting and enduring. Couples may also find mental health professionals useful on an individual basis (outside their couples therapy) to help them get through the personal struggles related to reconciling.

If you've formally separated with an agreement, your agreement may have a provision about reconciliation or may become invalid upon reconciliation. In Colorado, for example, many couples who sign a separation agreement as a contract never finalize the divorce through the court. In these situations, the contract survives a reconciliation unless there are provisions within the agreement about reconciliation. Legal separations filed with the court and granted by the court typically contain language regarding reconciliation. But your particular court may differ from this. In New York, for example, you don't even have to file a legal separation agreement so long as it is in writing and properly executed with the necessary signatures and notarization. The agreement is treated like any other contract—and the courts couldn't care less until someone breaches the contract and files a complaint.

The Power of Counseling

To reiterate, do not underestimate the power of counseling as you go through a separation or a divorce. This may be the first time you've ever sought counseling or ever been to a mental health professional, and that's okay. For first-timers, the experience can be daunting and may seem unnecessary. Whether you opt for one-on-one counseling independently of your spouse or go together as a couple to marriage counseling, the process can benefit you in how you perceive yourself, your marriage, and your future.

Counseling is not only good for your relationship, but good for you as a person going through a tough time and trying to figure out what's best. Counseling can offer you more feedback and foster more critical self-evaluation than a friend or family member can. How? Counselors are third parties who don't already have a vested interest in your emotions and the outcome of your family life. No matter how much your family and friends love you and are there for you, it's hard for them to distinguish their own emotions with regard to your situation. They share in some of the grief, fear, shock, and sometimes anger that you feel. While it's important to have close friends and family members around you for support, be careful

> Close friends and family members can experience grief and shock as well upon hearing of
> your separation or divorce. They may also act strange and not know how to behave around
> you, your spouse, or both of you together. They have known you as a couple for so long that
> suddenly seeing you separated can be hurtful and troubling. You may not find it helpful to
> discuss all of your marital problems with these friends and family members who—for years—
> were very loyal to you *and* your spouse. Moreover, you don't want to force anyone to play
> favorites or side with one of you. While your friends and family members will want to be
> there for you in this difficult time, keep in mind that you may be better off seeking help from
> a noninterested third party, such as a marriage counselor, therapist, or any mental health
> professional. Believe it or not, these professionals can bring ideas and suggestions to the
> table that none of your friends and family members (who probably know you best!) can.

about how you filter and absorb what they say and suggest. They may not, for example, have
a true understanding of what exactly is wrong with your marriage or how to fix it. You also
don't want to alienate any friends or family members who've been close to both you and your
spouse for a long time.

Finding the right marriage counselor and/or a professional for you as an individual is a
task in itself. If you've been keeping your marital problems a secret and you don't want to
divulge your situation until you and your spouse know what you are going to do, you may
resist asking your friends and family members for referrals. If this is the case, start by asking
your primary physician for referrals. Also call your health insurance company to ask about
potential therapists covered under your plan (often called *preferred service providers*). Be
sure to ask about limits on counseling, in case your insurance will cover only a fixed number
of sessions a month or year.

The most important aspect in finding the right counselor is finding one whom you like and
can feel comfortable with during your sessions. If you and your spouse are together in marriage counseling, both of you need to feel good about your choice and willing to share your
most intimate thoughts and problems with this person. It may take a couple of sample sessions
with potential counselors before you find one that you like. Don't worry about making your
first counselor happy by signing up with that person. Counselors know how difficult and
important finding the perfect match can be; they want to click with you as much as you should
click with them. It's like finding a shoe that fits ideally—you'll know when you find it.

Annulment

People are regularly confused by this concept of annulment. To annul a marriage means to
nullify and void it, as if it never happened and was never valid. Divorce, on the other hand,
terminates a valid marriage. Historically, annulments are associated with the Roman Catholic
Church and are granted if certain circumstances make the marriage invalid from the start. A
legal annulment from your state is not the same thing as a religious annulment from your
church. Both procedures dissolve a marriage by basically saying it never happened, but they
do not always honor one another's recognition of an annulment. In other words, you cannot
assume that by getting a legal annulment, your church will acknowledge that annulment without your going through its own system. For example, if you are Catholic and seek a divorce,
you will not be able to remarry in the Catholic Church without first getting that marriage

annulled *through the church.* Also, if the church declares your marriage invalid through its annulment process, your state may still view you as married until you get a legal annulment or legal divorce.

The annulment process is not so easy, either through a church or the state. Not all states offer legal annulments, but for religious conservatives, getting a church annulment in addition to a civil divorce is important for purposes of participating in church-related practices and being recognized as single again (that is, remarrying in the church, receiving the sacraments, and having the church acknowledge you as not married anymore). If your state offers legal annulments, you may find that you'll have to go through another procedure in your church so it can declare your marriage invalid within the church and not just the state. The more conservative your church, the more hurdles you have to clear to get your marriage annulled.

Legal Annulments

Legal annulments are not so popular now that divorce has lost much of its social stigma (since 50 percent of Americans get divorced, it cannot keep its negative image forever). And if an annulment is desired for religious reasons, a couple can obtain a religious annulment through their church after getting a civil divorce.

Proving that your marriage is invalid in the court requires meeting specific criteria. In most states, the most often cited grounds for civil annulments are fraud or misrepresentation, concealment, refusal or inability to consummate the marriage, and general misunderstanding.

Examples that fall under these criteria include the following:

- You were under the influence of drugs or alcohol at the time of your marriage.

- Your spouse withheld the truth about important facts that would have changed your mind about marriage, such as intentions or capacity to have children; an addiction to drugs or alcohol; a history of violence, arrests, or conviction of a felony; children from a previous relationship; infection with a disease; or an inability or refusal to engage in sexual relations.

- Your spouse was not of legal age at the time of the marriage or was already married.

- You were forced into the marriage.

Any of these reasons may be grounds for an annulment in your state, but the process will vary from state to state and may not be available in all states. The grounds required by your church may also vary, but generally they tend to be very similar to these examples.

Religious Annulments

If you cannot seek a legal (civil) annulment, you can always seek an annulment in your Catholic church by first going to your local pastor or parish priest and asking about the procedure. Every church diocese will have its own methodical steps for achieving the annulment, but it may not be as straightforward as getting a divorce through the civil courts. You will have to submit your marriage license, divorce decree (assuming you've already obtained a civil divorce), baptismal certificate, and other related documents. The church will set up a council of at least three judges—called a *tribunal*—at which you'll be subject to questions about your marriage and the reasons you seek an annulment. This questioning can get very personal, as the church probes the details of your life, including your experience before marriage, your

Most annulments take place after a couple has been married briefly. Brief marriages involve little or no assets or debts to divide, and the marriage has not produced any children for whom custody, visitation, and child support are a concern. When a long-term marriage is annulled, however, most states have provisions for dividing property and debts, as well as determining custody, visitation, child support, and alimony. Children of an annulled marriage are not considered illegitimate. Annulments do not in any way nullify or void any parental responsibilities.

life after divorce, and how you anticipate your future life with a partner. Witnesses will have to testify on your behalf about your marriage by either appearing before the tribunal or submitting written statements. If your ex-spouse raises any objections to your annulment, this can stop or prolong the annulment process.

Here's an example: You get married when you are 20 and divorced when you are 28. You want to get married again when you are 34, but your fiancé is Catholic and wants to get married in the church. So he asks that you go back and get your first marriage annulled by the church. When you try to obtain that annulment, your former spouse says you have no grounds to annul the marriage, and the church denies your annulment. (This does not prevent you from getting married again because in the law's eyes, you are divorced. But you may not be able to remarry in the church.)

You can appeal a denied annulment and hope that it gets settled before reaching the Vatican. Religious annulments are uphill battles, but they are battles people are willing to fight for the sake of their religious beliefs. You may also find that it costs you a lot—in time, effort, and friendly donations to the church—to move your case along. The quicker you can supply the information the church needs to decide on your case and the better your witnesses and former spouse cooperate, the sooner you can obtain an annulment. Britney Spears got her annulment within a couple of weeks, but she was married only a few short hours. For most, annulments take months to years and are completed long after the civil courts grant you a civil divorce.

Many people wrongly assume that getting an annulment is easier than getting a divorce. That is not always the case. However, an alternative to divorce in some states that does offer an easier route to ending your marriage may be available. States have different names for this type of simplified divorce, such as *summary* divorce. Check with your state for more information.

In California, a couple can get a summary divorce (an easier and quicker type of divorce) if the couple qualifies using the following parameters:

- They were married less than five years from the date of filing.
- There were no minor children from the marriage (and the wife is not now pregnant).
- The parties own no real property.
- Community property is valued at less than $25,000 (excluding cars).
- Community debt is less than $5,000.
- No spousal support will be paid.
- Both parties agree to sign the joint petition.

Getting Help Right Away

Not every divorce or separation is a peaceful or well-planned experience. If your spouse leaves you abruptly and you are vulnerable to running out of money or fear that your spouse will act in a manner that may harm you and your children, you must seek help from the courts right away. If you cannot trust your spouse to help support you and your children (assuming your spouse was the breadwinner), you may not be able to wait until the separation or divorce agreement gets hammered out and enforced by a court. Furthermore, if you worry that your spouse may try to take your children, lock you out of the house, or refuse to let you use shared assets that you need for living, such as your car, you have reasons to seek the court's help. Don't wait until you get desperate. If you sense that trouble is around the corner, it's best to get the court's help now.

Temporary Orders

If your relationship with your spouse is so horrendous that you must seek temporary orders from the court to ensure your and your children's safety, you simply have to ask the court (through specific papers that you can obtain at the court) for what you want. Any or all of the following are typical temporary orders:

- Ordering your spouse not to come near or contact you (or if he or she hasn't already done so, ordering your spouse to move out of the family home), otherwise known as a *restraining order*
- Establishing child custody and visiting arrangements
- Providing for spousal support and/or child support payments
- Ordering your spouse not to sell valuable assets (also called a *restraining order*)

Temporary orders are usually valid until the court holds another hearing or until you and your spouse arrive at your own settlement through negotiation or mediation.

Even in amicable separations and divorces, couples may want to obtain temporary orders just so they have a clear understanding of what needs to be taken care of as soon as that separation or contemplation of divorce commences. If your children will be staying with you, file for custody and child support. Assuming you do not make a good enough living to support yourself and your children (because your spouse was the main source of income), the court will award the proper amount of child support and acknowledge that you live with the children. This also prevents your spouse from claiming that you kidnapped the children, an allegation that could sabotage your attempt to obtain sole custody in the later divorce proceeding. None of these actions are extreme. They are smart actions to take and do not leave

The family courts have ways of settling urgent and necessary needs of couples in contentious breakups, especially when the breakup leaves one spouse financially or physically vulnerable. Some decisions between arguing couples should be made as soon as possible, such as temporary orders regarding who gets the children, who stays in the home, and how one spouse can obtain temporary support while the terms of a separation or divorce are figured out. The court will conduct an informal hearing within days or weeks to settle such issues. This can happen before a formal divorce petition is filed.

any room for misbehavior. If you feel these actions are excessive, radical, severe, or uncharacteristic of you or your spouse, bear in mind that people can act foolishly or in the extreme when under stressful circumstances.

Filling Out the Paperwork. Visit your local family court as soon as you can and fill out the proper paperwork. Go to www.wethepeopleforms.com for quick and easy access to your state's online sites for downloading forms. You may also access these links at www.wiley .com/go/wethepeopleforms. If you find it difficult to navigate your court's web site, or your local family law court in particular, pay a visit to the courthouse that handles divorce cases in your area. (Refer to chapter 5 for tips on locating that courthouse.) Your formal petition for a temporary order will consist of a small set of several documents. Your court may also have help available to guide you through the process of completing the paperwork properly. If not, ask for the forms and take your time reading through the instructions and filling them out as best you can. The clerk will review your forms and request any information you failed to include. (Some courts have self-help law centers for family law cases, which are intended to help people fill out these forms. Ask the court clerk if your court has such a center at your disposal.)

The most important documents to obtain are called the Application for Order to Show Cause (OSC) and the actual Order to Show Cause, which can also be called a *motion*. What these documents say is "I want a hearing to ask for something from the court." An Order to Show Cause is a simple, fill-in-the-boxes legal form or short typed legal document that sets out what you are asking for, such as a temporary order for spousal support. The document orders your spouse to come to court at a specific date and time and explain (show cause) why the court should not grant this request.

You will also need to provide a declaration—a document that states "here's what I want and why I should get it." This written statement sets out the facts of your request for the temporary order. Chapter 4 will guide you through writing such a statement and give you some examples of real statements used in the courts. Your statement must be given under penalty of perjury ("Honest, I'm not lying"). You can also submit declarations from other people who have firsthand knowledge of the facts.

Two additional documents you may need to complete your filing are a proposed temporary order that grants you your request (the family law judge will sign this order to grant your request) and a proof of service. A *proof of service* is a document that says someone has given copies of all the papers you've filed at the court to your spouse. This document proves to the court that you have formally notified your spouse about your request(s) with copies of the relevant information.

When serving important papers to your spouse, send them according to your court's rules. Your proof of service form may suggest that you send paperwork one particular way, such as by U.S. Postal Service Certified Mail. If in doubt, ask the clerk what is required to deliver your papers.

Depending on the kind of temporary order(s) you are seeking, you may have to provide a few additional documents that will help the judge make a fair decision. For example, if you are requesting spousal and/or child support, you should prepare a document that describes your sources of income and how that income gets used up on monthly living expenses for you and your children. Ask the clerk if the court has any recommendations for providing this kind of information.

Once you have filed orders for temporary relief, you may have to attend a hearing where a family law judge listens to your request and rules on it. These hearings generally last

TIME OUT! *I Don't Understand What You Mean By . . .*

Order   A court ruling that tells (orders) someone to do or not do something. Orders can also establish certain rights and responsibilities of a person under the order.

Temporary order   A court ruling that tells (orders) someone to do something or not do something for a specified (temporary) period of time, such as pay child support or spousal support until the divorce agreement is finalized.

Restraining order   A court ruling that tells (orders) someone to hold back (restrain) from doing something, such as contacting and/or coming within a certain distance of another person, or selling assets, or draining a bank account.

Proof of service   A document that someone signs telling the court that they delivered copies of all the court-filed papers. It can also be called a *certificate of service.*

Order to Show Cause hearing.   A hearing at the family court where you have filed temporary orders and need a family law judge to rule on your request(s). The document that declares this hearing is called the *Order to Show Cause document* and it officially tells your spouse to come to court at a specific date and time and explain (show cause) why the court should not grant the request listed on the document.

---

about 20 minutes and may not necessarily take place in a formal courtroom. Depending on the court's calendar, your hearing may take place within a few days or a couple of weeks. How your case gets heard will depend on the judge assigned to your case. The judge's tasks include reviewing all the relevant details of your case, asking any questions, and obtaining both sides of the story if your spouse shows up to defend him- or herself. The judge may not have the time to sit and listen to everyone who shows up—such as you, your spouse, and any witnesses. And even though you filed the request, you may not have the opportunity to speak to the judge and present your side of the story. Instead, the judge might only accept the papers you gave at the court to arrive at a decision. Be prepared, however, to know exactly what you want and have the evidence to prove that what you are asking for is fair. This may entail that you provide copies of your budget, a statement that reflects your income and expenses, and any other relevant information. Judges do not rule haphazardly on child support; they follow state guidelines that recommend certain support figures, given your particular situation—who has the children and how much money each spouse makes.

At the close of the hearing, the judge will rule on your request by either issuing your order as is, making some changes, or denying your request.

Paternity

Paternity means "fatherhood." To establish legal paternity (*legal* means that papers are filed in the court) is to give the

> The three (other) ways to get unhooked—besides divorce—are
>
> 1. Annulment
> 2. Legal separation
> 3. Paternity
>
> These options accomplish pretty much the same thing as a divorce.

child of unmarried parents a legal father. (Parents who were married to each other when the child was born do not have to establish legal paternity.) Paternity cases are no longer unique because out-of-wedlock births are commonplace. In 2003, about 1.6 million paternities were established and acknowledged. Of these, nearly 700,000 were voluntarily acknowledged in a hospital at the time of birth. In fact, paternity cases outnumber divorce filings in many courts.

By taking steps to establish legal paternity, a mother gives her child a right to the same benefits as children of married parents. Establishing legal paternity gives a child access to the following benefits:

- *Right of inheritance:* Rights of survivorship are important. If the father dies, the child could qualify for death benefits, including Social Security benefits, veteran's benefits, life insurance, pension, and inheritance rights. Unless legal paternity has been established, a child may not be able to claim these benefits from his or her father.

- *A sense of identity:* A child can have the father's name on his or her birth certificate. A child then has a sense of full identity by knowing the father and his family. A child has a right to know both mother and father and, wherever possible, to be supported by both.

- *Access to father's medical history:* This can help prevent or treat diseases and health conditions passed from father to child.

- *Financial support by father:* This includes regular cash payments and health insurance benefits.

Many fathers voluntarily acknowledge paternity, which also leads to the father wanting a personal relationship with his son or daughter—a priceless bond. In a disputed case, father, mother, and child can be required to submit to genetic tests. The genetic test results are highly accurate. States must have procedures that allow paternity to be established up to the child's eighteenth birthday. Hospitals must provide fathers the opportunity to acknowledge paternity voluntarily at the time of birth.

If the alleged father signs a voluntary acknowledgment of paternity, the courts do not have to decide parentage, but custody, visitation, and child support often remain at issue. However, if legal paternity is at issue—that is, the alleged father (and sometimes the mother) denies paternity—the parent who wishes to establish paternity must bring a paternity suit or action. You do this by filing specific papers with the court, asking the court to determine paternity. In California, for example, the main paper is called a Complaint to Establish Parental Relationship. It gets filed along with other paperwork, which prompts the court to set a hearing date, at which time the parent can request orders for support, custody, and/or visitation. If both parents are cooperating, they may not need to appear in court and the court will enter a judgment.

Paternity cases are handled very much like divorces. The only difference is that paternity does not deal with assets and debts. Paternity cases deal only with children, legally establishing the father as the parent. Either parent can file the suit, and issues of support, custody, and visitation typically lead to orders from the court.

Unlike more conventional legal cases, contested paternity actions are decided primarily on the scientific evidence of DNA testing. Therefore, if biological fatherhood is in question, one's first step is to conduct a paternity test. If parents do not agree to the test, the court will order it. These genetic test results are often conclusive, although courts may allow contradicting evidence, such as proof that the alleged father had no physical access to the mother at the time of conception.

Custody, child support payments, and visitation schedules are often decided after paternity is established, whether contested or uncontested. Although mothers and fathers of children born to married parents have equal rights consistent with the "best interest of the child," many states favor mothers' rights when children are born to unmarried parents.

When you file your paperwork to initiate a paternity case, you will have to provide information that may seem intimate to you. Each state has its own requirements for establishing paternity, but here are examples of questions you may encounter:

> In 2003, nearly 35 percent of all births were to unmarried women, according to the Health and Human Service's National Center for Health Statistics. That's up from 11 percent in 1970, though the rate of increase has slowed since 1995, when 32 percent of births were out of wedlock. Births to unmarried teens have declined since the mid-1990s.

- When (during what time period) did you engage in sexual intercourse with the other party?
- When did you give birth to X out of wedlock?
- Are you pregnant and expect to give birth out of wedlock?
- Were you married at the time of conception?
- Has the other party acknowledged paternity and/or provided support?
- Have you applied for child support services with the local department of social services?
- Is the child a Native American subject to the Indian Child Welfare Act of 1978?
- Who has custody of the child, and what percentage of the time does each parent have custody?
- Who will provide medical/dental insurance for the child?
- What is your visitation schedule?
- What kind of parenting plan will you have?

Again, the information you'll have to provide to the court will depend on your court's specific requirements. You may have to submit a parenting plan (see chapter 4) that the court will enforce by making it an order. The plan should detail exactly how the other parent will be involved with the child or children. A visitation schedule should be set, which can simply be stated as "reasonable visitation," or you can articulate exactly when those visitations will occur (especially if there is one problem parent and you want to limit visitation). An example of a carefully worded suggested visitation schedule is the following:

> The _____ shall have visitation on the first, third, and fifth weekends of each month, commencing at 6:00 P.M. Friday and ending at 6:00 P.M. on Sunday; on (Mother's or Father's) Day, and on _____'s birthday from 9:00 A.M. until 6:00 P.M. (providing there is no conflict with regular school hours); and on alternating major holidays, comprised of Easter, Thanksgiving, Christmas Eve, and Christmas day, from 9:00 A.M. until 7:00 P.M. (Christmas Eve and Christmas day shall be considered separate holidays for the purpose of visitation). _____ is to have the children for two consecutive weeks during summer vacation. Each visit is to be confirmed at least twelve (12) hours prior to its occurrence.

Paternity papers can be filed even if the parents decide to stay together. It's always in the best interest of the child to legally establish fatherhood, so no matter what happens to the parents, the child's father has been legally acknowledged. Chapter 4 will explore how parenting plans work and why they are essential to any agreement package you submit to a court when

Some states, like Missouri, require that a paternity action be filed before a divorce if there are children of the parties who were born prior to their marriage.

children are involved. Whether you are married or not, you need a specific plan that suits the current and future needs of your children. The only way to legally enforce anything you ask the court to grant you is to create a plan and get a judge to sign it. You may, for example, be a father who wants visitation rights to your son who was born out of wedlock last year and whose mother will not let you see him. You won't be able to get a court to enforce anything until you've filed a paternity case and gotten the court to make an order. So remember: Children deserve the legal right to both parents. They also deserve a well-thought-out plan for their emotional, physical, and financial well-being.

Conclusion

You have options to consider before filing for divorce. Your particular state may limit these options, but for the most part, all states allow you to separate and obtain temporary orders for ensuring your livelihood while you and your spouse work through your differences and perhaps prepare for divorce. How you prepare for divorce is just as important as how to proceed through divorce one day at a time. Separating can be just as powerful a step as actually filing for divorce, and its impact on children who don't understand what's going on—and have no say in the matter—is huge. As mentioned, do not undervalue the importance of keeping your emotions in check through counseling or some form of therapy.

Depending on the age of your children, you may also want to consider therapy for them so they can begin to heal their pain and understand the emotions moving through them. Talk with their teachers to make sure they are continuing to do well in school and are maintaining their bonds with friends and fellow classmates. As much as you would like to withdraw from the world to settle your problems alone, they, too, may be withdrawing from their own lives but to a much greater degree. Keep an open dialogue with your children, and don't be afraid to speak sincerely to them about your situation. Be honest and realistic. You'd be surprised just how much information and emotion a young child can retain and understand, especially since that child has probably been a witness to your marriage for a long time. Just be careful not to take your frustrations and anger out on them when you really wish to direct those feelings to your spouse. Never share hatred, disgust, or negative feelings with your children about their mother or father. They don't want to pick sides and they don't want to be the football tossed between the two sides, either. Learn to recognize the signs of trouble and know when you need to put all of your efforts into listening to your children and taking care of their emotions.

Acquiring the right coping skills for separation and divorce is a process that takes patience, self-evaluation, hard work, and time. Your children will be acquiring their own set of coping skills, as well. They will carry these skills for the rest of their lives. In chapter 3, we'll give you some tips for broaching the topic of divorce with your spouse and begin to discuss how your children figure into your negotiations when it comes to custody, visitation, and support. We'll also detail how you can reach certain agreements, find a mediator if you need one, and prepare financially for divorce.

Preparing for Divorce

O nce you've decided to proceed to divorce, your next step is reaching agreements—if you can—with your spouse and filing the paperwork with the court. We cannot stress enough the importance of reaching as many agreements as you can without the help or intervention of the court. This keeps you in control of your divorce and more likely to get what you want. If the court must make decisions for you and your spouse, those decisions may not reflect your wishes and you may find yourself exceedingly disappointed and frustrated.

If you have children, you must put them first and consider where they fit into the new life that you begin to create the moment you and your spouse decide to divorce. Unfortunately, children often become financial pawns in a divorce when it comes to child custody issues. Make sure they know it is not their fault and that just because you are getting a divorce from the other parent, neither parent is divorcing the children. Remind them as often as you can that your love for them is unconditional and will not change because of the divorce. And even though one parent will move from the home, that parent will not be removed from the children's lives forever.

As briefly outlined in the previous chapters, many aspects of divorce must be considered, including custody, visitation, and support, and financial issues such as alimony, taxes, pensions, and insurance. Before you can begin to discuss these issues, however, you must have a realistic idea of where you stand financially. This chapter guides you through finding the documents and financial data you need to analyze before coming together and making decisions about who gets what and how much one may need from the other to maintain a certain

As you can imagine, the rate of divorce varies across the United States. In some states, divorce (and marriage) is rampant. In others, divorce is less common and people tend to stick it out for the long haul no matter what. Do you live in a divorce-friendly or -unfriendly state? Take your guesses: Try to list the top five states where divorce is the most common. Or on the reverse end, try to come up with the states where residents are least likely to get divorced. The answers might surprise you. (Turn to chapter 5 for the answers.)

standard of living. This will ultimately prepare you financially for your divorce and new life thereafter.

The Talk before the Negotiating

Timing is so much a part of life—including during a divorce. Timing has probably been a factor in your relationship since its beginning, and it cannot be ignored at its end. The decisions you make in your divorce, from the day you decide to divorce your spouse to the day you are unhooked legally from that person, may all come down to timing.

Not all divorces begin with two spouses who mutually decide to separate and divorce. You may want a divorce and have the added task of alerting your unsuspecting spouse about your feelings and intentions of filing for divorce. This may come as a surprise to your spouse, who had hoped you'd be able to work out your differences and repair your marriage. Do not expect to start negotiating the terms of your divorce before your spouse understands the situation and has time to recover from hearing the news that you want a divorce. If you and your spouse do mutually agree to separate, you may still need to give one another time to settle your emotions and gather your strengths before sitting down and discussing the terms of your divorce.

The time it takes to let the air clear before negotiating will differ for every couple. It will also depend on whether you and your spouse separate, for how long, and the exact condition of your relationship. This may entail weeks or months. If you can come to the negotiating table with the same patience and compassion that you practice while you and your spouse await those negotiations, you'll be in a better position for arriving at good decisions and reaching fair agreements. During your waiting period, think about what you want and how you are going to ask for it. Remember, the three most important items to consider are assets, debts, and kids (ADK). Have a plan in mind before approaching your spouse in the negotiating phase. Hopefully, your spouse will also have thought about the ADK and have a plan in mind that can meet your expectations. If not, there are ways to still reach an agreement.

Some couples may not have the luxury of waiting a while before negotiating the exact terms of their divorce. Time, for example, may not do anything to settle anger, resentment, anxiety, remorse, or any other emotion one may experience. The shock and disbelief may subside, but if your spouse cannot manage his or her emotions and there is no indication that time will help matters (and the time may just prolong an ugly and undesirable situation), then it's best to proceed to the negotiating table sooner rather than later.

> Reaching agreements with your spouse once you decide to get a divorce often begins by having a talk before the actual negotiating talk. In between these two talks you allow yourselves a cooling-off waiting period during which you and your spouse each get time to absorb the reality of your divorce and contemplate the issues that you must soon agree upon.

Whether you and your spouse decide to negotiate now or later, talk about when you both want to have that discussion and agree to the best time, place, and date. It's the talk before the actual negotiating, during which you lay out your plan and set realistic goals for proceeding. If your spouse is unwilling to discuss anything when you bring up the topic, back off and try again at a later time. At some point, however, you will have to have a general discussion about your situation and find some common ground from which you can proceed. During this general discussion, try to agree to a schedule or time frame, and be sure to address the most critical issues that must get hammered out in your divorce. You do not need to negotiate or even discuss the details of these issues (remember:

ADK), but both of you need to be aware that when you do reconvene to negotiate, these are the issues that will be discussed.

Another key point to bring up when you have this talk is your desire to avoid lawyers and the court's intervention. Relay to your spouse the value of working through your divorce alone; should you need the help of a neutral third party, you can hire a mediator to help you resolve problems. You don't want your spouse to run out and hire a lawyer out of fear, which is why the style and tone of your approach are important. Be open-minded about your spouse's initial reaction and be ready to deal with unexpected and unsettling emotions—both within yourself and in your spouse.

Once you decide when is the best time to come together and start negotiating, have a clear understanding of how you can best have that discussion. You may want to meet in a place that will not allow either one of you to start fighting and raising your voice, such as a restaurant, hotel bar, or even a library that offers conference rooms. You also do not want to have this discussion in the presence of your children, so having it at the family home may be difficult, and it may surround you with too many memories. If the thought of getting everything figured out in one long session overwhelms you, you and your spouse can decide to negotiate in one- or two-hour sessions at a time, and let the outcome of your meetings dictate how many more sessions you need to come to all of your agreements.

The Financial Portrait

Having a clear picture of your finances is essential prior to negotiating. Most every decision made during a divorce is about money, so you must know where you stand with your money—your assets and debts. This will also allow you to plan for the future as a newly single person. The longer you have been married and the more you have mixed your separate assets and debts with those of your spouse, the harder this step in the process may be, but it's an important step regardless.

Start by taking inventory of your assets, which is everything you own together with your spouse. Don't worry about assets that you owned separately before your marriage, that you inherited during your marriage, or that were gifts to you, and you alone, during your marriage. Sometimes such assets do become shared, but for purposes of this exercise, just worry about the property you know you share with your spouse. Later this chapter gives you instructions for placing values on these items. Here are the items to consider:

Total Assets (What You Own)

- ☑ Cash
- ☑ Basic bank accounts (checking and savings)
- ☑ Security deposits held by utilities or landlord
- ☑ Money market accounts
- ☑ Certificates of deposit
- ☑ Treasury bills or notes
- ☑ Safety deposit boxes
- ☑ Retirement accounts—IRAs, SEPs, 401(k)s
- ☑ Brokerage accounts (stocks and bonds, including options)
- ☑ Government bonds and securities

☑ Insurance policies, including life insurance proceeds

☑ Real estate

☑ Automobiles, boats, airplanes, other recreational vehicles

☑ Household items, furniture, jewelry, clothing (that mink coat)

☑ Books, pictures, artwork, antiques, and collectibles

☑ Records, CDs

☑ Electronics and appliances

☑ Sports/photographic/hobby equipment, firearms/gadgets

☑ Cash value in insurance policies

☑ Annuities

☑ Interest in pension or profit-sharing plans

☑ Patents, copyrights, and other intellectual property

☑ Interest in partnerships, joint ventures, or other business

☑ Stocks and interests in incorporated/unincorporated business

☑ Tools and equipment

☑ Valuable animals or livestock

☑ Money owed you

☑ Other investments or valuable property

If you and your spouse started a business or own a franchise, you'll have those assets to contend with, such as office equipment and supplies, inventory, licenses, machinery and fixtures, and accounts receivable. You will also have to figure out how you will continue to run the business—whether you decide to split it into two parts, sell the business, liquidate the business (close up shop and sell the business's assets), or sell your half to your spouse.

Hopefully, you already have your financial papers organized and ready for review. If not, this exercise will force you to put all of your financial paperwork in one place. Be sure to check your usual hiding places, such as your safety deposit box, your home office, a safe, and your desk drawer or filing cabinet at work. Find those papers that identify ownership and gather those documents into one big file. Include all deeds, titles, certificates, wills, living trusts, and other important documents.

Total Debts/Liabilities (What You Owe)

☑ Mortgage or home equity loans

☑ Credit cards

☑ Auto leases/loans

☑ Tax obligations

☑ Student or business loans

☑ Medical and dental bills

☑ Judgments against you

☑ Other personal loans or debts

You can use the first worksheet in appendix C to map out your financial portrait. The goal of this exercise is to realize what you and your spouse own and what you and your spouse still owe. You must also include your monthly overhead expenses for daily living, such as phone, utilities, cable, Internet, food, and gas. These costs will get factored in when you consider spousal and child support.

Locating all of the relevant documents may sound daunting, but this will get you organized in a manner that you should practice in your new life after divorce. There are huge benefits to having your financial paperwork orderly and accessible at any time, not just in divorce. The documents—or copies of documents—in particular that you should hunt down include the following:

- ☑ Any prenuptial or postnuptial agreement
- ☑ Ownership papers (titles, deeds, warranties)
- ☑ Real estate tax bills
- ☑ Bank statements and loan applications
- ☑ Insurance policies, including life
- ☑ Bank or broker statements regarding stocks, bonds, mutual funds, and retirement accounts
- ☑ Will and/or trusts, including a living trust
- ☑ Business papers that reflect profit and loss for any business you and your spouse own
- ☑ Partnership agreements
- ☑ Articles of incorporation

Once you find all of your documents, make extra copies of them.

Living Expenses

The next step is to create a more formal income and expense report for yourself. This will show how much income you make and where your money goes on a daily or monthly basis. Both you and your spouse will have to do this exercise and arrive at numbers for each of your net incomes. Your income must include all sources of income, including take-home pay, income from rentals, investments, pensions, inheritance, trusts, bonuses, child support from a previous marriage, and any other source. Appendix C contains an additional copy of the worksheet in Figure 3.1. If you've already done the first worksheet (also in appendix C), you can use that to complete this one, which is a little more tailored.

Your expense worksheet will probably be longer and more detailed than your income report. Many household expenses are shared, such as rent or mortgage payments, utilities, car payments, cable, and phone bills. Don't forget to include those periodic bills, such as insurance premiums, tuition, taxes, subscriptions, and averages for entertainment, holiday, and miscellaneous expenses. You can also break down your expenses into those owed by you, by your spouse, and by both of you jointly. For example, you may—once you complete the overall worksheet—do another exercise and create an income and expense report with three columns. One column will be labeled "Wife," another will be "Husband," and the last will be "H/W" or your jointly held assets and obligations. However, start with the worksheet in Figure 3.1 and see where it takes you.

TOTAL-GROSS WAGES RECV'D LAST 12 MO.	$	
YOUR **MONTHLY** INCOME & list your average monthly income (divide total income by 12)	**Last month**	**Average** (divide your total inc. & taxes by 12)
Gross **MONTHLY INCOME** (BEFORE taxes)	$	$
Overtime - gross		
Commissions or bonuses		
Public assistance (TANF, SSI, GA/GR)		
Spousal support ❐ from this marriage/ ❐ from different marriage		
Pension/retirement payments		
Social Security retirement payments (not SSI)		
❐ Disability ❐ Social Security ❐ SDI ❐ private		
Unemployment compensation		
Workers compensation		
Other		
INVESTMENT INCOME		
Dividends/interest		
Rental property income		
Trust income		
Other (specify)		
SELF EMPLOYMENT INCOME - after business expenses		
I am the ❐ owner/sole owner ❐ partner ❐ other		
# of years in this business_____ Name of business		
Type of business _____		
ADDITIONAL INCOME		
other money you received in the last 12 months describe_____		
DEDUCTIONS	LAST MONTH	
Mandatory Union Dues (monthly)	$	
Mandatory retirement/pension fund contributions	$	
Court ordered child support (NOT this relationship)	$	
ASSETS	VALUE	
Cash/checking/savings/credit union/money market etc	$	
stocks/bonds/other assets you can sell	$	
all other property ❐ real or ❐ personal (less loans)	$	
	$	
	$	

Figure 3.1 Income and Expense Worksheet

List all persons living in your home whose **expenses you pay and are included below** (include their income)

NAME	AGE	RELATIONSHIP	INCOME

Other people living in your home

NAME	AGE	RELATIONSHIP	INCOME

MONTHLY EXPENSES

EXPENSE	AMOUNT	EXPENSE	AMOUNT
RENT { } MORTGAGE { } If mortgage average principle average interest real prop. taxes home insurance Maintenance and repair	$_____ $_____ $_____ $_____ $_____	EDUCATION - (specify)	$
HEALTH CARE not paid by insurance	$	ENTERTAINMENT, GIFTS, VACATION	$
CHILD CARE	$	AUTO TRANSPORTATION EXP. (gas, repairs etc)	$
GROCERIES AND household supplies	$	LIFE/ACCIDENT INS.	$
FOOD - EATING OUT		SAVINGS AND INVESTMENTS	$
UTILITIES	$	CHARITABLE CONTRIB.	$
TELEPHONE/Cell/Email	$	MONTHLY PAYMENTS listed below - ENTER TOTAL HERE	$
LAUNDRY AND CLEANING		OTHER - (specify)	$
CLOTHING	$		$
	$		$

MONTHLY INSTALLMENT PAYMENTS

CREDITOR	PAYMENT FOR	MONTHLY PAYMENT	BALANCE	DATE LAST PAID
		$	$	
		$	$	
		$	$	
		$	$	
		$	$	
		$	$	
		$	$	

Figure 3.1 (Continued).

COMPLETE THIS PAGE **IF CHILD SUPPORT** IS AN ISSUE

HEALTH INS. FOR MY CHILDREN { } IS   { } IS NOT AVAILABLE THRU MY EMPLOYER
            MONTHLY COST PAID BY ME $_____
            NAME OF CARRIER _____
            ADDRESS   _____
                               _____
            POLICY #   _____

% OF TIME EACH PARENT HAS PRIMARY PHYSICAL RESPONSIBILITY FOR THE CHILDREN
       MOTHER _____%   FATHER _____%

ADDITIONAL CHILD SUPPORT TO BE REQUESTED

{ } Child care costs related to employment (also state amount currently paid and by who)

{ } Uninsured health care costs for children (state monthly amount and paid by who)

{ } Special educational needs of the children - describe

{ } Travel expense for visitation (amount and who pays now)

{ } Hardship deductions - (expenses that are extreme hardships)

Extraordinary health care   Amount paid: $ _____ need to pay until _____
Uninsured catastrophic losses $_____ need to pay until _____
Living expenses of <u>dependent</u>
 minor children who live with you $_____ need to pay until _____
(list names and ages)

Figure 3.1   (Continued).

Numbers don't lie. Once you have a clear picture of your finances, you'll be better equipped to not only negotiate but understand your status with regard to your financial security. Can you afford to live the way you do? Will you need to consider a new job or career? What kinds of adjustments will you have to make? These are hard questions to ask yourself, but they are essential.

Looking at the numbers may be alarming, but it's a necessary and healthy step in moving forward with your divorce. Numbers are hard to fake, so much of your negotiating can be facilitated by referring to the concrete numbers and agreeing on how they fit into your and your spouse's future lives. These numbers compel you to consider what your life will be like after divorce and how you will adjust to your new financial situation. No one escapes from a divorce without making a few changes in the way he or she lived when married. But that doesn't mean you cannot rebuild your life and get back to the way you lived during your marriage.

As you arrive at those numbers, your mind should already be planning your future. You may need to consider new living arrangements, a new job, and a cheaper standard of living. Think about what you are willing to lose or give up in your divorce and what you want to ask for and are willing to fight for.

Projecting Your Future

A list of goals should accompany your income and expense worksheets. On this list, write down what you want to get out of your divorce and the reasons why. Also include an estimate for your future living expenses. This may entail another round of income and expense reporting for yourself using figures that you anticipate in your postdivorce life. You may find yourself writing down goals unrelated to your divorce, such as more personal goals about your potential to earn a bigger income in the future and where you want to be in five years. Don't restrict your goal writing. See what comes out of you and don't be afraid of what emerges on paper.

You may have to revisit this list of divorce priorities a few times, because initially you may bring a lot of anger and spite into the exercise. When it comes time to ask the court to grant you your wishes, the judge may ask you for the reasons behind your requests, so be ready to defend them. All of your requests should be within reason.

Now may be the time to start opening accounts in your own name so you can begin to set aside money for yourself and get used to managing money on your own. If you've never had good credit in your name (without the help of your spouse), now is also the time to build your own credit history, so think about opening a credit card in your own name, too. If you do have a lot of shared credit card debt with your spouse already on joint cards, you may not necessarily want to have another credit card. But you can notify the three big credit bureaus—Equifax, Experian, and TransUnion—that you want each of them to establish a credit file in your own name. Request that if you are named as Mrs. Jonathan Sample, you'd rather they refer to you as Judy Sample. Be careful if you and your spouse have racked up a poor credit history. Before you decide how to build your credit and maintain financial health, it's wise to obtain copies of your credit report from each of the three credit bureaus.

The Big Three Credit Bureaus

Equifax (www.equifax.com)

- To order a credit report, call 800-685-1111.
- To place a fraud alert, call 888-766-0008.
- Or mail correspondence to Equifax Credit Information Services, Inc., P.O. Box 740241, Atlanta, GA 30374.

Experian (www.experian.com)

- To order a credit report, call 888-397-3742, or write to P.O. Box 9066, Allen, TX 75013.
- To dispute information in your report, call the number displayed on your report or request a dispute online. You can also start by calling the main line.

TransUnion (www.tuc.com)

- To order a credit report, call 800-916-8800, or order online at the web site. Written correspondence (general inquiries) can be sent to TransUnion LLC, P.O. Box 2000, Chester, PA 19022.
- To dispute information in your report, call 800-916-8800 or refer to the web site for both online and mail-in dispute correspondence.

Getting Your Credit Report

Credit reports used to come with a small fee, unless you were unemployed, were on welfare, or were recently denied credit, or if your report was inaccurate because of fraud. New laws, however, make it easier to obtain credit reports for free once a year; the federal government initiated the program that allows everyone to receive a free credit report from each of the three credit agencies. Go to www.annualcreditreport.com for more information. You can also request your report by calling 877-322-8228, or by mail by filling out the request form online and mailing it to Annual Credit Report Request Service, P.O. Box 105281, Atlanta, GA 30348-5281.

It's a good idea to check your credit at least once a year, looking for mistakes and errors. In preparation for getting a divorce, it's imperative that you see what's on your credit report.

Good FICO = Good Credit. Another site to check out is www.myfico.com. In this information-based economy, FICO scores are essential personal information. FICO stands for Fair, Isaac and Company, which develops the mathematical formula used to obtain snapshots of your credit risk at a given point in time. These scores are the most widely used and recognized credit ratings. FICO scores are calculated by the three major credit reporting agencies (Experian, TransUnion, and Equifax), and your score determines how easily you can obtain credit or apply for a loan. Factors that determine your FICO score include payment history, amount owed, length of credit history, new credit, and types of credit in use. FICO scores are like SAT scores for adults. Just as SAT scores facilitate the passage into college and beyond, FICO scores facilitate the passage into adulthood with the purchase of large assets (think houses) and good lines of credit (think credit cards and loans).

Having your (and perhaps your spouse's) credit scores available will help you make decisions and fiscally sound plans. You should know what the credit bureaus say about you and your spouse, as this will affect just about everything you try to do in the future when it comes to money. Your credit report can also tell you whether you should distance yourself from your spouse's finances as much as possible or use your spouse's creditworthiness to help establish good credit in your name, so when you do break away from your spouse you'll have the ability to apply for loans and credit with fewer hassles.

Another alternative to getting a new credit card in your own name for building credit is to apply for a small unsecured bank loan. The loan is unsecured because you are not putting up any asset, such as a home, as collateral to back the loan. If you do not qualify for such a loan (which usually will depend on your relationship with the bank), you can ask for a *secured* loan, which means you prepay the loan with a cash payment. These types of loans can be small, such as $500 or $1,000. With secured loans, the bank will require that you keep a certain minimum amount in a savings account to back the loan, or purchase a certificate of deposit. If you default on the loan, the bank will take the money in the account or the CD as payment. Other types of credit to consider include store cards, a gasoline card, or a prepaid cell phone plan.

> The goal is to establish credit in your name—and your name only. Be sure to use any new cards wisely, and avoid getting into any new debt by failing to pay off all bills each and every month. Use your credit to build a history, not to amass debt.

You can learn how to read a credit report by contacting the credit bureaus or simply doing a search online for advice. In addition to your debts and payment history, credit reporting agencies also provide general data (name, social security number, marital status, addresses past and present), employer's name and address, inquiries of your credit file, and public record information such as bankruptcies and liens. Credit reporting agencies do not, however, maintain files regarding your race, religion, medical history, or criminal record, if any.

Review your report carefully to make sure no unauthorized charges were made on your existing accounts and that no fraudulent accounts or loans were established in your name. Should there be errors on your report, contact the credit bureaus and start the process of correcting the information. Having erroneous negative information about you on your file should be cleared up as soon as possible because such information can do long-term damage on your report and will complicate your attempts to repay your debts or proceed in a bankruptcy. You can find information about reporting errors on the Federal Trade Commission's web site (www.ftc.gov) or by contacting the credit bureaus.

Choosing a Credit Card

When you are ready to apply for a credit card in your name, don't pick the first solicitation that comes in your mail. Do your research and find one that fits your needs. Understand the credit terms and conditions of any card you choose. Compare terms and fees before you agree to a certain card. Know how a particular credit card company calculates balances, including finance charges, transaction fees, and annual percentage rates. The way in which credit card companies compute balances when you maintain a balance over time can get confusing. Do your best to understand your statements; if you pay off every balance each month, your statements should be easy to read. Watch out for cash advance features, as they are often costly and don't come with grace periods for payment.

Credit card companies want your business, so you have more leverage than you think. You can negotiate interest rates and limits. Calling the credit card companies and talking with a representative over the phone easily accomplishes this. If you encounter trouble

Once you have a credit card, continue to negotiate terms for its use. If you misplace a bill and fail to submit your payment in time, you can argue your finance charge. Don't be afraid to get on the phone and argue any fees you find on your bill, unless you've chosen a card that has an annual fee. Explain to them that you missed your payment by mistake and never meant to miss it. If you're in good standing with the company, they should remove that charge. Or you can threaten to cancel the card.

negotiating, hang up and try another. There are hundreds of credit card companies seeking customers. One will respond to your wishes. You can find the best credit card rate at www.bankrate.com. For more general information, check out www.smartmoney.com/debt.

To assist you in good money management, you can find lots of information and advice online, in a bookstore, and at community centers or colleges that offer classes. Learn money managing skills by taking classes or self-teaching through books, seminars, audiotapes, and even friends and contacts.

Coming to Agreement

You and your spouse have a lot to discuss by now. You'll have to decide how to divide your assets and debts—a "he gets/she gets" list. This is not the easiest task, and this is where you may need the help of outside third parties. If you thought gathering all of your documents and information was exhausting, dividing up assets (and debts) requires patience, time,

---

 I Don't Understand What You Mean By . . .

Tangible property   Tangible assets are things that are literally tangible—things that you can touch. They are physical articles (things) as distinguished from things you can't necessarily touch such as rights, patents, copyrights, and franchises. Examples of tangible property are homes, cars, furniture, electronics, jewelry, and household goods. These items have value in and of themselves.

Intangible property   Assets that do have value but that you cannot necessarily touch, such as stock in a company, retirement benefits, a pension, or bonds.

Separate property   Assets that you own independently of your spouse. In community-property states (California, Texas, Arizona, Idaho, Louisiana, New Mexico, Nevada, Washington, and Alaska by agreement), separate property is any property owned by one spouse that he or she acquired before marriage, by inheritance, as a gift, or as property the spouses agree is separate property.

Marital property   Assets that are owned by both spouses jointly. These are typically assets that you acquire together during your marriage. In community-property states, no matter who contributed more to the acquisition of an asset, the asset becomes half owned by one spouse and half owned by the other. A few exceptions may apply. For example, separate property brought into the marriage (e.g., a house) can become a gift to the marriage if it is deeded to both spouses and becomes marital property. In many states, the appreciated value of separate assets may be considered marital even though the base value of the asset at the time of the marriage may be considered separate.

thought, and debate. How you decide to divide your stuff has both short-term and long-term consequences for you and your spouse.

In chapter 6 we'll help you understand how assets like pension plans, retirement accounts, stocks, and bonds should be divided. These are *intangible* assets. Here we focus on the *tangible* items you and your spouse have. These are the things you own that you can literally touch and that have intrinsic value, such as a house, a car, a set of golf clubs.

> Even property held in the sole name of one spouse is considered to be owned by both spouses if it meets the definition of marital property in the state where the parties are getting divorced.

Before you can come to an agreement about your assets and debts, you must have a clear understanding of who owns what—and who is responsible for what. As we outlined in chapter 1, the property laws of your state will determine how your assets are designated legally, but any prenuptial or postnuptial agreement in place can change that designation. You also have lots of room to negotiate. You can decide to take one shared asset while giving your spouse another. The property laws may apply only if you land in court and a judge must decide who gets what, using state-specific guidelines.

Placing a Value on Your Assets

Assigning a dollar value to your assets is your next step. If you started a list of your assets using the preceding checklist, go back to that list and try to place a value on each item. Some things are easier to value than others. For large-ticket items, such as a home or collectible, you may need the help of a neutral appraiser or a certified public accountant (CPA). Outside help is beneficial when you and your spouse cannot agree on a fair market value for a certain item. Use the worksheet in Figure 3.2 to record your main marital assets.

Fair market values are what you want to get. Consider the fair market value of any item as the price you would get if you didn't have to sell it and you had a willing buyer. The

> Depending on your state, you may have to submit a declaration of disclosure, which lists full and accurate information about your property, debts, income, and expenses to the other party (your spouse). Spouses must always be completely open and honest in their dealings with each other. In California, for example, within 60 days of serving the petition, each spouse must serve on the other (by mail is easiest) a preliminary declaration of disclosure. This lists all assets and debts in which the spouse has an interest, along with a completed income and expense declaration. At or before the time you enter into any final agreement for support or the division of property, each spouse serves on the other spouse a final declaration of disclosure. In other words, you are telling the court that you have complied with the disclosure law. In some counties, you and your spouse can waive the final declaration of disclosure in your marital settlement agreement (MSA).
>
> Even if your state does not require a declaration of disclosure, it's a good idea to create a document that details your assets and debts and who is responsible for what. You and your spouse should share this list, agree to its details, initial, date, and sign it. Therefore, if there is any question in the future about your assets, debts, and any other items you feel it is important to list, you have a document to prove what you and your spouse agreed to.

ASSET	APPROXIMATE VALUE
CASH	
BANK ACCOUNTS	
SECURITY DEPOSITS	
MONEY MARKET ACCOUNTS	
CERTIFICATES OF DEPOSIT	
TREASURY BILLS OR NOTES	
SAFETY DEPOSIT BOX	
RETIREMENT ACCOUNTS	
BROKERAGE ACCOUNTS	
GOV'T BONDS AND SECURITIES	
REAL ESTATE	
AUTOMOBILES, BOATS, RECREATIONAL VEHICLES	
HOUSEHOLD ITEMS, FURNITURE	
JEWELRY/CLOTHING	
BOOKS, PICTURES, ARTWORK, ANTIQUES, COLLECTIBLES	
RECORDS, CDS	
ELECTRONICS & APPLIANCES	
SPORTS, PHOTO & HOBBY EQUIPMENT, FIREARMS, GADGETS	
CASH VALUE IN INSURANCE POLICIES	
ANNUITIES	
INTEREST IN PENSION OR PROFIT SHARING PLANS	
PATENTS, COPYRIGHTS, TRADEMARKS	
INTEREST IN PARTNERSHIPS, JOINT VENTURES, BUSINESSES	
TOOLS & EQUIPMENT	
VALUABLE ANIMALS OR LIVESTOCK	
MONEY OWED YOU	
OTHER INVESTMENTS OR VALUABLE PROPERTY	

Figure 3.2 List of Your Marital Assets (Stuff)

Internet can play a big role in finding honest values. You can find fair values for cars, for example, by reading classifieds (in your local newspaper), an auto trader publication, or Kelley Blue Books, or by checking online at sites like www.Edmunds.com, www.eBay.com, or www.kbb.com (this is Kelley Blue Book's site). Given the vast number of items bought and sold today on the Web, online auction and retail sites can provide values for just about anything these days. And if you don't have easy access to the Internet, then the old-fashioned way of looking through your local classifieds or trade magazines or calling pawnshops works. (Hopefully, you won't need to do this kind of homework for all of your assets, but for those items that you either do not know how to evaluate or for which you and your spouse cannot reach an agreement, there are many options that will give you an answer.)

> If attorneys and/or a judge enter the scene to help you divide your property, don't assume that this will get you more of what you want or think you deserve. Once you let others intervene in your agreement, you become vulnerable to your state's property laws, any property division laws practiced by the court, and any additional prejudices or preferences practiced by the judge who hears and rules on your case.

Once you figure out the values for all of your assets, you and your spouse must agree to split up the value of those assets. This can be done by using the property law or divorce law guidelines of your state, or by agreeing on some kind of fair division system with your spouse. Coming up with a fair way to divide your assets with your spouse is the best way to go, because if you rely on the court's ruling, you and your spouse are less likely to get what you want.

The Elements of Fair Asset Division

You have a lot to consider once you get down to the nitty-gritty details of deciding who gets what. Keep your overall goals in mind when you work through these decisions, including how you plan to live after your divorce and what your financial needs may be now and in the future. A checklist of elements to include in your decision-making process should consist of the following:

- ☑ Your age, health, and the length of your marriage
- ☑ How much you contribute(d) to your marriage, your combined assets, and your debts
- ☑ Your current standard of living
- ☑ How much you and your spouse earn now
- ☑ How much you and your spouse can potentially make in the future (future earning power)
- ☑ The value of your separate assets

These factors take into account a wide range of situations. For example, when you consider your contribution to your marriage, you must include all forms of contributions to a marriage, which may entail supporting a spouse through graduate or professional school, being a stay-at-home parent, paying the bills, postponing higher education while your spouse pursued a further degree and began a practice, or taking an extra job to help pay for a spouse's entrepreneurial endeavors. Whether you contributed significantly to the household debt

A good rule of thumb at the negotiating table: Don't nickel-and-dime every single asset. You have assets that you know you want to keep or that you cannot live without. Fight for those assets and don't worry so much about losing a few assets that you don't really care about. Worry about the big stuff, and let go of the rest. If the home is something you insist on getting, focus your efforts on keeping that asset but be willing to give up other items—or hand over a huge chunk of change—for the right to keep the house. In other words, pick your battles. Don't lose sight of the big picture. The same holds true for the issues: Pick the issues you think are most important to you and fight for them. (Your children should be among those issues.)

through credit card abuse, poor business choices, or perpetual risky investments and money squandering or gambling will affect your ability to get what you want. Moreover, your ability to make money both now and in the future will have an impact on a judge's decision to give you more or less from the settlement. As can be expected, if you earn less or have the potential to earn less, you will be entitled to more from the property division. A judge may also factor in your education level, mental and physical health, and any other factors that affect your ability to earn a good living.

In the end—no matter where you live—a judge wants to arrive at a fair and equitable distribution of assets. (This means you should try to arrive at a fair and equitable division of assets before needing the court's help.) The longer you are married and the more each of you has contributed to the marriage overall, the more likely you'll get a distribution that's pretty much 50/50. A judge will do his or her best to preserve both your and your spouse's standard of living, assuming your spouse has not done anything too egregious and does not need to be punished for abusing money, carrying enormous debt, or committing some act that inserts fault into your divorce. For example, in *Faram v. Gervitz Faram,* a 1995 Texas litigated case, the husband was awarded only 27.1 percent, while the wife got 72.9 percent of their shared estate, due to the husband's violent and abusive nature, his steady income, and his waste of their shared estate after the separation.

Creating Your Own Way of Dividing Property

As already stated, creating your own system for dividing property is the best way to a mutually fair and reasonable settlement. But you still must have some guidelines, for which an understanding of your state's laws may help. If you end up having to use a judge to settle property disputes, he or she will use your state's laws and property division guidelines to determine what is fair and equitable. Always remember: Focus on the assets that are most dear to you and that you want. Pick your battles when you come to the negotiating table. Be willing to lose a few items that don't mean much to you if letting them go means you get to keep what you really want.

Non-Community-Property States. If you live in a non-community-property state, you are entitled to your fair share of your marital assets. This can mean 50/50 for some assets, but 60/40 or 30/70 for other assets, depending on whatever you (or a judge) thinks is fair, given your particular circumstances. If you're having a hard time dividing assets, it's best to follow the same guidelines that a judge in your state would use. If you're negotiating with your

Among the myths perpetuated in the 1980s was the one that said the average standard of living of divorced women declines 73 percent, while that of a divorced man rises a whopping 42 percent. This poorly founded but then-famous divorce statistic was broadcast far and wide by the media and was the prop upon which much of the child support legislation of the 1980s rested. This statistic, however, was fundamentally wrong, and when sociologists revisited the test, they arrived at new numbers: a 27 percent decrease in standard of living for women and a 10 percent increase for men in the first year after divorce.

spouse toward an agreement, you can split your stuff however you want (assuming you can both agree), but adhering to the same guidelines a judge would use is usually easier—and it prevents serious arguments.

Community-Property States. If you live in a community-property state, the law says you are entitled to a 50 percent interest in all assets acquired during your marriage—no matter who paid for most of those assets. A judge, however, may use some leeway when deciding who gets what and go beyond the 50/50 exact split to take other circumstances into consideration. A judge, in fact, can divide property at his or her discretion such that it does not matter whether you live in a community-property state. However, if you live in California, Louisiana, or New Mexico, a judge is more likely to adhere to the strict 50/50 rule. As with splitting in a non-community-property state, you can negotiate the split with your spouse however you both like, but using the same guidelines as a judge would use in your state may alleviate some of the problems you might encounter in your negotiations.

You do not need to swap apples for apples in your division of property. You can, for example, allow your spouse to take the antique bedroom armoire if you want to take the online investment account—assuming they are of similar value. If you feel that the time you spent raising the children and delaying your reentry into the workforce has value, then you can argue that you deserve more than a swap of one item for another. For example, you can ask for a specific amount of cash as payment for all your years of service in your marriage. We'll visit the issues related to pension funds and so-called qualified domestic relations orders (QDROs) in chapter 6. These orders permit a spouse to take a certain share of a pension or retirement fund based on the number of years married.

Use the worksheet in Figure 3.3 to write down your "he gets/she gets" ideas. You can make copies of this worksheet and redo your list through your negotiations.

Don't underestimate the value of advice from a certified public accountant, tax advisor, or financial planner. For couples who share a large estate (they have lots of assets), these specialists can further assist you in understanding how your division of property will ultimately affect you and your spouse in the long term. They may also be able to analyze your current situation so you can more fairly divide that property. Sometimes, a couple's estate can be so large as to make it impossible to predict how a division of those assets will affect each one in the future. But with special financial software tools, mathematical models, and personal expertise, the advice of a professional trained in evaluating a couple's specific situation can be beneficial.

Example: 1999 Honda Civic, VIN # 1234567

ASSET	APPROX. VALUE	TO WIFE	TO HUSBAND
	$		

Figure 3.3 He Gets/She Gets List

Who Gets the House?

The family home can be the hardest asset to part with or abandon. Homes become such a part of family life that they sometimes become members of the family, like people. People also tie so many emotions to a home that it can be hard to separate the emotional decisions from the financial ones at divorce.

If you'll have primary custody of the children, you may want to remain in the home so that you minimize the impact on them. But to do so, you must make sure that this is a financially realistic endeavor. With potentially one less earner contributing equally to the home and its maintenance, you must decide if you can handle the future costs related to keeping the home.

You basically have three options: (1) You and your spouse sell the house, (2) you and your spouse keep the house with one person remaining in the house, or (3) one person keeps the house and agrees to buy out the other spouse. All of these options have different but serious financial consequences to both spouses. Given the costs related to getting divorced, some couples decide to sell a home and try to take some money from it to help give them a cushion in their new lives. Selling a home is sometimes the only option for some couples who cannot afford to keep a home and get through a divorce at the same time. Unless you are certain that you know exactly what you want to do with the home, your first step should be to find out how much your home is worth (or how much *equity* you have in your home, which is the money value of your home that does not include the lender's portion of the value). To find out this value, look at your lender's statement and compare what you owe on the mortgage or loan to what you could get today if you sold the house. In other words, consider your home's sale price less what you owe. You can find current purchase prices by asking local real estate agents or searching online for similar homes in your area. (You can also hire an appraiser from your bank, but this will cost you.)

For couples that have considerable assets, one spouse may take the home if the other receives an asset of equal value. Or one spouse can buy out the other's interest in the home over time by receiving a warranty deed from the spouse who will give up his or her interest. The spouse who assumes the mortgage loan must give the other spouse a deed of trust that says the mortgage will be paid by that one spouse. Generally, a mortgage company will hold both spouses liable on a debt if both signed the mortgage originally, and that mortgage company may proceed against a spouse even though one spouse took responsibility for the debt in their divorce settlement. Because of this possibility, it's best to have the mortgage

If your spouse asks to keep the home and buy your interest from you over time, you have to be careful about your spouse defaulting on the loan in the future with your name still tied to the original mortgage or deed. When discussing your agreement to sell your interest, you can ask for certain provisions to be inserted, such as a *hold harmless agreement,* which will help protect you in the event your spouse defaults and the mortgage lender comes after you. With a hold harmless provision, you retain the right to sue your former spouse for money you owe the original lender. You may never get this money, but at least you do your best to protect yourself from the start. You can also request special language in your agreement that, in the event your former spouse defaults, will allow you to remove your former spouse from the home, rent the home to someone else, or sell it in order to get rid of your legal and financial responsibility still tied to the home.

Real Estate Terminology

Equity   The money value of your property, such as a home, that does not include the lender's portion of the value. Example: Your home is worth $250,000. You owe your lender $200,000; therefore, your equity is $50,000.

Interest   Your financial right, title, or legal share in something, such as a piece of land or a business. Example: You and your wife own a home in a community-property state. You have 50 percent interest in your house. Your wife has the other 50 percent interest.

Foreclosure   The forced sale of real estate to pay off a loan on which the owner of the property has defaulted (payments haven't been made).

Deed of trust   A document that pledges real property to secure a loan. The state of Georgia calls these documents a "deed to secure debt." The property is deeded by the titleholder (trustor) to a trustee (often a title or escrow company), which holds the title in trust for the beneficiary (the lender of the money).

Security interest   A generic term for the property rights of a lender or creditor whose right to collect a debt is secured by property or asset. Example: Your mortgage company has a security interest in your home. The lender can take the security (the house) if payments are not made.

refinanced to get the one spouse's name off. The spouse who takes on the mortgage must be careful when making this decision and factor in all the costs linked to keeping and maintaining the home—taxes, upkeep, mortgage payments, insurance, and so on. Speaking with a tax or accounting specialist when considering this option is a good idea.

Because of the complications that can arise with one spouse taking on responsibility for a mortgage, it's best to have one spouse refinance the mortgage to get the other spouse's name off and then transfer ownership of the property completely to the spouse who will be keeping the house. (This is usually done via a quitclaim deed that gets filed with the county land record's office.) Although you can include a provision whereby one spouse accepts all liability on the debt (in terms of the other), it does not bind the mortgage company, which will sue both spouses if their names are on the mortgage.

Some couples with children will do anything to keep the home and allow the children to grow up in the same place. If both of you decide to keep the same amount of interest in the property for the sake of keeping the home and selling it later or allowing children to remain until they become legal adults, it's wise to draft a document that sets out your arrangement clearly. Both of you must remain responsible for the home, whether its mortgage has already been paid off or not. Items to address in this agreement include the following:

- Who remains in the home

- How much interest each spouse retains

- How the costs related to the home will be paid each month, including mortgage, insurance, major and minor repairs, and general upkeep (e.g., gardening, trash removal, city taxes)

Transferring Ownership of Assets

For small assets to which there is no paperwork attached, you will not need to do anything but give (or accept from) your spouse that asset and call it a day. However, for larger assets, to which you have a deed, title, or some other formal paperwork, you'll need to fill out and submit extra paperwork that recognizes the transfer of ownership. To transfer titles to homes, you simply create a new deed and register it with the county land records office where the property is located. In the case of bank or brokerage accounts, contact the agent or company with whom you deal for that particular asset and inquire about renaming your accounts to reflect how you and your spouse will be dividing the asset. For cars, contact the Department of Motor Vehicles to change the name on the title. All of these places will have specific rules and procedures to follow.

- How the property taxes will be paid
- When, if, and how the home will be sold

The costs related to the upkeep of a home can be huge. Couples used to sharing these costs during a marriage might not understand how much effort keeping a home can be until one is trying to do it all on his or her own. Mortgage and taxes are one chunk of change, but another chunk of change must go to the daily, monthly, and yearly repair and maintenance costs, which can vary widely from year to year. Utilities, water, sewage, trash removal, city taxes, insurance, and other related costs of homeownership are often forgotten, as these are generally larger bills for homeowners than for renters.

Whatever you and your spouse decide to do with your home, make sure that the terms of your decision are clearly indicated in your divorce agreement. If one spouse takes on the responsibility of taking care of the home and the mortgage, and hopes to buy out the other spouse over time, this option should especially be clearly spelled out in the divorce agreement. That way, should there be any problems in the future related to the home and its loan, creditors who attempt to go after the spouse who gave up his or her interest in the home will have at least one way to defend him- or herself.

Who Takes Care of the Debts?

If you're like most divorcing couples, you do have some debts . . . and you may have a lot of debts. In fact, your debts may outweigh your assets, so this is where the true debate about who gets what (debt) begins. To review the two kinds of debts you probably have:

1. *Secured debt:* Debts where the assets securing the debt can be repossessed or foreclosed on, such as your home mortgage, car loan, or rented furniture. A secured creditor is one who holds an item of yours as security for the debt. The bank that loaned you the money to buy your house holds a mortgage or trust deed lien on your house as security for the loan; therefore, the mortgage company is a *secured creditor.*

2. *Unsecured debt:* A debt that is not tied to any asset. Credit card debts are classic unsecured debts. Others include personal loans and medical bills. An unsecured creditor is one who holds no security or collateral for the loan. In other words, your credit card company cannot reclaim the things you've purchased on the card to help pay for the

money it is owed. Unsecured debts generally are characterized as those debts for which credit was extended based solely on the creditor's assessment of your future ability to pay.

If money was ever tight and you and/or your spouse used your credit cards to pay for everyday living, such as food, gas, vacations, holiday gifts, or eating out, you may have a lot of unsecured credit card debt to contend with. In a divorce, such debt can create more conflict and friction, compounding your problems. Just as you negotiate how you want to deal with your assets, you must do the same with your debts. This may entail any of the following:

- *Paying off all of your marital debts* with money generated through your divorce, such as through the *sale of your home* or other assets.

- *Paying off all of your marital debts* by using *shared funds or savings* before your divorce is final.

- *Dividing the debts* as you would the assets. Each of you takes a fair share of the debts and is responsible for paying those debts off. For example, if two credit cards contain a similar dollar amount owed, each of you takes one card and becomes responsible for it. However, if one spouse accepts more assets than the other, that division does not have to be equal; the spouse who keeps more of the assets must also agree to keep more of the debt. The spouse who accepts fewer assets can also accept less debt.

- *Paying off all of your marital debts after your divorce* through an agreement that clearly states how and when both of you will fulfill your duties of contributing to the debt payoff. You also don't know how your relationship will change after your divorce, making it harder to communicate and cooperate in taking care of the old—and haunting—debt.

Your state will dictate who is responsible for debts incurred during a separation period. Most states' laws say that all debts incurred during a marriage—whether or not you are separated—are joint until a divorce is final. But some states do consider debts from a separation as a separate category of debt, unless that debt resulted from basic living expenses such as food, shelter, and clothing.

> No matter what your divorce agreement says, creditors can still come after both you and your spouse for assets originally tied to both of you. A divorce cannot sever your financial and legal responsibility to a debt incurred during your marriage. Marital debt can survive a divorce and remain marital debt in the eyes of the creditors.

If a judge must intervene and make the decisions regarding your debts for you, he or she will employ the same rules and guidelines that would be used for the division of assets. You should not, however, be responsible for any debts that your spouse incurred before your marriage. If your spouse squandered money during your marriage, this can help sway a judge to rule in your favor, giving you the benefit of fewer debts. A judge will also take into consideration the ability of each of you to pay down the debts.

Finding a Mediator to Help Out

Coming to an agreement about your assets and debts can be a challenge. We haven't even begun to discuss the issues of alimony and child support, which we'll tackle in chapter 4.

If you're finding yourself arguing to no end before getting to the point of asking for financial support in the form of spousal or child support, now may be the time to get a mediator to help out.

Mediators help you and your spouse get over the emotional barriers to negotiation and help you devise a sensible divorce agreement that meets the needs of both of you. Unlike lawyers, mediators work with both spouses at the same time. They don't represent the individual spouses' interests the way a lawyer does. Instead, mediators facilitate an ongoing negotiation between the spouses which, in well over 80 percent of cases, results in an agreement that is satisfactory to both sides.

Mediators are neutral third parties who will work hard to get you and your spouse to come to a mutual understanding through cooperation and problem solving.

> Mediators do not provide legal advice. While they sometimes do referee bitter debates and arguments, their goals are to keep the discussion moving forward in an organized and methodical manner. They can provide legal information, but they will in no way act as lawyers, take sides, or antagonize your efforts to reach a solution to your disagreement. Mediators are like coaches, providing the path on which you can more easily reach your own personal goals in your divorce.

Who They Are and What They Do

Mediators come in all shapes and sizes. They can be volunteers, counselors, mental health professionals, financial advisors, members of the clergy, or social workers—and they can also be attorneys. But if an attorney takes on the role of mediator, he or she cannot give any legal advice. Mediators do not make decisions for you—they facilitate the decision-making process for you by engendering an environment conducive to you and your spouse getting along and working through your most troubling issues.

Your mediators will set ground rules, articulate the issues you want to resolve, and try to find the common ground from which you can reach an agreement with your spouse. Your mediator can also set an agenda, and once he or she gets to know how you and your spouse communicate and function, your mediator can set a schedule or agenda that maps out your mediation work from beginning to end. You may need one mediation session or you may need many. It will just depend on how many issues you have to resolve and how near or far you are from resolving them. As a process, mediation is structured, but it is nonbinding without the consent of the disputants and/or a court of law.

Not all mediators are the same, nor do they structure mediation sessions the same way, because there are different styles of mediation. The typical stages of a problem-solving style of mediation are as follows:

1. The opening stage in which the mediator describes the meaning of mediation, the mediator's role (impartiality, confidentiality, etc.), and a bit about what to expect from the process.

2. Each client has a few minutes of uninterrupted time to share his or her views about the dispute.

3. An exchange phase takes place in which both parties freely converse with each other (often with high emotion and loud words) to further identify issues, interests, and needs. When appropriate, the mediator intervenes with questions, restatements, and so on.

4. This stage opens the door to potential options, which generates more discussion and negotiation.

5. Finally, the parties formulate their agreements and write them down.

Because of the long and difficult process of litigation, mediation is often a preferred alternative to courts and attorneys. Mediation is an effective, efficient, and productive way of resolving disputes, even those that are very difficult and seem unsolvable. Mediators are trained to deal with emotions and to help people navigate their way through sometimes complex and multifaceted disputes. Mediations take place in offices and rooms with a professional and comfortable atmosphere and ample resources such as copier, fax machine, and phones.

Preferably the mediator is mostly an active listener, but as stated, there are different styles of mediation. The whole idea is to empower people to create their own solutions rather than to have them imposed by a judge or lawyers.

Most mediation sessions are task oriented, looking at how to resolve disputes rather than at causes of conflict. Mediation focuses on the present with future results in mind, rather than being concerned with the past. It is finite and short term, but disputing parties may decide to revisit the process from time to time.

The services of mediators do not come for free, but they do cost a lot less than attorneys' services and they also can help you avoid going to court and litigating your differences at a cost of thousands of dollars. Mediators' fees range widely depending on whom you choose and where you live. A popular mediator in New York City may run you a few hundred dollars an hour, while a mediator in a small town may cost less than $100 an hour. Courts can also provide referrals to low-cost mediation.

We cannot overstate the value of mediation for couples who cannot come to an agreement about their divorce. Mediation can help resolve your toughest disputes, all the while keeping you in control of your own divorce and saving you the pain, anguish, frustration, and money related to the all-out battle in court. Television shows tend to dramatize divorce court as if it were easy, quick, cheap, and doable. Few couples require the help of the court, however. For most, mediation gets both spouses more of what they want sooner and with much less stress. This, in turn, helps ensure that the agreements made will be honored in the future.

What's more, mediation can give you the room to breathe and figure out over the course of many sessions how best to deal with your children, the division of your assets and debts, and any support that one spouse or the children need from the other spouse. You can take as long as you like using mediation to come to a fair and sensible agreement. The flexibility and informality of mediation also allow you to explore all of your options so you don't arrive at any decisions in a hasty or anger-filled manner. If later on you do need the court to step in and resolve a few last issues, it can.

Perhaps the most attractive aspect of mediation is the privacy it provides. Once you land in court, your problems will be public information. Mediation sessions are kept private, so no one will be able to witness your sessions.

How to Find a Mediator

Mediators exist for a variety of situations, not just for families going through divorce. However, you should seek a mediator who specializes in family law and has experience in helping couples reach agreements during divorce. The mediator need not have a background in family law or be a lawyer, but he or she should have all the qualifications of a mediator and be familiar with the laws of your state and your options as a couple contemplating divorce. Put simply, you'd rather have a mediator who has helped dozens of couples reach a divorce agreement rather than one who usually deals with business mediation or conflict resolution in educational settings.

Both you and your spouse must agree on your mediator and feel comfortable with the person you choose. Many courts have mediation services in the court itself. Some courts actually require use of their preferred mediation services in certain situations (such as figuring out issues related to children). Many of these services charge a very reasonable fee or offer sliding-scale payment arrangements, as opposed to private mediators. If you want to find a private mediator and you have friends who have already experienced mediation and divorce, you can start by asking them for referrals to good, trustworthy mediators in your area. Or you can contact the Academy of Family Mediators, which is now part of a larger organization called the Association for Conflict Resolution.

The Academy of Family Mediators has been an international professional organization for family mediators over the past 20 years. In 2001 it merged with the two other national organizations for alternative dispute resolution: SPIDR (Society for Professionals in Dispute Resolution) and CREnet (Conflict Resolution Education Network). The new amalgam organization is now the largest membership association in the conflict resolution field, and has as its mission ". . . to promote peaceful, effective conflict resolution."

Visit their web site at www.mediate.com or contact them at P.O. Box 51090, Eugene, OR 97405; 541-345-1629. You can also e-mail them at admin@mediate.com for more information.

Questions to Ask Your Mediator before Beginning

- How much do you charge and how do your fees work?
- What experience do you have in family mediation, specifically divorce?
- What are your qualifications and educational background?
- Are you a member of the Academy of Family Mediators?
- How do you usually work with couples? What is your particular style?
- Are there any issues that you don't feel comfortable mediating, such as child custody?
- What is your success rate?

If mediation does not work, then you can proceed to court. However, if it does work for you (which in most cases happens), then your mediator will draft an agreement that sets out the solutions you and your spouse arrived at, and you will make that agreement part of your final divorce agreement. The written agreement made by your mediator will eventually get filed with the court, and once your divorce is final you become legally bound to the agreement.

Another option—arbitration—will be briefly mentioned in chapter 5. Arbitration is a way to resolve marital disputes short of going to court. It's more formal than mediation, but it's not quite like stepping inside divorce court.

Conclusion

We've covered a lot in this chapter, but we haven't even gotten to child custody, alimony, and other issues, such as splitting up retirement benefits and sharing pension plans. Hopefully by now you've got a handle on your financial situation and can see your options, as well as your future, more clearly.

We leave this chapter with two important reminders. First, if looking at your finances worries you immensely because you see yourself having a hard time staying afloat through and after your divorce, now is the time to think about your job and your employability—especially if you were the one staying at home and raising a family while your spouse generated the income and supported you. We talked about establishing good credit in this chapter, but equally important to having a good credit report to your name is having the job skills you need to be employed in today's market. Don't be afraid to start investigating new options for yourself careerwise, which might entail reeducation, going back to school, and training in a new field. In fact, a shift in your working life may be just what you need to move forward and embrace your new life overall.

Second, because of the tax implications that may accompany the division of your property—and particularly the sale or buy-sell agreement you make with your spouse for your house—you should consult a tax specialist or financial planning expert who can provide the advice you need to make those agreements realistic. A tax expert can help you minimize the tax burdens related to some of your large assets. Otherwise, you and your spouse may find yourself making an agreement that has serious consequences later that cost lots of money.

Let's move on and get to talking about alimony, child support, and custody.

CHAPTER 4

Alimony, Child Support, and Custody

Determining how much support you may need from your spouse (if any at all), who gets the children most of the time, and whether or not extra support must be provided for the children are difficult decisions to make. They are difficult because you and your spouse may not agree on the right kind of support—how much, for how long, and under what circumstances. You may have had an easy time divvying up the physical property and debts but get to this point and find yourselves in much need of outside help and guidance for determining what's best for everyone. This can be the toughest part of your divorce. It's okay if your negotiations temporarily slow down or even break down at this stage. You can always use a mediator to get you through it. Just because you reach more impasses at this point, you are not necessarily doomed to a litigated court case.

Now that women are more likely to earn a good living on their own and work outside the home, the old days of the man making enormous alimony payments and losing custody of the children in a divorce are over. Courts now tend to look at both parents as equals when it comes to setting alimony and deciding who gets to have primary custody of the children (unless they decide on joint custody). Judges will weigh the man's ability to generate an income and take care of the children as much as the woman's. It's not uncommon, for example, to find men getting custody of the children *and* receiving alimony from their former wives. Permanent alimony is also a thing of the past; as ex-spouses move forward in their lives, earn more income, and perhaps remarry, they are no longer entitled to those alimony payments from their previous marriage. Unless you are getting divorced after a very long marriage and never commence a serious relationship with another person—and you still can prove that you need that check from your former spouse—you will not be able to rely on your former spouse financially for the rest of your life.

In this chapter we'll explore how alimony, child support, and custody issues work. We'll also give you some tips for creating a parenting plan and including that in your paperwork with the court.

Every state has public programs to assist parents in establishing paternity, obtaining support orders, and enforcing those orders. These programs have existed since the late 1970s and serve a substantial proportion of custodial parents and their children. Despite these efforts, nearly $72 billion in unpaid child support is reported to be owed in cases using the public system. Not all of this $72 million is due to deadbeat parents, but a large number of custodial parents never receive their routine checks from the noncustodial parent who's been ordered to pay. States and the federal government continue to work hard at establishing programs that assist parents in getting the support they deserve from their former spouses.

Types of Alimony

Generally, alimony is awarded to either spouse in an effort to maintain the standard of living that both parties were accustomed to during the marriage. But because traditional alimony has changed so much with society's own evolution and the changing roles of husband and wife, *alimony,* or spousal support, has gradually been replaced by *rehabilitative maintenance* or *rehabilitative alimony.* It's better to think of alimony as temporary payments designed to help the lower-earning spouse get back on his or her feet. In fact, the shift in how alimony works today has been so great that some divorce lawyers insist that a lump-sum payment is better for both parties than a routine check that goes out on a weekly, monthly, or bimonthly basis. The recipient gets a healthy nest egg for moving forward, making the necessary changes to his or her life to eventually support him- or herself, and avoiding any reliance on the ex-spouse. This method also reduces the risk of default (nonpayment), which is currently hovering at around 50 percent. How much you are entitled to receive depends on a variety of factors, including the following:

- Your immediate financial needs
- Your future financial needs and your ability to generate an income
- Your education, health, mental and emotional condition, and job experience
- How many marital assets and debts you are accepting in your divorce
- How long you were married and how you contributed to your marriage (this is where being a stay-at-home parent or supporter of a spouse's pursuit of a career counts)
- Your children's needs and how you and your spouse will continue to support them financially and emotionally

Other factors may be considered as well. A mom who gave up her career to raise children and who finds herself in divorce may have a particularly hard time adjusting to singlehood again and making ends meet. The court will place a value on her time at home spent caring for the family and running the household. She will likely get some support until she finds a way to support herself after divorce. As time moves on and she gains work skills and more lucrative jobs, those payments may diminish and eventually end. It's a double-edged sword for the woman who decides to be a stay-at-home mother and wife. While she's not in the job market, she loses considerable ground in advancing her career and will probably be granted a greater amount of alimony while she restructures her financial life and gets back into the game. But if she keeps her skills and experience updated throughout her marriage (or if she works part-time), she's less likely to get substantial alimony—if any.

Basic Types of Alimony

Permanent   This type of alimony is to be paid until either the death of the payor or the remarriage of the recipient. Some agreements may include a "cohabitation" clause stating that alimony ends when the recipient cohabits with another person in the avoidance of marriage. Permanent alimony settlements are, generally speaking, a thing of the past.

Lump sum   This type of alimony is one payment of alimony instead of periodic (usually weekly or monthly) payments.

Temporary   This type of alimony lasts for a specific period of time, usually one to two years. It may be awarded when the persons involved are on almost equal ground but due to certain circumstances one person may need financial assistance in order to get on his or her feet.

Rehabilitative   This type of alimony is the most commonly awarded alimony. It is awarded in a situation where the recipient is younger or able to eventually enter or return to the workforce and become financially self-supporting. Rehabilitative alimony may include payments for the education necessary to enable the recipient to become self-supporting.

How Much Alimony Can One Get?

Unlike child support, there is no guarantee that alimony will be granted . . . and no guarantee that it will be paid regularly. What's more, there are no strict guidelines for granting alimony at either the federal or the state level. Your specific state may offer some guidelines, but usually it's up to the judge's discretion to determine how much is necessary, fair, and reasonable. Hopefully, you and your spouse can work out a deal between the two of you—without having to go before a judge. When discussing alimony with your spouse, it's a good idea to become familiar with how a judge would evaluate the situation. The following are issues you need to consider in contemplation of asking for alimony.

In ordering spousal support, the court may consider all of the following circumstances (this is taken from one court's guidelines):

(a) The extent to which the earning capacity of each party is sufficient to maintain the standard of living established during the marriage, taking into account all of the following:
   (1) The marketable skills of the supported party; the job market for those skills; the time and expenses required for the supported party to acquire the appropriate education or training to develop those skills; and the possible need for retraining or education to acquire other, more marketable skills or employment.
   (2) The extent to which the supported party's present or future earning capacity is impaired by periods of unemployment that were incurred during the marriage to permit the supported party to devote time to domestic duties.
(b) The extent to which the supported party contributed to the attainment of an education, training, a career position, or a license by the supporting party.

(c) The ability of the supporting party to pay spousal support, taking into account the supporting party's earning capacity, earned and unearned income, assets, and standard of living.

(d) The needs of each party based on the standard of living established during the marriage.

(e) The obligations and assets, including the separate property, of each party.

(f) The duration of the marriage.

(g) The ability of the supported party to engage in gainful employment without unduly interfering with the interests of dependent children in the custody of the party.

(h) The age and health of the parties.

(i) The immediate and specific tax consequences to each party.

(j) The balance of the hardships to each party.

(k) The goal that the supported party shall be self-supporting within a reasonable period of time.

[In this court's state, the definition of "reasonable period of time" is given as follows: Except in the case of a marriage of long duration as described in Section 4336, a "reasonable period of time" for purposes of this section generally shall be one-half the length of the marriage. However, nothing in this section is intended to limit the court's discretion to order support for a greater or lesser length of time, based on any of the other factors listed in this section, Section 4336, and the circumstances of the parties.]

(l) Any other factors the court determines are just and equitable.

Your emotional state should also be factored into your situation. The ultimate question is: After your divorce can you continue to live as you had in your marriage, if your spouse's contribution to your family's bottom line is gone? For most, the answer is no. Most people do have to make some changes in their lifestyles immediately following a divorce. But there is nothing wrong with asking for a little support during your transition if you are seriously in need of financial help. Unless you were married to a monster, your spouse most likely will not want to see you out on the streets a month after your divorce—especially if you have children. It is up to you and your spouse, however, to arrive at a fair number, as well as the specifics of how it will be paid, for how long, and when. If a judge has to intervene, he or she will use a set of criteria to calculate the amount of alimony payments. As with any other aspect of your divorce, it's always best to negotiate alimony rather than have a judge arbitrarily determine whether your situation is one that will include alimony and how much will be awarded.

Enforcing alimony payments is not as easy as enforcing child support payments. If you don't think your spouse will live up to your agreement, you may want to ask for a lump-sum payment (mentioned previously). Keep in mind, however, that a lump-sum payment will have

Beware of conditions attached to your alimony. Avoid any agreement that places any conditions on your support, such as a promise to make dinner for your ex-spouse once a week or a stipulation that you cannot meet and date new people. You want your arrangement to be fair and reasonable. Keep it simple, too. You only need to figure out how much, when, for how long, and under what circumstances the alimony should end. For example, if after three months of alimony you get a huge job promotion or win the lottery, your alimony should end.

Alimony payments are tax deductions for the payor. But they are claimed as income for the recipient. How you accept your alimony may affect your taxes, so consult with a tax specialist or CPA, who can advise you on the best way to minimize those taxes in light of the alimony. Remember that if you are awarded any type of alimony, it will cease at the death of the payor. You may want to consider a life and disability insurance policy in an amount sufficient to replace any alimony lost at the death or disability of your paying former spouse. Because you have an insurable interest in the person being insured, you are able to buy the policy yourself. Other options include an annuity. This could be money well spent in the event that life and disability insurance are not part of your agreement. Every state has its own criteria for determining the need and extent of alimony. For information about annuities and insurance, speak with a financial or estate planner.

tax consequences for which you should consult a tax specialist before accepting the lump sum. Also, if you are not that good with money and you worry that you will run through a lump-sum payment quickly, this may not be the best route for you.

Alimony is never written in stone. Payments can change depending on both spouses' particular circumstances. This change can occur at the request of you and your spouse, or at the order of the court. If the court orders a change in payment, be prepared to provide the reason. For example, if you were just in a car accident and suffered serious injuries that prevent you from generating the same income you had previously, your request for more support may be granted by the court. Conversely, if you're responsible for paying alimony and you just declared your small business as bankrupt, you can ask the court to lower your payments. Generally, your circumstances must change for the court to grant a modification to your support, but it may be harder in some states than others to get that modification.

Pendente Lite Alimony

Alimony awarded prior to the divorce is called *pendente lite alimony*. It is taxable income to the recipient and tax deductible to the payor. If your primary goal at the onset of divorce negotiations is to get the support you need while you and your spouse figure out your divorce

Tax Tips

When getting divorced, you cannot forget about the potential tax burdens you face. Taxes should be part of your discussion when you negotiate with your spouse. For example, if you are due any type of joint tax refund, determine how it will be split. If you cannot reach an agreement, often those funds end up in an escrow account until the issue is settled.

If you are keeping a home, you must determine who will take the tax deduction for the mortgage interest and real estate taxes if you file separately. Usually it is the person who is paying the mortgage; however, if one person needs the deduction and the other doesn't need it, this could be a good negotiating point.

If you have children, you must determine who will take the tax deduction for them if you file separately. Usually the spouse paying the support would be allowed to claim one or more of the children, depending on the amount of support being paid. Once again, however, if one person can use the deduction and the other doesn't need it, this could be a good negotiating point.

How to Tell the Court Your Story

If you need to ask the court to order support, custody, and/or visitation, you should provide a declaration that says what you want and why you should get it. Declarations typically get filed with the court when and if one spouse needs something from the other spouse before the divorce gets finalized—and you can't reach an agreement. They may also get filed after your divorce once circumstances change and you must ask the court to modify a previous order, such as child support. If you need a court hearing, you need to first provide the court with your side of the story. A judge will review your declaration and consider your request at the hearing. Keep the following tips in mind when crafting your declaration:

1. *Be brief:* The judge has dozens of files and will not take the time to read a declaration that goes on for pages. Try to keep your declaration to a maximum of two pages.

2. *Be specific:* Include dates and relevant details; do not use generalities ("he is violent"); instead, relate specific incidents that demonstrate the trait ("on 1/2/05 he punched me in the nose").

3. *Use the most recent information:* The judge will be less interested in what happened 10 years ago than in what happened last week.

4. *Stay focused:* If the issue is visitation, don't go off on a tangent about property division.

5. *Don't name-call:* The judge doesn't want to hear that she is a "drunken witch"; let the judge come to that conclusion for him- or herself based on your facts.

Type your declaration and use clean, plain paper. Some courts will provide room on your form for you to write your statement. If you must use an attachment to your form, be sure to include your name, the name of your spouse or ex-spouse, and your case or file number at the top. Do not try to use fancy language or unusual sentence structures. The declaration does not need to be a Hemingway masterpiece or in legalese, but it does need to be in your own words. Make your declaration understandable, to the point, and clear. Check with your court how best to present your declaration; ask about the preferred type of paper and format. Some courts, for example, require pleading paper (special paper with numbers on the side). Your court may be able to give you this paper (or a form that can be used for a declaration) or tell you where to go to obtain the preferred paper.

Figures 4.1 and 4.2 are samples of two different declarations from two different states.

agreement, you can ask the court to order your spouse to pay you a set amount of money. This order may be part of your separation agreement (and is sometimes called a *pendente lite* order). It's a formal agreement that provides for the support and other financial conditions until your divorce is final.

It's best to get any such order from the court and not rely entirely on an informal agreement with your spouse; otherwise, the agreement may not be binding. Additionally, if there are alimony payments, you cannot file a joint return. Discuss this with an accountant. Depending upon the situation, it may be better to not allocate the funds as alimony.

Getting the court order should not be too difficult so long as you and your spouse agree to its terms. Your appearance in court will be minimal as well. All you need to do is appear before the judge and get him or her to sign the written agreement that you and your spouse have already signed. The judge's signature makes it a court order. Some courts don't even require your appearance if you have an agreement. The court will issue its decision and make your agreement an order, and you'll be done (and divorced).

Petitioner/plaintiff: Jane Doe-Smith
Respondent/defendant: Travis Smith
Case number: V-1234567-5

Declaration:
I want child support for Emily and Sarah to be a minimum of $1800.00
each, with my having physical custody 95 percent of the time.

In the previous order, we were receiving family support that was taxable
to me as income. I felt I had to agree to an amount that was considerably
less than what the calculations suggested because the negotiations were
going nowhere. After 4 years, he would not agree to release any of our
savings to me unless I settled. I feel Emily and Sarah have suffered greatly
because of this decision and now that family support has been
terminated, I d like to see them get the support that is consistent with a
father who has an income of approximately $185,000.00 a year.

I was making the estimated $3000.00 per month, but have not been able
to find a permanent position with benefits and have not been able to put
anything aside for retirement. I have experienced that being 47 with
arthritis has contributed to the difficulty of finding employment. Since
4/19/04, I've been on disability and according to the calculations given
to me by the State Department, will be making $1,331.00 a month. I
think it is unfair for Emily and Sarah to go without because they choose
to live with me. Emily and Sarah have both been anxiously awaiting the
opportunity to have their voices heard regarding visitation. It is my main
objective to see that their wishes are granted therefore, I am requesting
that the visitation, which is currently stated as "every other weekend," be
changed to "a mutually agreed upon time and date" and for Emily and
Sarah to have a say in their availability. During the past 4 years they have
been visiting their father at a mutually agreed upon time and date and it
has consistently become less frequent and has never been the equivalent
to "every other weekend." I'd like to see this made into an order and be
taken in to consideration in their support.

Jane Doe-Smith

Figure 4.1   Sample Attachment to Petition for Modifying Child Support

STATE OF MICHIGAN
IN THE CIRCUIT COURT FOR THE COUNTY OF KENT

File No: 96-01234-DM

BRIAN JOHN SAMPLE
Plaintiff,

Vs.   **Declaration in Support**
                                                         of Modification of Child
                                                         Custody and Support.

SHEILA G. SAMPLE   HON:
Defendant,

_____

Brian John Sample
302 Blue Oak Dr.
Coopersville, MI 49404
(555) 123-4567
Sheila Gay Sample
3265 Olivet
Grandville, MI 49418
(123) 555-4567   /
_____

I, Brian John Sample, the Plaintiff in the above entitled matter declare the following:

CHILD CUSTODY:
I am requesting a change in custody of my son Brian John Sample, Jr., born 04/21/89, because he asked me to. The last two years while living at his mom's he has failed the 7th and 8th grades. Both summers I contacted the school and got him enrolled and paid for his summer sessions. Both times he passed these summer school classes that he had failed while living at his mom's. Brian and his mom fight and argue all the time. I feel it would be better for him and her if he was to come live with me. I got a call at work one day, and was asked to stop by because Sheila was having a problem with Brian. When I entered the house I noticed the two of them at the bottom of the stairs. Sheila was lying on top of Brian and had him in a headlock. I think I can control Brian better than his mom can. I think it would be better for him if Brian was to come live with me.

CHILD SUPPORT:
I am requesting to modify the current child support payments in the amount of $768.00 per month payable to the defendant be changed to a reserved order. Since I am requesting a change in custody the child support payments for the minor child Brian John Sample, Jr. should be changed as well

Dated: _____, 2005.

                                        _____
                                        BRIAN JOHN SAMPLE, Plaintiff

Figure 4.2a   Michigan Declaration

AFFIDAVIT

STATE OF MICHIGAN   )
) SS.

COUNTY OF _____)

I, the below undersigned, being duly sworn, deposes and says:

         1. That the said Defendant was personally served with process in said action, as appears from the acknowledgment of service on file.

         2. That the said Defendant has not filed or served an Answer to Complaint, or taken such other action as may be permitted by law, although more than 21 days have elapsed since said date of service.

         3. That the defaulted party is not in the military service and is not an infant or incompetent person.

_____

Subscribed and sworn to before me on _____ , 2005.

_____
Notary Public,

_____ County, Michigan
               My commission expires:

DEFAULT

The default of SGS, Defendant, in the above-named action is hereby entered for the reason that the said Defendant has failed to plead or otherwise defend as permitted by law within the time prescribed by summons as appears from the court file and attached affidavit.

Dated: _____, 2005.

_____
               Deputy Clerk, Circuit Court

Figure 4.2b

Most states look at both parents as equals in their parenting responsibilities. Courts encourage both parents to be involved with their children's lives and upbringing. In a sense, courts assume that both parents are "innocent until proven guilty" when evaluating whether they are good parents. But if custody decisions must be made by the court and ugly accusations emerge about one parent's failure to be actively involved in his or her children's lives—and those accusations are successfully proven in court—the court will not grant equal custody rights to both parents. Mothers usually end up having primary custody because they usually are the primary caretakers during a marriage. But if a father can prove otherwise, the court can grant him the right to have primary custody—whatever is in the best interests of the children.

The Children

The first thing to keep in mind when it comes to making decisions about the children is that *their interests are more important than yours.* You and your spouse must make decisions based on what's best for your children, and not for you or your spouse. As with all the other decisions you must make in your divorce, if you can come to an agreement with your spouse in regard to your children, your entire family will be better off. Courts do not like to make custody decisions, and if they must, you are less likely to be happy with the outcome. More-over, custody battles are time consuming, costly, and emotionally draining. Once you enter a custody battle with your spouse, you may never be able to emerge from it without holding a lifetime of resentment against your spouse, which will not help your children's recovery and the quality of their future family life.

Before we get to the details of custody issues, you should understand the difference between legal custody and physical custody. *Legal custody* refers to your rights and obligations as a parent toward your children, especially with regard to making decisions on their behalf. Examples of decisions you make about legal custody include how they will be raised, where they go to school, how they receive medical care, and what religion they practice. *Physical custody,* however, refers only to which parent physically has the children in their possession at any given time. Both parents typically have legal and physical custody to some degree after divorce. The extent to which each parent has legal and physical custody will depend on each spouse's particular circumstances. A parent who was more involved in the parenting prior to divorce will mostly likely have greater legal and physical custody after divorce. Conversely, a parent who was not as involved in the parenting and emotional support of the children before divorce is not as likely to get an equal amount of legal and physical custody as the other spouse after divorce.

There are 12 million single parents in the United States. Roughly 84 percent of children who live with one parent live with their mother. The number of single mothers has remained constant, while the number of single fathers grew 25 percent in three years to 2.1 million in 1998. Men constitute one-sixth of the nation's single parents.*

---

*U.S. Census Bureau, 2000.

The parent who has greater legal and physical custody is said to have *primary custody.* However, many parents today share joint custody, meaning each parent is more or less equally involved in the parenting and support of their children.

According to a 1997 U.S. Census Bureau brief, most single-parent children live in metropolitan areas and 6 in 10 of them are in cities with populations of 1 million or more.

Joint Custody

If you and your spouse can share your children relatively equally after divorce, this is the healthiest arrangement for your children's sake. Of course, this option also demands that you and your spouse can communicate effectively and can find common ground from which to share your children successfully. If you are significantly at odds with your spouse, having to deal with him or her every time the children switch residences, may not be in your children's best interests. Moreover, if making decisions together as parents has been troublesome in the past, it will be more troublesome after divorce. Have a realistic and clear understanding of what's best from the start—before you agree to joint custody or before you ask the court to rule.

You and your spouse may not want to split the physical custody 50/50 because it's too much for your children to shuttle between two different places, but you can each have equal rights for making decisions on their behalf. You can, however, try to make the physical custody somewhat equal by having the children live with one spouse during the school year and the other during vacations and summer months. It's up to you and your spouse to devise a plan that is fair and mutually agreeable and, as always, in the best interests of the children.

The optimal form of custody for the children is joint legal and primary physical custody. This means both of you share the important decision making for your children's lives (you both have legal custody), but the children remain under the physical care of one parent primarily. This prevents the instability created by constantly handing the children back and forth between two households.

Another option under joint—or shared—custody is to give one spouse primary physical custody but set no limitations on the other spouse's visiting rights. If you choose this option, be clear about who has more decision-making rights and in what areas. For example, you may want each of you to continue to share all of the major decision making, but what if you cannot agree? Which parent gets to have his or her way? You may want to list the types of decisions you can allow the other to liberally make, but for some decisions, you and your spouse must have a discussion. If you spell out exactly what the rules are for making decisions on your children's behalf, you will be better able to avoid heated arguments and problems later on. Typical decisions that parents have to make include the following:

- Health-related decisions, including dental, psychological, and even so-called unnecessary medical treatment such as orthodontia and cosmetic surgery
- Education-related decisions, such as where a child goes to school and who pays the tuition bills
- Consenting to a child's personal choices, especially when they affect their well-being and future (e.g., entering the military, getting married, dropping out of school, picking up an expensive hobby or sport that requires the parents' financial support)

The way in which you and your spouse design a joint custody plan will be unique to you and your family's situation. Your goal is to minimize the effect your custody split will have on

> Remember: You may not like your spouse anymore, but your children do! You won't always be your spouse's spouse, but your children will always be your spouse's children.

your children. If you and your spouse will be living far apart, you must consider the effect of this reality on your children's ability to maintain their studies in school, keep up with friends, and generally feel like they have a permanent home somewhere. This becomes especially important as the children get older and enter their teenage years. They may not want to play by your and your spouse's ground rules as they mature, so be ready to adjust your parenting plans as their needs and interests change.

Beyond the predictability and routines that children crave, they also need—and subconsciously want—discipline. A show of discipline is a show of your caring and concern for their needs and best interests. Do not let the divorce guilt you or your spouse into thinking that discipline should now be lessened or avoided. They may need more discipline in the early years following divorce. You may also need to give them the space and time to adjust to your divorced life (and their new life) before they articulate their true wishes and feelings. Be patient with them. Reinforce your love and concern for them. And do not bring your issues with your former spouse into your relationship with your children. This will always backfire.

State Specifics

Your state may have specific laws regarding custody. Most all states recognize joint custody, and some prefer it to the other options. In states where joint custody is preferred, a judge can order joint custody. He or she can also order both parents to accept certain rights and responsibilities, and delineate those rights and obligations based on who has primary custody and when. For example, a judge can order both parents to communicate when a decision must be made about invasive medical treatment, but allow the parent who has physical custody at the time to make a decision about noninvasive medical treatment.

Among the forms you'll fill out for issues related to your children will be one that contains references to the Uniform Child Custody Jurisdiction and Enforcement Act (UCCJEA). The purpose of the UCCJEA is to avoid conflicting custody orders and simultaneous custody proceedings in different states and to comply with the Parental Kidnapping Prevention Act, which was enacted by the federal government in 1980. The UCCJEA provides states with basic rules encouraging them to honor custody decisions made by other states as part of their constitutional duty under the "full faith and credit" clause of the U.S. Constitution. What this

> As your children mature into thoughtful and productive adults, do your best to consider their preferences when you make custody decisions. You may also need to adjust your custody situation as they age and their preferences and lives change. Some courts will listen to a child as young as 10, while others consider a child's choices if he or she is a teenager.
>
> Remember that children—at whatever age—like predictability. They also like routines and will not enjoy constant shifts in their lifestyle. Be as supportive and open-minded about their ideas and concerns as you can.

form actually does, therefore, is declare that the court in that jurisdiction has authority to make decisions related to the children. The form establishes the court's authority over matters related to the children. For example, if a divorcing couple in California have two children who live with their grandparents in the Philippines, where they attend school, the family court in California may not have the authority to rule on issues related to the children if the children have been living abroad for more than six months.

Figure 4.3 shows a sample of this form. Take note of the information that these pages contain—namely, where the children live, how long they've lived there, and what the relationship is between the children and their primary caretaker. Most states' UCCJEA forms will be similar. Remember, you can use our web site at www.wethepeopleforms.com to link you to your own state's court web site. Many states' court web sites have forms available to download and print, which can also be found at www.wiley.com/go/wethepeopleforms.

Split Custody

This is an unusual arrangement: You and your spouse literally split up your children between the two of you, so one parent has custody of one or more of the children and the other parent has custody of the other children. This should be considered only if one parent must provide special care for a child, such as special medical, psychological, or educational needs. Children do not like to be separated from their siblings, and this kind of an arrangement can do lasting damage to the children. A split custody arrangement can happen on a temporary basis, however, if one or more of the children needs extra attention or special care, such as the case when an accident has happened or a child gets involved with drugs, alcohol, or bad behavior and you want to separate that child from the other children.

Primary Custody

If you and your spouse decide that one of you should have primary custody, that person will have the children under his or her care most of the time. But you can structure your primary custody arrangement however you like and either give the parent with primary custody the legal right to make all important decisions or opt to split the decision-making process to some degree. It's up to you how you want to formulate your agreement. You will also have to factor in child support payments and medical care, more so than with joint custody.

Visitation Rights. Your arrangement should also address the time spent with the children by the *noncustodial parent,* the one who does not have primary custody. There are no set rules for making this arrangement, so do what you can to accommodate yourself, your spouse, and your children's schedules. You may want your spouse to have the kids only on the weekends, or every other weekend, or include some nights a week in that arrangement. Also make plans for holidays, birthdays, vacations, and summers.

You may also want to create some flex room for unexpected events, such as a special occasion on one side of the family, school-sponsored events, or other situations that may emerge and change your predetermined schedule. For example, if your sister gets married and wants your children in the wedding, you may have to ask permission to take them that weekend if it falls on a weekend when your spouse would normally have the children. Another example: Your son made it to the Little League finals and the championship game lands on a weekend when he's supposed to be with the other parent. Your arrangement should allow you to discuss

ATTORNEY OR PARTY WITHOUT ATTORNEY *(Name and Mailing Address):*	TELEPHONE NO.:	*FOR COURT USE ONLY*

ATTORNEY FOR *(Name):*

SUPERIOR COURT OF CALIFORNIA, COUNTY OF

STREET ADDRESS:

MAILING ADDRESS:

CITY AND ZIP CODE:

BRANCH NAME:

CASE NAME:

DECLARATION UNDER UNIFORM CHILD CUSTODY JURISDICTION AND ENFORCEMENT ACT (UCCJEA)	CASE NUMBER:

1. **I am a party** to this proceeding to determine custody of a child.

2. ☐ Declarant's present address is not disclosed. It is confidential under Family Code section 3429. The address of children presently residing with declarant is identified on this declaration as confidential.

3. *(Number):* _____ minor children are subject to this proceeding as follows:

(Insert the information requested below. The residence information must be given for the last FIVE years.)

a. Child's name	Place of birth	Date of birth	Sex

Period of residence	Address	Person child lived with (name and present address)	Relationship
to present	☐ Confidential		
to			
to			
to			

b. Child's name	Place of birth	Date of birth	Sex

☐ Residence information is the same as given above for child **a.**
(If NOT the same, provide the information below.)

Period of residence	Address	Person child lived with (name and present address)	Relationship
to present	☐ Confidential		
to			
to			

c. ☐ Additional children are listed on Attachment 3c. *(Provide requested information for additional children on an attachment.)*

Page 1 of 2

Form Approved for Optional Use
Judicial Council of California
FL-105/GC-120 [Rev. January 1, 2003]
**DECLARATION UNDER UNIFORM CHILD CUSTODY
JURISDICTION AND ENFORCEMENT ACT (UCCJEA)**
Family Code, § 3400 et seq.
Probate Code, §§ 1510(f), 1512

Figure 4.3a   UCCJEA Form for California

SHORT TITLE:	CASE NUMBER:

4. Have you participated as a party or a witness or in some other capacity in another litigation or custody proceeding, in California or elsewhere, concerning custody of a child subject to this proceeding?

   ☐ No   ☐ Yes *(If yes, provide the following information:)*

  a. Name of each child:

  b. Capacity of declarant: ☐ party ☐ witness ☐ other *(specify):*
  c. Court *(specify name, state, location):*

  d. Court order or judgment *(date):*

5. Do you have information about a custody proceeding pending in a California court or any other court concerning a child subject to this proceeding, other than that stated in item 4?

   ☐ No   ☐ Yes *(If yes, provide the following information:)*

  a. Name of each child:

  b. Nature of proceeding: ☐ dissolution or divorce ☐ guardianship ☐ adoption ☐ other *(specify):*

  c. Court *(specify name, state, location):*

  d. Status of proceeding:

6. Do you know of any person who is not a party to this proceeding who has physical custody or claims to have custody of or visitation rights with any child subject to this proceeding?

   ☐ No   ☐ Yes *(If yes, provide the following information:)*

a. Name and address of person	b. Name and address of person	c. Name and address of person
☐ Has physical custody ☐ Claims custody rights ☐ Claims visitation rights	☐ Has physical custody ☐ Claims custody rights ☐ Claims visitation rights	☐ Has physical custody ☐ Claims custody rights ☐ Claims visitation rights
Name of each child	Name of each child	Name of each child

I declare under penalty of perjury under the laws of the State of California that the foregoing is true and correct.
Date:

▶

_____
(TYPE OR PRINT NAME)

_____
(SIGNATURE OF DECLARANT)

7. ☐ Number of pages attached after this page:

NOTICE TO DECLARANT: You have a continuing duty to inform this court if you obtain any information about a custody proceeding in a California court or any other court concerning a child subject to this proceeding.

FL-105/GC-120 [Rev. January 1, 2003]   **DECLARATION UNDER UNIFORM CHILD CUSTODY**   Page 2 of 2
JURISDICTION AND ENFORCEMENT ACT (UCCJEA)

Figure 4.3b

Tax Tips

Children present tax concerns for both parents. Include in your agreement how you and your spouse will deal with these tax issues—especially if you are sharing joint custody. For example, decide who will file as head of the household. Consider alternating this beneficial way of filing year after year—you get to file as head of household one year, and your ex-spouse gets to file as head of household the next year. Or if you have more than one child, you can split up the children so at least one lives with you for 51 percent of the time. That way, both of you can file as head of household. The point is to share the tax deduction through the years. Include your arrangement in your agreement.

The tax credits you can get for children are large enough to make a difference in many people's tax bills, especially if the parent's income is low. You can also share this credit yearly but switch off who gets to claim it. Child tax credits are available only to parents with children under 13 years old.

Both you and your spouse can claim the deductions for medical expenses paid for your children. The sum of your expenses, however, must be greater than a certain percentage of your adjusted gross income.

---

these unexpected situations when they emerge. (This will, of course, depend on the relationship you have with your spouse. Hopefully, it's friendly enough to allow for such flexibility.) We'll give you more tips for establishing visitation schedules in chapter 7.

Legal Rights. Just because one spouse has primary custody does not mean that the other spouse automatically gets excluded from all decisions and daily dealings. You may opt to have one parent assume primary custody because it's in the best interests of the children (that is, they don't have to shuttle between two living quarters), but you can also agree to mutually make the important decisions and ensure that the other parent is as equally involved with the parenting as possible. It's up to you, however, to make sure you share such responsibilities, as courts will not necessarily enforce the arrangement. Noncustodial parents do have more rights today than they did years ago, and many states allow them to have a say and make important decisions on their children's behalf.

Parents are not the only people who seek custody and visitation rights upon a divorce. Grandparents can also ask the court to allow visitation and, in extreme circumstances (that is, both parents are proven to be unfit to raise the children), they may also win primary custody. Again, the rule of thumb is that whatever is in the best interests of the children is how the court will decide. Thus, you can also determine what's best for your children—aside from your potentially contentious relationship with your spouse—and come to an agreement without the court's help.

Problem Parents. If your spouse is a huge thorn in your side and you cannot imagine having to deal with him or her in your postdivorce life, this can be a problem if you have children and you must share them. Visitation is not easy to work out between two warring parents who cannot act civilly toward one another. This also sets the stage for each parent to use their children as pawns for getting back at the other spouse, either by being extremely difficult with the visitation arrangement or by withholding child support. If the court must rule on your visitation schedule because you and your spouse are uncommunicative, be prepared to accept a schedule that reflects your state's established guidelines, which may or may not be what you had wanted. A judge may not dictate exactly how the arrangement will work down to the number of days and hours, but in some extreme circumstances a judge will set a minimum amount of time that the noncustodial parent can spend with the children.

If you fear that your ex-spouse may harm or endanger your children while they are under his or her care, you can ask the court to limit visitation rights or request that another adult be present whenever your ex-spouse is with the children. For example, if your ex-spouse is abusive, mentally or emotionally unstable, or addicted to a substance, or has committed a crime, you will not want your children to be under his or her care exclusively at any time. However, you have to prove to the court that your allegations about your ex-spouse are true and that the court should take them into consideration when ordering custody and visitation rights. Typically, the court will appoint someone, either a guardian or an attorney, to investigate the allegations and represent the children. That person will also prepare a written report for the judge to review before ruling. For more information about these and other unusual situations, see chapter 7, which gives some information about how to deal with a spouse you fear will hurt you and/or your children.

Child Support

As we discussed at the beginning of this book, divorce does not change your relationship with your children. You remain legally responsible for their support while they are minors, which means you must provide the basics for them—food, clothing, shelter, an education up to a certain age, and other necessities such as access to medical care when needed. Both parents should share the cost of raising children. This entails providing child support, or a fixed amount of money that is intended to go solely toward the children's upbringing. Despite the giant uphill battle you feel that child support negotiations present, it's possible to work through the issues and deal with child support in a realistic manner. Hopefully, some of the math you did on your financial life in chapter 3 will help when you and your spouse sit down to discuss child support.

Joint Custody versus Primary Custody

The amount of child support that is necessary will depend on your custody arrangement. If both you and your spouse will be sharing the children equally, as in joint custody, neither of you may have to pay any child support. This assumes that you and your spouse contribute equally to your children's support by being fully responsible for their needs when each of you has the children under your care. However, exceptions to this rule apply if one parent does not have the children in his or her care 50 percent of the time, or if one parent makes considerably more money than the other parent. If the court has to decide child support issues, it will take both parents' income into consideration, as well as how much time each parent intends to spend with the children.

For parents who do not share custody equally in an arrangement whereby one parent is the designated primary caretaker, then the noncustodial parent typically pays the custodial parent some child support. The noncustodial parent's income will be the biggest factor when determining child support. Once his or her basic living expenses are met, the remainder becomes subject to child support payments.

Child support payments are not tax deductible. If you are paying child support, you may want to give more in child support payments and request that you get to take the tax exemptions and deductions. Another way to save tax dollars is to pay child support payments as alimony, which is tax deductible, so long as you can be certain that your spouse will put that money to use for the children. If you and your spouse allow for extra expenses in your child support payments (which is a good idea), the spouse paying child support can consider that extra money as alimony so he or she can take the tax deduction. The spouse who receives that extra support as alimony must declare it as income, however, so both spouses must find a balance between benefiting one person and helping the other. There are tax consequences for both spouses.

How to Calculate the Amount of Child Support. Each state has its own specific formula for calculating child support. Generally speaking, the two most important criteria for determining child support in all states are (1) the incomes of both parties and (2) who has physical custody most of the time.

Child support is about dollars and cents, and how those dollars and cents reflect the particular circumstances of both parents. How much, if any, child support can be expected may also factor in any special needs of the children and the living expenses of both parents.

To find out how your state computes child support, ask your local family court clerk for the information. A public family law center tied to your court will also have this information. And if a We The People store is located in your area, we can help you to understand your state's support guidelines.

Although alimony payments are less defined in the law books, child support gets a lot of attention and in most states is clearly laid out. These guidelines usually spell out the formula for child support based on income—expressing the amount as a percentage of a parent's income. But keep in mind that every state will determine child support differently. Your state, for example, may define income as your gross income (not net) and might not include your income from other sources, such as investments and trusts, when it calculates child support. Your state may also consider the income of the noncustodial parent only and set different percentages for different levels of income. Also, how many minor children you have will affect the formula for configuring child support. A judge may order the noncustodial

If the only custody issues you and your spouse have to work out are in relation to your pet pooch or feline friend, you're not alone. A combination of a vigorous divorce industry and an equally vigorous pet industry—spending on pet products and services hit a record $34.3 billion in 2004—has led to a dramatic increase in pet custody disputes during the last decade. Some experts believe there has been a hundredfold increase in the frequency of such cases since 1990. Dogs, for example, have been traded in divorce settlements for sums of up to $30,000, as well as for part of a pension plan, for a fraction of the cost of a house, and for jewelry! To win a pet custody dispute, either reach an agreement or expect to hire a neutral vet or "animal evaluator," and an attorney. And expect to pay more in the custody battle than the animal—or *chattle*, according to the law books—is worth. Like children, what's in the best interest of the pet will dictate what should happen to him or her (or it).

parent of several children to pay out a lump sum for all children, pay out an amount per child, or buy an annuity that's calculated to cover the expenses of the children, or it may order the parent to set aside assets that can be used to benefit the children in the future. A judge can also order the noncustodial parent to carry out a combination of these options.

Child support payments can be altered by asking the court to increase or decrease the payments. If the custodial parent loses a job and cannot make ends meet, or decides to move to another state that has a higher cost of living, that parent can ask the court to reconfigure the child support payments. (More on modifications in chapter 6.)

> If you are the one paying child support and cannot make ends meet to cover your living expenses and child support, it's in your best interest—and the interests of the children—to go to the court and ask it to change your child support order. The court can grant you a temporary modification and, depending on your particular circumstances, may change your entire child support obligation.

If Your Ex-Spouse Falls behind on Payments. The courts act more seriously about enforcing child support payments than they do alimony payments. Each installment of court-ordered child support must be paid on the date required by the order. If your ex-spouse fails to meet that order, the overdue payments are called *arrearages* and the person is said to be *in arrears* (late) on payments. Judges have become very strict about enforcing child support orders and collecting arrearages. If your spouse falls behind, he or she will not be able to erase that debt owed to your children. A judge will order the parent to pay up in full, either right away or in installments.

Similarly, if a parent falls behind in payments and eventually asks the court to reduce his or her obligation, a judge will not erase the payments already owed. Judges in most states are prohibited by law from retroactively modifying a child support obligation.

It's more than likely that your local district attorney has a child support collection department. Under the Child Support Enforcement Act of 1984, the district attorneys or state attorneys of every state must help you collect child support owed by your ex-spouse. Sometimes this means that the DA will serve your ex-spouse with papers requiring him or her to meet with the DA to arrange a payment schedule and saying that if the ex-spouse refuses to meet or pay, he or she could go to jail. If your ex-spouse has moved out of state, you or the district attorney can use legal procedures to locate him or her and seek payment. Federal and state parent locator services can also assist in locating missing parents.

In 1998 Congress passed the Deadbeat Parents Punishment Act (DPPA), making it a felony to willfully refuse to pay out-of-state child support. If you and your ex-spouse live in different states, you may use the Uniform Interstate Family Support Act (UIFSA) to enforce a child support order. Under this law, you can

- Ask a court in your state to force your former spouse to pay (but your state must have legal authority over your ex-spouse, otherwise known as *personal jurisdiction*)

- Ask a court in your state to forward the child support order to a court in the state where your ex-spouse lives and have that state's courts and agencies enforce the order

- File an enforcement request directly in the state where your ex-spouse lives

- Forward the order to your ex-spouse's employer and ask the employer to withhold the support amounts from your ex-spouse's paycheck

If your ex-spouse files for bankruptcy, this does not excuse him or her from paying child support. Bankruptcy does not wipe out a child support debt. Federal laws exist to protect child support payments, which may mean your ex-spouse's tax refunds can be intercepted to pay child support or wages can be garnished (seized) and assets can be taken. The government can also suspend the business or occupational license of a parent who is supposed to pay, or revoke his or her driver's license. Your state's district attorney will use any one of these methods in an attempt to help you collect from your ex-spouse.

Nearly every state has an agency that can help you with child support enforcement at little or no cost to you. For a list of links to these agencies, see www.ncsea.org/resources/links.php3.

As a last resort, the court can hold your ex-spouse in contempt and in the absence of a reasonable explanation for the delinquency, impose a jail term. This contempt power is exercised sparingly in most states, primarily because most judges would rather keep the payor out of jail so that he or she has a chance of earning the income necessary to pay the support.

Examples of helpful sites for information are www.childsupportdirectory.com, www.ancpr.org (the Alliance for Non-Custodial Parents Rights), and the federal Office of Child Support Enforcement at www.acf.dhhs.gov, which is part of the U.S. Department of Health and Human Services. The Child Support Enforcement Program provides four major services: locating noncustodial parents, establishing paternity, establishing support orders, and collecting support payments. The program also provides services to noncustodial parents. (States offer access and visitation services through federal grants.)

Making Room for the Extras. As with anything in life, you must take into account many extra expenses that will be incurred as your children grow up and need additional support. There's a lot more to life than food, shelter, and clothing. Examples of added expenses include college or trade school tuition, unexpected medical care, orthodontia, eyeglasses, psychological counseling, club sports, summer camp, after-school activities, tutoring, SAT classes, annual gifts for holidays, general entertainment, birthdays, special events, traveling expenses, vacation expenses, that journey to Europe when your daughter turns 18, and that entertainment system (computer included) that your son wants when he turns 15. There are a lot of extras that come into play when you are raising children. Your child support payments may meet only basic needs, which will not be enough to cover all that your children will expect or require.

When you figure out your child support agreement, you should build these expenses into the agreement so you and your spouse are ready to deal with them as they emerge. At the

Many factors change child support amounts. Changes in income, deductions, custody, emancipation age, or even time can make a significant difference in your child support payment or obligation. Child support is an important part of your monthly budget. Some web sites have calculators you can use to help you figure out how much child support you should be paying (or receiving). Software is also available that can help you calculate support payments (in California, it's called DissoMaster).

In 1988, the government required states to set guidelines for basic child support, which set monetary amounts for food and clothing. Since then, the battle over who's paying for the children's necessities has become less contentious. But there are still plenty of battles over who is going to pick up that bill from a prestigious summer internship or private university.

If you and your ex-spouse are amicable, the burden of footing any excessive bills can be divided equally between you. One option is for both of you to put money aside in a joint account or set up a minor's trust—preferably one that's irrevocable—to shelter the money from estate taxes if one parent should die. If drafted properly, an irrevocable trust can also shield money from creditors, in case you or your ex-spouse should lapse on your mortgages. If your ex-spouse is unwilling to spring for half of a college education, you may be able to trade off the cost of tuition for some other asset.

least, you should talk about how you and your spouse will discuss the needs of your children as they age and demand more from you. Agree to which extras both you and your spouse are willing to help pay, and reach an agreement on how you and your spouse will pay for these extras, especially the very expensive items such as the tuition to a private high school or college or an automobile when your child turns 16. You can calculate the split in the same manner as you calculated your rough child support payments: Base the contribution on your income as a percentage of your combined income. So if your income accounts for 40 percent of the combined income of you and your ex-spouse, then you should pay for 40 percent of the extra costs.

You and your ex-spouse may decide to create a fund that holds all the money for the extras, and each of you designates a set amount to that account a year. Of course, this assumes that you and your former spouse trust one another to be financially responsible, manage that money well, and not abuse this account. You can also choose to have only one parent, typically the one with primary custody, have access to this special account.

Optimally, you would contribute a certain percentage of your income each year to the account, and your ex-spouse would do the same (or give you the money to put toward that account). If this kind of an arrangement is not possible, you'll need to have another set plan for dealing with extra expenses. It's your call; the court is not going to rule on any request for extra payment that goes beyond the basic necessities.

Types of Insurance. Other means by which you can help provide for the financial support of your children include the use of insurance policies, which may not have anything to do with child support checks per se. You may want to consider getting a life insurance policy and disability insurance for the what-ifs that may happen and ultimately impact your children. A judge may also order you to obtain certain insurance so that your children have the added security.

In chapter 6 we'll detail what happens with health insurance in a divorce and how you can ensure your children remain covered even if your ex-spouse was the means through which you and your children obtained medical insurance. Many fear losing medical coverage in a divorce, but there are avenues you can take to prevent that from happening. For more information about how insurance can help you further protect yourself and your children, consult an experienced insurance broker or a financial planner who can help you find the right kind of insurance for you—and at the right price.

A Parenting Plan

Creating a parenting plan is one of the best things you can do. A parenting plan is a written pact with your spouse that lays out exactly your intentions and plans for your children—from custody arrangements and precise visitation schedules to how their medical and dental care will be covered and who can make important decisions about invasive treatment. They almost always accompany or are part of a separation agreement or marital settlement agreement. If your spouse won't let you see your own children, you need a parenting plan that the court legally acknowledges and enforces.

> The parenting plan may be the most important matter you deal with in your divorce and it can sometimes be the most difficult. The parenting plan refers to all of the arrangements for the children and how you will share responsibility for their care and upbringing. If you cannot agree about the parenting plan, the matter will be decided in court. But before a custody dispute can get to trial, you may be required to meet with a court counselor, who will attempt to mediate.

A parenting plan will make your arrangement(s) perfectly clear and will bolster your other agreements with the court. Drafting a parenting plan might also give you and your spouse the perspective you need to make the right decisions about what's best for your children. Moreover, as you discuss your goals and intentions as parents, you may find yourselves solving future problems as parents now instead of later. All of your issues related to being a divorced parent can come out and be addressed.

Parenting plans work best for parents who are sharing custody or for parents who will be taking an active role in their children's lives even if one parent has primary custody. You can make your plan as detailed as you like, and the more detailed you get, the better. As with all the agreements you make in your divorce, keep your plan simple, straightforward, and clear. Avoid ambiguity or inflexibility.

We've already touched upon most of the following topics, but here's a concise list of issues to address in your written parenting plan:

- ☑ How you will share parenting responsibilities—specifically (who will be responsible for what)
- ☑ How you will physically share your children
- ☑ How you will deal with holidays, birthdays, vacations, summers, and the haphazard events that may change your custody or visitation schedule
- ☑ How you will share the decision-making process for both day-to-day decisions and the major ones like school, medical treatment, religion, and as many general upbringing issues as you want to address
- ☑ How to deal with problems with your children (that is, how to punish or discipline them if they get into trouble)
- ☑ How to set boundaries for your children and deal with their adolescent-related years, especially with regard to alcohol use, smoking, drugs, dating and sex, staying out late, getting involved with the wrong crowd, doing poorly in school, and so on
- ☑ How you will handle illness or injury in your children
- ☑ How to deal with an emergency (that is, who will leave work to respond)

Try to predict what you may face as a parent in the future, and do your best to address those issues in your parenting plan. Remember: Your plans can be modified in the future as your circumstances change.

You can be as specific or as open-ended as you like in your plan. Tailor it to your needs and concerns. How defined you want your plan to be will depend on your relationship with your (soon-to-be) ex-spouse as well as your children's relationship with your ex-spouse. For example, you may want your ex-spouse to have "reasonable visitation" rights to your children. You can also be very specific about your visitation schedule, down to dates. If you want your kids to be with your ex-spouse only "every other Tuesday," specify the date when visitation begins so there is no confusion over which Tuesday means "every other Tuesday." Say "every other Tuesday starting June 7." No matter how you decide to craft your plan, be clear about exactly what you mean.

As mentioned, flexibility is key to the overall integrity of your parenting plan. If your plan is too rigid and strict, you may have a hard time following it through. If, however, you create a flexible plan that allows sensitivity to unexpected situations and changes in life, you and your spouse have a greater chance at living out your plan successfully. If you and your spouse negotiate all of your parenting responsibilities—custody, spousal support (if needed), and child support (if needed)—you will be better positioned to account for changes in your plan and make those changes accordingly as the future dictates. You want to be able to modify and reconsider your plan to accommodate the changes life will bring not only to you and your spouse but also to your children. You know that your and your spouse's income levels will change, and so will the expectations and goals of your children. A plan that provides for these changes and can jibe with the ebb and flow of your family's life is optimal. Try to anticipate future problems and attempt to resolve them or at least prepare for them now as you craft your parenting plan.

Figure 4.4 is a sample parenting plan.

Child support payments typically end when the child reaches legal adulthood, which is 18 years of age in most states. However, exceptions to this rule may apply if, for example, your state permits child support payments to continue when the child is a full-time college student or is matriculated in a trade or vocational school. This obligation usually ends once the child reaches his or her early 20s. Other circumstances that end child support obligations include the following:

Don't assume that child support payments automatically end when the child reaches the age of legal majority (usually 18). You may have to go back to court to formally terminate the order; otherwise, you may still be on the hook for child support payments. If there is no clear language in your court papers about how and when an order for child support ends, contact your family court and ask.

- Death of the paying parent
- Entrance to the military by the child
- Marriage of the child
- Full-time employment by the child
- Emancipation of the child

A child becomes *emancipated* if he or she wishes to be considered a legal adult in the eyes of the law and has not reached the legal age of adulthood, which can be 18 or 21, depending on the state. To become an emancipated adult, the child must meet specific legal requirements and go through a court process.

a.   **Joint legal custody with primary physical custody:** Petitioner and Respondent shall jointly share the legal custody of the minor child of the parties, and Petitioner shall have the primary physical custody of said child. Our parenting relationship shall be guided by the following plan:

b.   Both Parties agree that this Court has jurisdiction to make child custody orders in this case pursuant to the Uniform Child Custody Jurisdiction and Enforcement Act. Both parties agree California is the child's home state. Both parties were personally present at the execution of the attached custody agreement, both have knowledge of their right to a hearing in this matter and both waive their right to the hearing based upon the attached custody and visitation agreement. The parties agree the habitual residence of the child is the U.S.A. Both parties acknowledge being advised that any violation of this order may result in civil or criminal penalties, or both. Each party declares under penalty of perjury pursuant to the laws of the State of California that the foregoing is true and correct.

c.   Respondent shall have visitation every other weekend by picking child up from school Friday before 5:30 PM and returning child to school or Petitioner's home by 8:30 AM Monday and a midweek visit on Wednesday by picking up child from school by 5:30 PM and returning child to school by 8:30 AM Thursday. Respondent shall have visitation on Father's Day from 8:30 AM to the following morning. Respondent shall have visitation every other year on Thanksgiving beginning in 2004. Each party will notify the other of plans as soon as possible for vacation during the summer. All visitation arrangements shall be confirmed at least 12 hours in advance. Neither parent shall remove the child from this State or the County of Los Angeles without prior written consent of other party. Respondent shall provide transportation for visitation.

d.   Neither parent shall conceal the child's whereabouts at any time.

e.   Each party shall keep the other party informed of his or her current address and telephone number and of the child's schools and day care providers, and shall notify the other within one day of any change of address or phone number.

f.   We recognize the unique contributions each of us has to offer our child. We recognize the need and right of our child to have frequent and continuing contact with both parents. We wish to provide our child with emotional security, physical well-being, intellectual stimulation and moral guidance.

Figure 4.4   Sample Parenting Plan (California)

TIME OUT! *I Don't Understand What You Mean By . . .*

Arrearages   Unpaid payments. If a spouse has not made the payments owed to the other spouse, those overdue payments are called *arrearages* and the person is said to be in *arrears* (behind) on payments.

Child support guidelines   The amount of child support to be paid, under normal circumstances, according to a schedule established by the state, based upon income. It is federally mandated that all states establish guidelines for child support.

Custodial parent   The parent with whom the child(ren) live most of the time. The *noncustodial parent* is the parent with whom the child(ren) do not live most of the time.

Disability insurance   A type of insurance that protects some of your income should you become unable to work due to illness or injury. If you become disabled, the policy will pay you a certain percentage of your income, which will help you maintain daily living and continue to care for your children. A court can require a self-employed parent, for example, to obtain some disability insurance.

Automatic wage reduction   To facilitate the payment of child support, court orders now include a provision for an automatic wage reduction, which takes the child support right out of the paycheck of a parent who is legally obligated to pay that support. That money then goes directly to the custodial parent. The law also sets limits on how much money can come from a person's paycheck. Employers receive the court order and must comply with the deduction. However, automatic wage reductions can be waived by two agreeing spouses who set up another plan in their divorce agreement. Whichever plan they decide to pick, this provision should be clearly stated in the agreement, which should describe backup plans in the event that those payments are not made. For example, if the paying spouse fails to meet those child support payments, a clause in the agreement can allow for the automatic wage deduction to activate.

A Note about Taxes

Throughout this chapter we've given you a few tips in relation to taxes. Tax consequences follow every decision made in a divorce, settlement agreement, or marital dispute resolution, often for many years. Whether there is a divorce, annulment, separate maintenance agreement, or dissolution, taxes need to be considered in making informed choices. Even when the choices are limited, knowledge of the tax problems created by the divorce may help achieve a better settlement. This is why discussing your concerns with a tax specialist can help you make better decisions about your divorce.

Before the divorce is even final, however, there are questions about taxes that must be addressed. Specifically, whether to file jointly or separately is among the first questions divorcing couples should discuss. If the atmosphere is one of mistrust, hostility, and anger, then having to make decisions about taxes can be excruciating but necessary. Avoiding the issue will only make Uncle Sam richer at your expense. You and your spouse will need to have as much extra money available as you can once each of you is on your own again and you are supporting separate households.

Ordinarily, joint returns produce a lower tax on the joint incomes of a husband and wife than filing separate tax returns. But in many instances, filing separate returns may actually produce a lower combined federal and state tax. So separate returns should always be computed. If by filing separate returns a lower combined tax results, one issue of disagreement can be resolved immediately by the filing of separate returns. Keep in mind, however, that this opens the door to other issues, such as who gets to claim the children as dependents and who gets to file as head of household. When deciding to file jointly or separately, you must take all the factors into consideration, such as the elections, credits, deductions, and exemptions you and your spouse may qualify for as joint filers or as separate filers. A tax specialist who can review your paperwork and numbers can best advise you which way to file to maximize your tax advantage.

Other, nontax issues could remain as well for joint filers. For example, a spouse may refuse to file a joint return because of hostility or vindictiveness—or fear of the resulting responsibility for tax, penalties, and interest that are actually due (whether or not correctly shown) on the return. Do your best to approach your tax situation as you would a business deal. You and your spouse need to reach a mutually beneficial agreement about how to deal with your tax liabilities (what you owe) or what you deserve to get back as a tax return. Think of it as a business deal in which you and your spouse are working together across the table from the government. It does you no good to fight with your spouse over taxes when arguing leads you nowhere but paying the government more money. The decision to file jointly or separately should be easy to make: You find out which method saves you and your spouse the most money, and you file accordingly.

Conclusion

The issues presented in this chapter are weighty but significant. Considering all of these issues may initially overwhelm you, but they are a crucial part of your divorce settlement. As a parent, you have a responsibility to prepare your children for their futures through careful planning now. We cannot reiterate enough how beneficial it is to do as much of the negotiating yourself with your spouse and come to an agreement about how the two of you can move forward and support one another in the transition to being single parents. The goal is to find a balance that considers every family member's needs, wishes, and limitations. This may surprise you, but some argue that almost all postdivorce violence is rooted in imbalanced custody arrangements.

Although parenting inequities may torment fathers, divorce has long been both an emotional and a financial blow to mothers suddenly raising children on their own. According to the state Department of Social and Health Services, in Washington state 95 percent of divorced mothers are named as their children's primary parents, and fathers owe some $1.7 billion in overdue support payments.

The tides are slowly shifting away from old patterns in which children typically live with their mothers and spend alternate weekends with their fathers. But some fathers do feel that the system sides with mothers first. At the Divorce Center, a Massachusetts-based nonprofit organization, staff mediators, therapists, and attorneys report that 30 percent of all divorced parents remain bitter and hostile years after the split. Hopefully, you can limit the amount of hostility you feel toward your spouse by assuming that you are equals in the negotiating phase, and that you can be equally responsible parents in your children's future. New laws may emerge that further presume more equitable parenting plans.

If you and your spouse cannot reach an agreement on your own, try mediation or speak with a counselor, therapist, or member of the clergy to try to work out your differences and reach that oh-so-important agreement.

You can always rely on a judge to make custody decisions for you, but here's your warning: Not only might a judge rule against your wishes, but he or she may force you to reach an agreement with your spouse through other means, such as mediation. Courts do not like to make decisions for parents when it comes to their children. A court will do all it can to get parents to arrive at their own decision and set forth a plan. They might also require that you attend parenting classes so you gain some new skills for being a divorced parent.

Helping your children through the divorce is a topic all its own, and because we do not go into detail about dealing with your children's emotions and knowing when they need special attention, we suggest the following books for further reading:

Helping Children Cope with Divorce, by Edward Teyber (Jossey-Bass, 2001)

We're Still Family: What Grown Children Have to Say About Their Parents' Divorce, by Constance Ahrons (HarperCollins, 2004)

Helping Your Kids Cope with Divorce the Sandcastles Way, by M. Gary Neuman with Patricia Romanowski (Random House, 1999)

The Truth About Children and Divorce: Dealing with the Emotions So You and Your Children Can Thrive, by Robert E. Emery, Ph.D. (Viking, 2004)

Chapter 5 takes you through the actual court process, from the how-tos of filing your paperwork to actually appearing in court and responding to requests from the court. Whether you and your spouse are cooperating through your divorce or you face a bitterly contested divorce that gets settled in the courtroom, you will have to deal with the courts on some level. Knowing what to expect and how to act can lessen much of the stress and anxiety.

CHAPTER 5

Divorce Court

The courtroom is one of the most intimidating places you may ever be. Once you enter into the courtroom you give control of your divorce to someone you have never seen or met before—a judge. The extent to which you can control your divorce and the decision-making power you have are now limited, as all decisions will now be made by the judge. This person is not infallible; like people, judges are prone to mood swings, illogical thinking, and feelings of superiority, and they bring their own set of values and ideas into their decision-making process, which may not reflect your own. We've been stressing the importance of doing as much of the negotiating yourself and reaching as many agreements as you can with your spouse before resorting to using the courts to settle your dispute. People tend to underestimate the true cost of going to court and having a judge do all the heavy lifting in your divorce. It's not the easier, simpler, or less stressful way to go. But for some, it's necessary when two spouses cannot come to terms with their issues and must rely on the court to help them settle their divorce. Only about 5 percent of divorcing couples fall into that category. The remaining 95 percent of couples can work their way to a divorce agreement and be done with it.

On some level, you will have to deal with your local courthouse that handles family law cases even if you never set foot in a real courtroom. This can also be an intimidating experience for those who've never even been close to a courthouse and who are unfamiliar with the legal system, how courts work, all the forms that they require, and what you need to do to get

Here's the answer to the question posed in chapter 3: As you would expect, Nevada (hint: Las Vegas and Reno) wins for granting the most divorces per capita than any other state. Following Nevada, in order, are Indiana, Tennessee, New Mexico, and Alabama. Those who win for granting the *least* number of divorces per capita a year are, in order, Massachusetts, Maryland, Pennsylvania, Connecticut, and New Jersey. Religious differences and population dynamics—including demographics and mobility—may explain why those states with the lowest divorce rate tend to be in the Northeast and Mid-Atlantic.

Nevada, and especially Reno, was long a divorce center. Many came to "take the cure," as they called it. "I'm on my way to Reno," sang Billy Murray in 1910, declaring Reno's easy divorces under Nevada state law. This dry, barren land in the West became an oasis of hope for those seeking relief from their marriage. Though other states offered divorces to varying degrees, Reno's mix of the quick and practical divorce quickly gained the city a reputation as the undisputed leader in convenient divorces. Reno also played a key role in the dramatic increase of marriages at the outset of World War II, with its instant marriage services. It's only fitting that Reno would help people reverse their hasty decisions.

things done. Most people feel so put off by the thought of going to a courthouse that they begin to ask questions like What do I wear? How do I act? What if someone asks me questions I cannot answer? These are all good questions.

In this chapter, we'll take the mystery out of the courthouse and give you the information you need to navigate your local divorce court successfully. We'll also guide you through the how-tos of completing and filing your paperwork, dealing with motions, giving copies to your spouse, and responding to the court if you're the one who's been given copies of the divorce papers. Last, we'll give you some tips should your divorce turn sour and become a lit-igated case.

The Court System

We don't want to take you back to high school government and history class, but we do want to give you some idea of how the court system works on a practical level, and what it means for you as a person who needs to access and use the courts to get something done, such as file for divorce. You are more likely to land in court throughout your life than be hospitalized. Unless you're well versed in the lingo of the judicial system or work for a court, you probably don't know much about the courts—on either a federal or a state level—and the thought of dealing with them is scary. That's okay. You don't have to be an expert on the law and you don't have to understand the system all that much to get what you need. Many of our customers use our services for the simple reason that they don't want to do even the filing themselves, because they prefer to stay away from the courts as much as possible. It's hard enough to deal with going through a divorce; dealing with the courts is an added stress.

Courts are public places. You can go and listen to someone else's case in preparation for your own. If you know you have to appear in your family court during your divorce, spend some time beforehand watching someone else's experience in the courtroom. It helps to see the process in action when you're not on center stage. You'll learn what to expect, which will lower your anxiety and ease your nerves.

We tell our customers that when it comes to needing something from the courts, all one must do is complete the proper paperwork and submit it (file it) with a particular court, such as your family law court. It's all about filing pieces of paper and waiting for the court to act upon your request. Each paper or document has its own particular title or name. (Later in this chapter we define some of the documents you may encounter.) A document may comprise 2 pages or be 15 pages long or more. You may have to get other people's signatures, such as that of a notary public or a witness. You may also have to attach documents to your paperwork that include other requested information. And you may have to present personal information, such as your paycheck stubs to prove the amount of your take-home pay or a bank statement to show your cash assets, to the judge who handles your case. Be prepared to submit whatever the court asks. It also pays to be honest, patient, and perpetually organized.

The number of forms you may have to fill out might seem outrageous, but just take your time with each document and complete them all to the best of your ability. Your court may also want you to complete worksheets of its own, such as a custody child support worksheet or a shared/split custody worksheet. If you've done similar worksheets on your own, you'll be able to use your worksheets as a reference guide for filling out the court's specific documents. This is when all that preparatory work you did before completing the official paperwork comes in handy.

Make copies of all forms both before and after you complete them (keep copies of *everything* you submit, including personal paperwork). If a judge or clerk asks you to redo a form, fill it out again using a fresh form. Some courts allow you to handwrite your forms (usually in black ink), but it's always best to type everything. If you cannot locate a typewriter (or you just don't trust yourself to use a typewriter well), you can hire a typist or a document preparer such as We The People to help you prepare your documents so they look professional, tidy, and ready for submission (We The People will also file the documents for you at the courthouse).

Your local family law court will have a few quirks of its own and request that you submit your paperwork in a particular order or bound in a particular way. You can find out about these local requirements by asking the court clerk or visiting your court's family law center (described later).

Remember: Neither you nor your spouse is on trial for murdering your marriage. The facts of your case will not send you to jail or impose an added filing fee on your divorce. You simply have to follow your local court's set rules to ensure a successful divorce. Do your best to meet all of the expectations of the court. You can do this alone. You don't need a lawyer by your side to coach you.

Your Local Divorce Court

Family law courts are sprinkled throughout the United States, but unlike federal bankruptcy courts, which are clearly labeled as such and are relatively uniform across the country, the place where you need to file your paperwork and/or appear in court may not be called family court or divorce court. Depending on where you live—both your state and your county—the name of the court that deals with divorces may be a circuit court, a state superior court, or a district court. In Arkansas, for example, couples must file in the chancery court. In Delaware, and in other states, the court is actually called family court. You should not have to go far, however, to find a court near you that handles divorces. (Due to the volume of courthouses in the United States that handle family law, it's impossible for us to list them all.)

> If you follow your local court's rules and show respect to whomever you encounter there—from the clerk to the judge—you will get what you want more easily and quickly. Act and look professional when you deal with the courts. Try to have all of your forms neatly typed and clearly written. If you are submitting any agreement or requests in writing, they should also be typed and neatly presented. A judge will respect the time and effort you took to complete your paperwork. He or she will return the respect by listening to you and doing his or her best to meet your wishes in light of the evidence you present.

STATE	COURT WEB SITES
Alabama	www.alacourt.gov
Alaska	www.state.ak.us/courts
Arizona	www.supreme.state.az.us
Arkansas	www.courts.state.ar.us
California	www.courtinfo.ca.gov
Colorado	www.courts.state.co.us
Connecticut	www.jud2.state.ct.us/webforms
Delaware	www.courts.state.de.us
Florida	www.flcourts.org
Georgia	www.georgiacourts.org
Hawaii	www.courts.state.hi.us
Idaho	www.isc.idaho.gov/judicial.htm
Illinois	www.illinoissecondcircuit.info/
Indiana	www.in.gov/judiciary/selfservice
Iowa	www.judicial.state.ia.us/families
Kansas	www.kscourts.org
Kentucky	www.kycourts.net/forms
Louisiana	www.state.la.us/
Maine	www.courts.state.me.us
Maryland	www.courts.state.md.us/courtforms
Massachusetts	http://mass.gov/courts/selfhelp
Michigan	www.courts.michigan.gov
Minnesota	www.courts.state.mn.us
Mississippi	Refer to your local court for information
Missouri	www.osca.state.mo.us
Montana	www.lawlibrary.state.mt.us
Nebraska	http://court.neb.org/courts.htm

Figure 5.1a State Web Sites for Court Forms and Procedures

Nevada	http://nvsupremecourt.us
New Hampshire	www.courts.state.nh.us
New Jersey	www.judiciary.state.nj.us
New Mexico	http://nmcourts.com
New York	www.courts.state.ny.us
North Carolina	www.nccourts.org
North Dakota	www.courts.state.nd.us
Ohio	www.sconet.state.oh.us
Oklahomo	www.oscn.net/static/forms/districtforms.asp
Oregon	www.ojd.state.or.us
Pennsylvania	www.courts.state.pa.us
Rhode Island	www.courts.state.ri.us
South Carolina	www.sccourts.org
South Dakota	www.sdjudicial.com
Tennessee	www.tsc.state.tn.us
Texas	www.co.travis.tx.us/records_communication/law_library/forms.asp
Utah	www.utcourts.gov
Vermont	www.vermontjudiciary.org
Virginia	www.courts.state.va.us
Washington	www.courts.wa.gov/forms
West Virginia	www.state.wv.us/wvsca
Wisconsin	www.courts.state.wi.us
Wyoming	http://courts.state.wy.us

Figure 5.1b

Finding Your Local Family Courthouse

Figure 5.1 presents a list of web sites that will help you find your state's court forms and procedures. Using these links can guide you directly to your local court, too. Your state's main site and your local court's main site post a wealth of trusted information that you can access as well. Once you learn how to navigate these sites through practice, you'll find them very helpful. Our web site (www.wethepeopleforms.com) also posts these links.

Another way to locate your local family law court is to call or visit your local courthouse and inquire about which court deals with family law cases. If you do not know where your nearest court is located, try an Internet search engine, such as Google, or refer to your phone

> Remember: A family court is one that has jurisdiction (authority) over family matters, such as divorce, child custody, paternity, alimony, and adoption. Your local family court may be within a district court, superior court, or circuit court.

book's listing of government addresses and numbers. (Government listings in phone books typically appear near the front and are divided by city, county, and state.) It's always easiest to let your fingers do the walking and call before you visit any court. Most courts have automated systems that relay information or people standing by to take calls and questions. You may even be able to speak to the clerk directly if your court is small. Your state's web site (.gov) may also have links that direct you to courthouses.

Getting Extra Help

Many family law courts have information centers open to the public that provide family law information, referrals, and general assistance. Many of these centers are referred to as *pro se* centers, which means "for yourself" centers. (If you are representing yourself—without a lawyer—in any legal action, you are said to be filing *pro se*.) These centers provide the legal forms you need and procedural guidance in many areas of family law, including divorce, legal separation, annulments, summary dissolutions, paternity, and domestic violence prevention cases. The office staff may consist of attorneys, paralegals, and support personnel, but none of them can give legal advice or represent you.

A good example of such a center is the Family Law Information Center (FLIC) in Los Angeles, which works in conjunction with other family law service providers at the court. The center can provide the following information:

- Explains the court process
- Provides instructional information regarding the preparation of documents in family law matters
- Provides court forms and information regarding local court rules
- Provides referrals to the family court services, the district attorney's offices, the family law facilitator's offices, various nonprofit family law organizations, guardianship clinics, and other community agencies
- Provides the viewing of instructional self-help videos with corresponding form packets
- Provides access to the Internet, reference materials, and SmartLaw, a project of the Los Angeles County Bar Association

Additionally, the center offers free divorce workshops at some of the courthouses around town. These kinds of services are not unique to Los Angeles. Your local courthouse may have a similar program set up to assist you in your divorce process—from obtaining the forms and learning how to fill them out, to calculating child support and determining a reasonable visitation schedule. Because divorce is so common today, you're likely to find lots of resources available to you—in places you may not have thought about; your local library or community center, for example, may also have programs or valuable information. Don't be afraid to use these resources; they exist to help make this process simpler and less costly. (Keep in mind that you're much better off using your local court's resources, where you have to eventually file anyhow, than anything you can find online.)

Preparing Your Paperwork and Filing

Once you've gathered all the appropriate forms and paperwork to fill out from the court, take your time completing everything. All divorces start out the same: A spouse files the first set of papers with the court, including a complaint or petition, and the other spouse waits to get copies of the filed papers.

Figures 5.2 and 5.3 are sample petitions from California and Georgia. Note: Even though these sample petitions are from two specific states, they generally exemplify the kind of information you'll need to provide on your own state's petition.

Types of Service

You can serve your spouse in a variety of ways. For couples doing their own divorce (without attorneys) and who can cooperate with one another (that is, the spouse who does not file will voluntarily accept being served), typically the spouse who files hires a neutral third party to deliver copies of the papers to the other spouse at an appropriate time. That neutral third party must be an adult, and can be a friend, relative, professional process server, constable, or a person from the local sheriff's office. The person who delivers the copies to the other spouse may have to get a signed and notarized *acknowledgment of service* (sometimes called an *admission of service*) from the other spouse who receives the papers, which gets submitted to the court along with another document called a *proof of service*. The acknowledgment of service says that the other spouse got the copies, and the proof of service proves to the court that the delivery person delivered the copies successfully. (Still another document—an *affidavit of service*—may also have to be signed in some circumstances, which entails a notary public.)

Some courts allow other methods of serving spouses that are not formal. For example, the other spouse may be able to sign a waiver of service, and the waiver becomes the acknowledgment that he or she is aware of the divorce filing. In some states, the divorcing couple can file as copetitioners to avoid the need of any service.

Though typically not preferred, the filing spouse may also deliver the copies in person and forgo getting a third party to do it. The filing spouse will still have to get a signed and notarized original acknowledgment of service from the other spouse, so this method does not necessarily make the transaction of delivering copies of the paperwork any easier. In fact, having to personally serve your spouse during this emotionally charged time is not always a good idea. If you know that your spouse will not voluntarily accept service, then service must be made in person by an adult other than you, and that person will take care of getting the notarized affidavit of service and either give this back to you or deliver it to the clerk of the court.

Generally speaking, when a spouse files the initial paperwork in court, the court returns to that spouse a packet that includes the acknowledgment of service and proof of service documents that are used by the third party who must deliver copies of the paperwork to the other spouse. Still other ways to deliver copies of the papers to the other spouse include the following:

- If the other party lives out of state, you need to find a professional process server in that state. You can serve anyone anywhere in the United States with divorce papers, as long as the papers are personally served and you have a properly executed affidavit of service (or some such document, depending on your court) to prove it. (To account for any

FL-100

ATTORNEY OR PARTY WITHOUT ATTORNEY (Name, State Bar number, and address):

DAVID A. MILLER
435 CARMEL DRIVE
LA MESA, CA 91941

TELEPHONE NO.: (619) 555-8284   FAX NO. (Optional):
E-MAIL ADDRESS (Optional):
ATTORNEY FOR (Name): IN PRO PER

FOR COURT USE ONLY

SUPERIOR COURT OF CALIFORNIA, COUNTY OF SAN DIEGO
STREET ADDRESS: 250 EAST MAIN STREET
MAILING ADDRESS: 250 EAST MAIN STREET
CITY AND ZIP CODE: EL CAJON, CA 92020-3913
BRANCH NAME: EAST

MARRIAGE OF
PETITIONER: DAVID A. MILLER

RESPONDENT: ANNA M. MILLER

PETITION FOR
[X] **Dissolution of Marriage**
[ ] **Legal Separation**
[ ] **Nullity of Marriage**   [ ] **AMENDED**

CASE NUMBER:

1. RESIDENCE (Dissolution only) [X] Petitioner [ ] Respondent has been a resident of this state for at least six months and of this county for at least three months immediately preceding the filing of this **Petition for Dissolution of Marriage.**

2. STATISTICAL FACTS
   a. Date of marriage: 12/10/89
   b. Date of separation: 10/28/04

   c. Time from date of marriage to date of separation (**specify**):
   Years: 14   Months: 10

3. DECLARATION REGARDING MINOR CHILDREN (**include children of this relationship born prior to or during the marriage or adopted during the marriage**):
   a. [ ] There are no minor children.
   b. [X] The minor children are:

Child's name	Birthdate	Age	Sex
SUSAN MILLER	8/10/95	10	F

   [ ] Continued on Attachment 3b.
   c. If there are minor children of the Petitioner and Respondent, a completed **Declaration Under Uniform Child Custody Jurisdiction and Enforcement Act (UCCJEA)** (form FL-105) must be attached.
   d. [ ] A completed voluntary declaration of paternity regarding minor children born to the Petitioner and Respondent prior to the marriage is attached.

4. SEPARATE PROPERTY
   Petitioner requests that the assets and debts listed [ ] in **Property Declaration** (form FL-160) [ ] in Attachment 4
   [ ] below be confirmed as separate property.

Item	Confirm to

NOTICE: You may redact (black out) social security numbers from any written material filed with the court in this case other than a form used to collect child or spousal support.

Page 1 of 2

Form Adopted for Mandatory Use
Judicial Council of California
FL-100 [Rev. January 1, 2005]

PETITION—MARRIAGE
(Family Law)

Family Code, §§ 2330, 3409

Figure 5.2a Petition—California.

MARRIAGE OF (last name, first name of parties): MILLER, DAVID A. and ANNA M.	CASE NUMBER:

5. DECLARATION REGARDING COMMUNITY AND QUASI-COMMUNITY ASSETS AND DEBTS AS CURRENTLY KNOWN

    a.   ☐   There are no such assets or debts subject to disposition by the court in this proceeding.

    b.   ☒   All such assets and debts are listed   ☐   in *Property Declaration*   (form FL-160)   ☐   in Attachment 5b.

          ☒   below *(specify):*

        THE FULL EXTENT OF THE PROPERTY IS UNKNOWN AT THIS TIME AND INCLUDES BUT IS NOT LIMITED TO: FAMILY HOME, MORTGAGE, AUTOMOBILE, BANK ACCOUNTS, PROMISSORY NOTES (DOT), STOCKS, RETIREMENT ACCOUNTS, AND MISCELLANEOUS HOUSEHOLD FURNISHINGS.

6. **Petitioner requests**

    a.   ☒   dissolution of the marriage based on   d.   ☐   nullity of voidable marriage based on

        (1)   ☒   irreconcilable differences. (Fam. Code, § 2310(a).)   (1)   ☐   petitioner's age at time of marriage.

        (2)   ☐   incurable insanity. (Fam. Code, § 2310(b).)   (Fam. Code, § 2210(a).)

    b.   ☐   legal separation of the parties based on   (2)   ☐   prior existing marriage.

        (1)   ☐   irreconcilable differences. (Fam. Code, § 2310(a).)   (Fam. Code, § 2210(b).)

        (2)   ☐   incurable insanity. (Fam. Code, § 2310(b).)   (3)   ☐   unsound mind. (Fam. Code, § 2210(c).)

    c.   ☐   nullity of void marriage based on   (4)   ☐   fraud. (Fam. Code, § 2210(d).)

        (1)   ☐   incestuous marriage. (Fam. Code, § 2200.)   (5)   ☐   force. (Fam. Code, § 2210(e).)

        (2)   ☐   bigamous marriage. (Fam. Code, § 2201.)   (6)   ☐   physical incapacity. (Fam. Code, § 2210(f).)

7. **Petitioner requests** that the court grant the above relief and make injunctive (including restraining) and other orders as follows:

		Petitioner	Respondent	Joint	Other
a.	Legal custody of children to	☐	☐	X	☐
b.	Physical custody of children to	☐	☐	X	☐
c.	Child visitation be granted to				

        As requested in form: ☐ FL-311   ☐ FL-312   ☐ FL-341(C)   ☐ FL-341(D)   ☐ FL-341(E)   ☐ Attachment 7c.

    d.   ☐   Determination of parentage of any children born to the Petitioner and Respondent prior to the marriage.

    e.   Attorney fees and costs payable by . . . .   ☐   ☐

    f.   Spousal support payable to (earnings assignment will be issued) . . . .   ☐   ☐

    g.   ☒   Terminate the court's jurisdiction (ability) to award spousal support to Respondent.

    h.   ☒   Property rights be determined.

    i.   ☐   Petitioner's former name be restored to *(specify):*

    j.   ☐   Other *(specify):*

        ☐   Continued on Attachment 7j.

8. **Child support**–If there are minor children born to or adopted by the Petitioner and Respondent before or during this marriage, the court will make orders for the support of the children upon request and submission of financial forms by the requesting party. An earnings assignment may be issued without further notice. Any party required to pay support must pay interest on overdue amounts at the "legal" rate, which is currently 10 percent.

9. **I HAVE READ THE RESTRAINING ORDERS ON THE BACK OF THE SUMMONS, AND I UNDERSTAND THAT THEY APPLY TO ME WHEN THIS PETITION IS FILED.**

I declare under penalty of perjury under the laws of the State of California that the foregoing is true and correct.

Date:

▶

DAVID A. MILLER
       (TYPE OR PRINT NAME)   (SIGNATURE OF PETITIONER)

Date:

▶

IN PRO PER
       (TYPE OR PRINT NAME)   (SIGNATURE OF ATTORNEY FOR PETITIONER)

NOTICE: Dissolution or legal separation may automatically cancel the rights of a spouse under the other spouse's will, trust, retirement plan, power of attorney, pay on death bank account, survivorship rights to any property owned in joint tenancy, and any other similar thing. It does not automatically cancel the right of a spouse as beneficiary of the other spouse's life insurance policy. You should review these matters, as well as any credit cards, other credit accounts, insurance polices, retirement plans, and credit reports to determine whether they should be changed or whether you should take any other actions. However, some changes may require the agreement of your spouse or a court order (see Family Code sections 231–235).

FL-100 [Rev. January 1, 2005]   **PETITION—MARRIAGE**   Page 2 of 2
                                 (Family Law)

Figure 5.2b

IN THE SUPERIOR COURT OF CLAYTON COUNTY

STATE OF GEORGIA

MARK MILLER,   )
)
    Petitioner,   )
)   CIVIL ACTION
v.   )
)   FILE NO. _____
SUSAN MILLER,   )
)
    Respondent.   )

COMPLAINT FOR DIVORCE

MARK MILLER, Petitioner, files this his Complaint for Divorce against SUSAN MILLER, Respondent, and shows as follows:

1.

Petitioner is a resident of Clayton County, Georgia, and has been a resident of the State of Georgia for at least six (6) months next preceding the filing of this Complaint.

2.

Respondent is a resident of Clayton County, Georgia, and is subject to the venue and jurisdiction of this Court.

(1) The Respondent has consented to the Jurisdiction of this Court and has acknowledged service of process and jurisdiction of this Court.

(2) The Respondent may be served at Respondent's residence address of 31 Creek Drive, Rex, GA 30273.

3.

Petitioner and Respondent were married on December 20, 1996.

Figure 5.3a   Petition–Georgia.

4.

The parties separated on or about May 3, 2003, and have lived in a bona fide state of separation since that date.

5.

There are 2 (two) minor children born as a result of this marriage; to wit: Tyler Jordan Miller, born July 3, 2000 and Kyle Louis Miller, born November 16, 2002.

6.

Petitioner is entitled to reasonable visitation with these children.

7.

The minor children currently reside at 31 Creek Drive, Rex, GA 30273, with Mother and Father. For the last five (5) years, the minor children have resided at the following addresses, with the following parties:

Birth to Present- 31 Creek Dr., Rex, GA 30273 (both parents), Clayton County, Georgia.

No proceeding other than this action has ever been initiated concerning the custody of said Children and Petitioner knows of no individual other than the parties to this action who has any claim of custody or visitation rights concerning said Children. The said minor Children are in the custody and control of Petitioner and Respondent. Once the house located at 31 Creek Dr., Rex, GA 30273 is sold, the children will be residing with the Mother at 262 Elm Tree Ct., Ellenwood, GA 30294.

8.

Petitioner has not participated as a party, witness, or in any capacity in any other litigation concerning the custody of the minor children in this or any other state. Petitioner does not know of any custody proceeding concerning the minor children which may be pending in a Court in this or any other state.

9.

Petitioner knows of no other person, not a party to this proceeding, who has physical custody of the children or claims to have custody or visitation rights with respect to the minor children.

10.

Petitioner is employed by Sheraton Hotels, Inc., earning $3,575.00 gross per month. The Petitioner is an able bodied person capable of earning sufficient money to support (the minor children). Respondent is employed by Shell Inc., earning $1,525.00 per month and Respondent is in need of financial assistance from the Petitioner for the support of the minor children.

Figure 5.3b

11.

a) Respondent should be ordered to maintain a policy for dental, medical, and hospitalization insurance for the minor children. Respondent should also be responsible for any other expenses for the children's medical or dental treatment, if such expenses are not covered by insurance policies.

b) Respondent and Petitioner should share the costs of dental, medical, and hospitalization insurance for the minor children.

12.

a) Respondent should be ordered to maintain life insurance for the benefit of the minor children.

13.

I am not seeking alimony because: N/A

14.

Respondent and Petitioner have already divided our marital property to our mutual satisfaction. The Respondent and Petitioner are selling the house located at 3107 Rock Creek Drive, Rex, GA 30273 and splitting the proceeds.

15.

Petitioner s grounds for an absolute divorce are:
a) The marriage is **irretrievably broken** Petitioner's Spouse and Petitioner can no longer live together.
There is no hope that the two of us will get back together.

Petitioner is entitled to a divorce from Respondent upon the ground that the marriage between the parties is irretrievably broken, as contemplated by O.C.G.A. '19-5-3(13), there being no reasonable hope of reconciliation.

Figure 5.3c

FOR THESE REASONS, Petitioner requests *(check all that apply)*

☐ (a) That she be awarded a total divorce from Respondent;
☐ (b) Temporary and Permanent Custody of the minor children;
☐ (c) Joint custody of the minor children;
☐ (d) Visitation with the minor children;
☐ (e) Child Support;
☐ (f) Medical, Dental and Hospitalization insurance for the children;
☐ (g) Life Insurance for the benefit of the minor children;
☐ (h) Alimony;
☐ (i) An award of the marital property listed in paragraph (14c);
☐ (j) Respondent to pay the joint debts listed in paragraph (15b);
☐ (k) That all issues of child support, health insurance for the minor children, life insurance for the minor children, alimony, division of property and debts be held in abeyance until such time as this court has personal jurisdiction over Petitioner's spouse;
☐ (l) A change back to Petitioner's former name
☐ (m) A restraining order to restrain and enjoin the Respondent from harassing, molesting or threatening me in any way whatsoever;
☐ (n) A total divorce, a vinculo matrimonii, from Respondent;
☐ (o) Respondent be served with a copy of Petitioner's Complaint for Divorce;

This the _____ day of _____, _____.
[date] [month] [year]
Respectfully submitted,

_____
(Sign your name here) PRO SE
Petitioner's name *(print or type)*: _____
Petitioner's address:
Petitioner's telephone number: (   ) _____

Figure 5.3d

TIME OUT! *I Don't Understand What You Mean By . . .*

Affidavit   "I promise the information on this page is true." A piece of paper (a document) that you sign saying that all the information on the document in question is true. An affidavit is a sworn statement in writing. You typically sign an affidavit to say that you have done something, such as filed paperwork or delivered paperwork to someone else. If you sign an *affidavit of service* in a divorce, you are promising that you've been given copies of the papers. It is an *acknowledgment of service.* The person who gives copies of the papers to your spouse will have to sign a *proof of service* document, which states that he or she gave copies of all the filed papers to your spouse. Affidavits may also be used to verify information, as in an *affidavit to verify income.* There are many different kinds of affidavit, and in a divorce you may find yourself obtaining many of these affidavits for many different reasons. There is no one affidavit to cover all the bases.

Summons   A call to court. A document issued by the court at the time a lawsuit (example: divorce) is filed, stating the name of both plaintiff (example: filing spouse) and defendant (example: other spouse), the title and file number of the case, the court and its address, the name and address of the plaintiff's attorney (if any), and instructions about the need to file a response to the complaint within a certain time (such as 30 days after service), usually with a form on the back on which information of service of summons and complaint is to be filled out and signed by the process server (the person who delivers the summons). A copy of the summons must be served on the other spouse at the same time as the complaint/petition to start the time running for the other spouse to answer. In divorce cases, once the filing spouse submits the initial paperwork, the court issues a summons to the other spouse, which alerts that spouse to the divorce

local laws you must follow if your have to serve your spouse out of state, be sure to ask your local family court the usual procedure.) Overseas, you usually need to have a lawyer do the serving to make sure it's done according to local laws.

• Only if personal service is not possible should you request the court to issue an order for service by publication. This happens if you cannot locate your spouse and you don't know how else to serve him or her. In such a situation, you will ask the court for permission to publish a notice of your divorce in a newspaper most likely to be seen by your spouse. You will need to tell the court what you have done to try to find your spouse in the last six months, such as checking with relatives, speaking to his or her last known employer, and presenting returned envelopes that you sent to his or her last address.

Keep in mind, if you serve by publication, the goal is to give actual notice to the defendant—your spouse. The notice informs your spouse that you have filed for divorce; it also outlines your spouse's legal rights. Publish in the newspaper most likely to accomplish that goal (that is, in the county where he or she was last known to live) and be prepared to explain to the judge why you chose that paper. The documents also must be mailed to the last known address most

proceeding and gives him or her time to respond with an answer to the court. A notice to appear in court due to the summons is also called a *citation*.

Motion   A formal request made to a judge for an order or judgment. Motions are made in court all the time for many purposes: to continue (postpone) a trial to a later date, to get a modification of an order, for temporary child support, for a judgment, for dismissal of the opposing party's case, for a rehearing, or for dozens of other purposes. Most motions require a written petition, a written statement of legal reasons for granting the motion (often called *points and authorities,* where you cite specific laws), written notice to the opposing party, and a hearing before a judge. However, during a trial or a hearing, an oral motion may be permitted.

Hearing   Any proceeding before a judge or other magistrate (such as a hearing officer or court commissioner) without a jury in which evidence and/or an argument is presented to determine some issue of fact or both issues of fact and law. In divorce cases, hearings are usually conducted with a family law judge listening to you and your spouse's cases in order to grant any motions or requests for custody, visitation, support, and so on.

Clerk   The person who does the intake and review of the documents before they are sent to a judge. An official or employee who handles the business of a court or a system of courts, maintains files of each case, and issues routine documents. Almost every county has a clerk of the courts or county clerk who fulfills those functions, and most courtrooms have a clerk to keep records and assist the judge in the management of the court. The clerk on duty when you file your divorce papers may be a good source of information.

likely to give notice, and proof of that mailing may be required at your default hearing. Publication must be for a period of time, such as four consecutive weeks, and the time for default runs from the last date of publication. If there is no response from your spouse, the court will grant you a default divorce (so you don't have to stay married to that person forever).

Default Divorce in Idaho as an Example

To demonstrate how divorce typically proceeds in court, we're going to take you through the steps couples experience in Idaho. We're also going to assume this is a default divorce, which means the other spouse does not respond to the lawsuit and the court rules based on what the filing spouse submits to court. Default divorces are common among couples who agree to get divorced; they discuss all the items stated in the complaint or petition, they reach a reasonable agreement on all the issues, and they pick one person to do the actual filing. The other spouse gets served copies of the papers and by not responding, tacitly agrees to what was detailed in the initial petition. In other words, the other spouse does not file an answer responding to or disputing items stated in the petition.

Fee waivers may be available if your income is very low. You'll have to fill out another form (a fee waiver application) to request a fee waiver from the court when you submit your paperwork. Ask your clerk how best to pay the filing fee, as some courts prefer cash and will not accept a credit card.

As you read through the following steps, don't forget that this reflects only one state's guidelines for default divorces. Your state will have a different procedure and may use different language for certain forms or documents. We've included some general information under these steps as well that broadly describe the purpose of each of the steps. All courts will practice some variation of these steps.

Step 1: Prepare a Verified Complaint for Divorce

This is the initial petition or complaint that must get filed with the court. The initial petition is where the couple establishes the facts and issues of their divorce—grounds for divorce, number of children, assets and debts, and so on—and the filing spouse indicates what he or she wants from the other spouse (if anything), such as alimony, child support, custody of the children, or visitation rights.

Petitions generally are more than one page and have many sections. In Idaho, for example, the Complaint for Divorce has two sections. The first section must include statements that clearly show (1) the names of both parties and all minor children of the relationship, (2) the date and place of the marriage, (3) your residency in Idaho for at least six weeks immediately before the date you file this complaint, (4) whether there are children, (5) whether there is any real property (land and things permanently attached, such as a house) to be divided, (6) what personal property (cars, furniture, etc.) and debt exist and how they can be fairly and equitably divided, (7) that you have irreconcilable differences, and (8) whether you want a former name restored and, if so, what that name is.

The second section is called a *prayer:* "I pray that I can get what I want." The prayer must specifically request what you want in the divorce decree and usually includes a divorce, a specific division of property and debt, and a name change. When there are children, the prayer *must* include a request for an order of custody and parenting schedule and an order for child support pursuant to the Idaho Child Support Guidelines. (The prayer often seems to repeat much of what is in the first section.) The court can only grant the relief specifically requested in your prayer.

Step 2: File the Verified Complaint for Divorce

Once you've completed the initial complaint and signed on all the dotted lines—which, in Idaho, requires a notary public—you'll make two copies of the entire set of documents, paperclip them to the originals, take the set to your county courthouse, and file it with the clerk of the court. You'll ask that a summons be issued (defined later), and you will pay the filing fee ($118 in Idaho).

The court will give you important orders (rulings you must follow): a joint preliminary injunction (things you can't do) for property, and, if there are children, you will also receive a joint preliminary injunction for children. These preliminary injunctions are court orders made in the early stages of the divorce that prohibit you and your spouse from doing anything related to what's in dispute—namely, your assets and children. The goal is to maintain the status quo until there is a final judgment. This means neither one of you, for example, can run off with the children to another state or sell the house immediately. In Idaho, the court also issues an order to attend a Focus on Children class.

The clerk will organize the documents with the summons according to its usual standard and give you any information the court readily provides. This is a good time to ask any questions you have about the process and what you must do next. For most, the next step will be getting your spouse served. The clerk will keep a set of original documents and return to you two copies—one for you and one for your spouse. The clerk may also have another document for you to take, such as a Certificate of Divorce, which indicates that your divorce action has been filed. But keep in mind that different courts have different ways of doing things, so your court may not have any such certificate.

Step 3: Serve the Other Party with Documents

The filing spouse delivers copies of the paperwork to the other spouse according to Idaho's preferred service methods. If hiring a professional server, the filing spouse must pay the server his or her fee for this service and tell the server how to find the other spouse and what time of day is optimal for reaching that spouse. The deputy or process server will then take care of serving the other spouse. After the spouse is served, the deputy or process server will fill out another form, sometimes called a *return of service,* which proves to the court that the job is done.

In our Idaho example, the papers to serve include the summons, the complaint, the joint preliminary injunction(s) and the order to attend the Focus on Children class (if there are children from the marriage). The spouse must follow any directions with regard to receiving the paperwork, such as signing an acknowledgment of service and getting it notarized. If the spouse wants to respond to the court (called *giving an answer*), he or she must follow the court's rules for doing so.

If you're the one getting served, you may opt to respond to the court even if you agree to the terms laid out in the paperwork. We said earlier that it's often a good idea to respond to the court so the court understands that you want to be a part of the case and that you intend to actively participate in its proceedings. Responding to a court usually entails filing a written, typed response. The packet of papers you receive should have instructions detailing how and why you need to respond. If you respond to your court, the case may no longer be considered a default divorce, but if you reach an agreement with your spouse, the process should be relatively easy. In some states, you may not have to appear in court; your agreement, which you and your spouse sign, will then get signed by the judge and your divorce will be final.

Step 4: File the Acknowledgment of Service or Affidavit of Service with the Clerk of the Court

The court needs to know that your spouse has received notice of your divorce case and copies of the paperwork. Each court will have a different way of getting that proof, but most request that another form—an affidavit or acknowledgment of service—gets signed by the person who gave the papers to your spouse and filed.

Step 5: In All Cases with Children, You Must Attend the Focus on Children Class

Mandatory parenting classes are becoming the norm in many courts across the country. They are not semester courses that have final exams, however; they typically take up an afternoon in a single three-hour session. Some are free; some come with small fees. Because divorce takes such an emotional toll on children and the courts want to do everything in their power (while they have it during a divorce case) to help ensure the safety and security of those children once they grant couples divorces, courts are increasingly encouraging parents to attend classes. These classes help parents prepare for their new roles in single parenthood. Parents will experience

To prepare for your own hearing, you may want to attend someone else's hearing first. You can attend as many of these public hearings as you like. Each judge approaches divorces differently, especially when couples represent themselves (again, this is called a *pro se* divorce). Many judges will walk you through the default procedure. Still, you should go to at least one default divorce session before yours is scheduled. That way you will hear the types of questions you will be asked and the types of answers you are expected to give. This will significantly reduce your anxiety at the time of your hearing.

an adjustment period during which they'll have to acquire new skills and get used to a different lifestyle. They may also have to accept and deal with many unexpected challenges, for which having some advance knowledge can be helpful.

You may initially find the obligation to attend parenting classes burdensome and unnecessary. But don't adopt a bad attitude about these classes or seminars. You may find that what you learn in these courses is what carries you through this transition in life and gives you the knowledge and skills you need to see your children pull through this tough time, too. In other words, don't underestimate the usefulness and value of mandatory parenting classes. They may surprise you—at a later date when you look back and realize how positive and effective they were.

Step 6: Schedule the Default Hearing

Twenty days (in Idaho) after the other party was served, and if the other party has not filed an appearance or answer (response) to the complaint, you will call the clerk and ask that the default hearing be scheduled. Proof that the other party has been served must be in the file in order to schedule a default hearing. In cases with children, you must attend the Focus on Children class prior to the date of your hearing.

Once your divorce is proceeding in court, it's important to watch the clock and calendar for waiting periods and filing deadlines. Mark dates on your calendar so you don't forget to respond to a request from the court or show up in court in response to a summons. The court will not accept many excuses for being forgetful, late, or difficult in general.

Step 7: Prepare the Documents Needed for the Default Hearing

Each court will have a different list of documents and items it wants you to bring to your hearing. Ask your clerk for this list and don't leave anything out or neglect any instructions. You may have to provide self-addressed stamped envelopes, for example. Be sure that you've made plenty of good copies of all your paperwork (usually two is enough; the court will keep the original), and that you've gotten the proper signatures on all the documents, including those from a notary public if necessary. Your case number and name should appear on every page. Ask your court about its preferred format and follow that.

Not all courts will require an appearance at such a hearing. Some default divorces proceed without anyone ever setting foot in a courtroom or similar setting. If you do have to appear in court, don't be shy about carrying as much supportive documentation as you can, such as financial statements that detail your income and expenses, records, worksheets, and agreements. You may find it useful to carry one folder filled with all the paperwork you think the court will want and another folder with copies of everything in the first folder, as well as any additional paperwork you think the court *may* want.

Step 8: Be on Time for Your Hearing on the Date Scheduled

By the time you attend your hearing, you will hopefully have thoroughly prepared yourself by knowing what to expect as well as how to act. As mentioned many times before, the more agreements you've made with your spouse before appearing before a judge, the easier this step will be. The judge will know, given your petition and other relevant documents, how well you and your spouse have cooperated and decided on matters.

The following are some tips to help prepare you for the courtroom:

- Do not expect the judge to make the "right" decision. There are three directions the judge can go when making a decision: your way, your spouse's way, or the judge's way. Two out of three are not in your favor.

- Try to settle as many issues as possible before entering the courtroom. (See the first bullet.)

- Avoid speaking unless addressed by the judge to do so.

- When addressing the judge, call him or her "Your Honor."

- Always thank the judge when you are finished speaking. Always be respectful.

- Never speak to or make comments to your spouse when you are before the judge.

- Leave all hostile and negative emotions at the door. Do not make faces or gestures when the judge, or your spouse, or your spouse's attorney is speaking. Judges see this and do not appreciate it.

- Dress appropriately. You should appear well-groomed, prepared, and serious about dealing with your divorce. You do not need to don a three-piece suit, but avoid being overly casual in threadbare jeans, a T-shirt, and open-toed shoes. Dress like you're going to a job interview.

- Take notes if you want to. You may need them in future dealings with your spouse and/or the court.

- Do not take children into the courtroom unless the judge requests it. This is your divorce—not your children's—and they should not hear what goes on in that room.

- Be prepared. Bring as much information and documentation and any other pertinent documents as you possibly can with you.

- Be patient, as you might have a long wait before your case is heard. While you're waiting, listen to other cases so you know what to expect.

- Remember: You can always ask the judge for clarification if you don't understand something that was said. You may have a very kind and patient judge, or you may have a grouchy judge who doesn't have a lot of extra patience. No matter your experience, don't ever be afraid to speak up and ask for more explanation.

As previously mentioned, not all states require hearings in default or no-fault divorces. You may not have to appear in court, or maybe only one of you will have to appear. The hearing is a formality that officially settles the case and essentially says "you are now divorced." You become legally divorced once the judge signs your divorce decree, which is the court's final written order for divorce and makes your decree, alongside your agreements, part of the court records.

Normally the judge will keep the court file at the end of the hearing. The clerk will receive it from the judge after all hearings have been completed. Usually later the same day (after your hearing), the clerk will mail out a certified copy of the Decree of Divorce to you and to your spouse.

Once the Decree of Divorce is filed for the record and copies are sent out, you are divorced. Your spouse will have a set number of days (42 in Idaho) to appeal the awards made in the decree. In most courts, you cannot change anything in the decree during those days, but once those days have passed and there has been no appeal, either party may request a modification to child support, custody, and visitation. Some courts can provide you with the forms for making these modifications. In courts where such forms are not readily available, ask the clerk what you should do. You may have to employ an attorney to help, or speak with a local We The People office for procedural information. To modify anything in your divorce decree, your circumstances must have changed, and you must prove this change to the judge. Modifications cannot be routinely changed just because you want to.

What to Do with Your Divorce Decree

As with any important documents, file your divorce decree in a safe place. You may need to present this document in the future to prove that you are, in fact, divorced. For example, if you apply for a marriage license again, you may need to show your divorce decree. Keep your decree in a place where you keep other documents, such as your birth certificate, passport, will, or living trust. All of these documents should be kept in a fireproof box. You should keep copies of all the agreements you made with your spouse, too. Note that you may have to go to court to get a certified copy of your decree, and extra copies can be provided with a small fee.

In your state, your divorce decree may have a different name. Other names for this document include Dissolution Order, Divorce Judgment, Dissolution Judgment, and Decree of

Notes from an Attorney

People often represent themselves *in propria persona* or *in pro per,* Latin for "in one's own proper person." Representing yourself in court is probably a new experience, exposing you to new circumstances in an unfamiliar environment. This can make you feel overwhelmed, nervous and scared and may make you want to go running from the courthouse. But fear not, the judge, bailiff, and court clerk are all there as part of a dispute resolution system designed to let you have your day in court. A few tips will help you through that first time in court.

- ☑ Dress appropriately. It isn't a black tie event, but it isn't a day at the beach, either. Proper dress lets the court know that you respect the process.
- ☑ Be prepared. Prepare in advance what you want to say and organize papers you think you may need. Try to be very concise with any statements you make to the court, the court prefers brief and succinct facts. Address any arguments to the judge rather than opposing parties and avoid arguing with the judge. Answer any questions the judge has and then listen carefully to what the judge says and take notes. You may ask questions of the judge if there is something you don't understand, but the judge cannot give you legal advice. When the judge is finished thank the judge and leave the court in an orderly manner. Follow these simple steps and your first day in court will feel like a day at the beach.

—Derek Thiele, Attorney-at-Law

Dissolution of Marriage. No matter what the document is called, it is an order from the court that ends your marriage.

Changes to Your Divorce Decree and Agreements

The settlement you make with your spouse, which gets signed by the judge and put into force, may not work for both of you in the long term. As life throws you changes and as the needs of your family—especially your children—change, you may need to revisit your agreement and make some modifications. How easily you can do that will depend on your relationship with your former spouse and whether the two of you can agree on the changes. However, if only one person wants to make a change and the other does not, you may find yourself back in the courtroom again and paying an attorney to help you get those changes signed by a judge.

The courts do not like to change divorce agreements liberally or without serious proof that your circumstances have changed. How serious must your circumstances be? Here are examples of situations that may merit changes:

- Increases or decreases in the income of the spouse paying or receiving alimony and/or child support
- A problem with the parent who has custody of the children, such as an illness, injury, substance abuse problem, criminal record, or inability to sufficiently care for them
- A problem with one or more of the children, such as an illness, injury, substance abuse problem, criminal record, or inability to be sufficiently cared for under the current divorce plan
- Serious conflict between the parent with custody and the children, such that their proper care is limited or sacrificed
- Contemplated relocation of one parent that makes former custody or visitation arrangements with the children more difficult, if not impossible

Reasons other than these may reflect your particular situation. Whatever your reasons are for making changes to your agreement, you must prove to the court that those reasons are valid and that the court should issue an order that modifies your divorce agreement. You're less likely to get a court to change your property settlement agreement than to your alimony, child support, and visitation arrangement. Some states prohibit the courts from changing property settlement agreements. But even those that do, allow such changes only within a certain time period.

To make changes, you must create a written, typed document (a declaration) that lays out what you want to change and why. Include any evidence that supports your request, such as a new income and expense report that demonstrates your need for more financial support. The court may also ask you to fill out other documents, such as an affidavit of income, which proves to the court how much you make.

In some states, you won't have to physically go to court if you and your ex-spouse can reach an agreement. In that case, your papers go to court and a judge ultimately signs them. You never set foot in the courthouse.

If you and your former spouse agree to making changes (and you also agree to exactly what should be changed), don't assume it's then okay to avoid the court's participation in issuing a formal order that reflects all of your changes. It's in your best interest, as well as your spouse's and your children's, to get a new court order so the court can enforce that order. Note that a

If you've taken the time to think through your divorce agreement and you've somewhat anticipated future problems or issues that you and your spouse will have to deal with, your need to make major changes in your agreement should be limited. Making changes to your divorce terms can be a big hassle, so this is more reason to ensure both you and your spouse agree to the terms of your divorce—before it becomes final.

judge can reject your and your spouse's request for changes if he or she thinks it's not in the best interests of your children.

Divorces that are settled by judges (*litigated divorces*) are very difficult to appeal. If a judge decides your divorce settlement and you are not happy with it, you face another round of obstacles that means more time, money, frustration, and another trial. You cannot file an appeal anytime you like, as each state has the appeal window open for only a certain time period following the decision. You must have a legal reason to file an appeal, and the process is not something you can do yourself (you will need an attorney). Appeals to litigated divorces are so "unappealing" on many levels that it's not even worth detailing the how-tos involved in this endeavor. Moreover, appeals come with no guarantees that they will get you what you want—other than a ticket to the poorhouse and severe depression. A judge is likely to say, "You asked for it!" when commenting on the outcome of a litigated divorce. If you cannot present an agreement to the court, you cannot expect to have your way and get exactly what you want. For any appeal attempt made on a litigated divorce, consult an experienced attorney.

Temporary Orders

We began talking about temporary orders in chapter 2. While you're going through your divorce procedure, you may need to get a temporary court order that spells out what you need while you and your spouse work out the details of your divorce. Temporary orders can apply to a variety of needs, some of which the court sees as needs. Here are some examples of what temporary orders usually cover:

- Who gets to keep the children (custody) for the time being
- How spousal support (if any) and child support can be expected
- How visitation will happen
- Freezing all assets so neither spouse can spend, sell, hide, or destroy anything
- Preventing a parent from selling or abusing assets, or taking the children
- Preventing an abusive parent from coming close to the other parent and children (also called a *temporary restraining order*)

If you are in dire need of having a temporary order granted and you cannot wait for a formal hearing at which your spouse is included, you can ask for *ex parte* orders. For example, if you fear for your safety and that of your children, you can ask the court to grant you temporary custody rights immediately—without having to inform the other spouse and await a hearing. *Ex parte* literally means "for one party," referring to motions, hearings, or orders granted on the request of and for the benefit of one person only. This is an exception to the basic rule of court procedure that both parties must be present at any argument before a judge. You may need an attorney to help you execute an *ex parte* order, but ask your court clerk if you can do this alone and how it can be done. *Ex parte* orders are very temporary; your spouse will be notified of the order and that a future hearing will be held to either extend the order or terminate it.

To protect both spouses during divorce procedures, your court will require that you follow certain rules and restrain yourselves from taking certain immediate actions. The following is an excerpt from a California summons for family law cases:

Standard Family Law Restraining Orders

Starting immediately, you and your spouse or domestic partner are restrained from

1. Removing the minor child or children of the parties, if any, from the state without the prior written consent of the other party or an order of the court;

2. Cashing, borrowing against, canceling, transferring, disposing of, or changing the beneficiaries of any insurance or other coverage, including life, health, automobile, and disability, held for the benefit of the parties and their minor child or children;

3. Transferring, encumbering, hypothecating, concealing, or in any way disposing of any property, real or personal, whether community, quasi-community, or separate, without the written consent of the other party or an order of the court, except in the usual course of business or for the necessities of life; and

4. Creating a nonprobate transfer or modifying a nonprobate transfer in a manner that affects the disposition of property subject to the transfer, without the written consent of the other party or an order of the court. Before revocation of a nonprobate transfer can take effect or a right of survivorship to property can be eliminated, notice of the change must be filed and served on the other party.

You must notify each other of any proposed extraordinary expenditures at least five business days prior to incurring these extraordinary expenditures and account to the court for all extraordinary expenditures made after these restraining orders are effective. However, you may use community property, quasi-community property, or your own separate property to pay an attorney to help you or to pay court costs.

Grinding It Out in Court

Because only 5 percent of divorcing couples end up battling it out in court, we won't be going into much detail about litigated divorces. But we will give you some information regarding what happens when you and your spouse decide to let the courts take control of your divorce.

Because the court-battled divorce is so nasty and generally undesirable, you have ample

If you let the courts settle your divorce for you (because you cannot come to any reasonable agreement with your spouse), you will lose control of your divorce and you risk not getting what you want. If you can agree to most everything related to your divorce but you need a judge's help in deciding a few final issues, you still risk losing control in that one area of your divorce. The point: Do your best to come to an agreement on all the issues before entering the court and asking a stranger to rule. In divorce court, somebody wins and somebody loses. It's not so much the two-way street that do-it-yourself divorces with cooperative and compromising spouses experience.

opportunity at every stage of your divorce proceeding to settle outside the courtroom and avoid having a judge making decisions. Only in extreme circumstances does a litigated divorce become essential to a clean getaway from your spouse. These are a few sample scenarios: if your spouse is totally uncooperative and refuses to negotiate with you despite your efforts; if your spouse is abusive, threatening, or uncompromising when it comes to alimony, custody, and the division of assets and debts; if your spouse refuses to pay much-needed financial support for you and your children; if you worry that your spouse has hidden or sold marital assets; and if your spouse has hired an attorney and instigated the court procedure already.

Moreover, if you've tried to go the do-it-yourself route and you've exhausted yourself through countless but unproductive mediation sessions, and time seems to only worsen your frustration and stress, then it may be necessary to haul your spouse into court and get things settled once and for all. This typically entails hiring a lawyer to help you through the process, especially if your spouse has already obtained his or her own legal counsel and intends to use that attorney to get all that he or she wants.

Why Does Litigation Cost So Much? People have misperceptions about the courts and how they operate. They also don't understand why it can cost so much to go to court and ask a judge to make decisions for them. Taking the formal legal route to divorce entails a litany of fees and expenses that go beyond attorneys' fees and filing fees. These include court reporter fees, discovery fees, subpoena fees, fees related to preparing exhibits, hiring experts for testimony, fees related to preparing witnesses, and the business-related fees of copying, postage and delivery of documents, phone calls, and so on. Attorney fees alone can cost you more than five figures. And let's not forget that because litigation takes so long, the monetary drain remains open. The fees will continue to mount. Your emotions and the level of stress you may have to endure will be off the charts.

Judge or Jury? Most litigated divorces are handled by a single judge. But in some states you may be able to have a jury settle your case or some of your issues. If you have this option, you should discuss this with an attorney to determine which way is better for your overall strategy. The trial process is the same for both a jury trial and a bench trial (a trial decided by a judge), but a jury will have to be selected prior to the trial beginning. The selection process further delays your divorce proceeding.

The Sequence of Events in Litigation

If you and your spouse have each obtained your own attorneys and you intend to go to court, expect the following sequence of events to occur:

1. Your attorney will file *pretrial motions,* which ask the court to take specific actions as soon as the initial filing of the petition has taken place. An example of a pretrial motion is asking for temporary orders.

2. Attorneys for both sides are given a period of time during which they can conduct their investigation into the case and collect as much evidence as possible to represent their clients as best they can. This period is called the *discovery process* and it can last from a few weeks to several months. If the exchange of information and relevant data needed to work out the terms of your divorce are trouble-free between the parties (and their

attorneys), then the discovery process can be relatively painless and easy to complete. However, if your divorce is so contentious that you require litigation, you probably won't have an easy and quick discovery process. What you may, in fact, need is a formal discovery process that entails subpoenas, depositions, interrogations, and questions about very personal matters that will become public. Anyone you know who can testify about your life with your spouse could be called to speak under oath and provide key information that may or may not be in your favor.

3. You'll experience a *pretrial hearing* or conference (also called a *pretrial settlement conference*), where you'll informally meet with a judge. The judge will listen to both sides and learn about any unresolved issues. He or she will then offer advice about reaching an agreement before going to trial, and encourage you (with lots of exclamation points for emphasis!!!) to settle with one another before letting the court rule. If no settlement is possible, the pretrial hearing allows your attorney (and your spouse's attorney) to review the facts of the case and prepare for trial. The judge you meet during this hearing may or may not be the judge who hears your case at trial.

4. At trial, the usual formalities of a case take place. This entails opening and closing statements from your attorneys, both sides presenting their case with witnesses and evidence, and the judge ultimately making a decision based on all that comes out during the trial.

When a judge enters his or her decisions, you become legally divorced (single again!) and legally bound by that decision. In cases where you and your spouse agree to the divorce terms and you avoid the litigation, your agreement becomes your judgment. Here, in a litigated divorce, the terms get set out by the judge and you have to accept them.

Settlement Offers

Think of a settlement offer as your chance to call a time-out and reach an agreement before a judge decides matters for you. It may be difficult at first to see a settlement offer as an agreement in your best interest, but keep in mind that you're more likely to get what you want in an out-of-court settlement offer than in court before a judge. If your spouse has an attorney, the attorney will draft an offer detailing the terms of your divorce, and you will continue to negotiate those terms until an agreement is reached. Assuming you have your own attorney, your attorney and your spouse's attorney may exchange several versions of the agreement in an attempt to arrive at some resolution and avoid the courtroom battle. The goal is to find a

If you're hell-bent on taking your divorce to trial, understand that you will encounter many barriers on your way to the courtroom, as every attempt will be made to avoid formal litigation. If you get as far as a pretrial conference, be prepared to listen to a judge urge you to reach an agreement. A judge can tell couples to discuss their issues further before returning and requesting a trial. A judge can also make his or her frustration clear by asking exactly why and how no settlement is possible. If you happen to experience a really tough and unrelenting judge, you just may surrender and decide to go back to the negotiating table with a settlement in mind.

reasonable and fair settlement, the same as if you had done all the negotiating yourself with your spouse.

The advantages to accepting a settlement offer are huge, simply because they avoid letting the court take control. However, it may be too difficult to reach an agreement if you and your spouse (and your attorneys) cannot see eye to eye and the costs of hammering out your differences continue to rise. You don't want to accept an agreement that you cannot live with, anyhow. Ask yourself the following questions when contemplating a settlement:

- Is the settlement fair?
- Am I getting what I asked for—or at least most of what I asked for?
- Will I regret making this decision in the future?
- Will the costs related to going to court outweigh the costs of continuing negotiations?
- How can I expect a judge to rule?
- How much more legal battle can I endure—emotionally, financially, physically?
- Does my attorney (if you have one) think this is a good idea or a bad one?
- What is in the best interests of my children?
- How much longer will a trial take than settling now?

These are all important questions to ask yourself. Your attorney should be able to help out by giving you a rough idea about timing, what a judge will likely do, the pros and cons based on the facts of your case in going to trial, and what you should do considering your particular circumstances. In the end, however, it's your decision.

Conclusion

After you've gathered all of your blank legal forms, personal documents, and other paperwork . . . and you're staring down at this mountain of work, wondering whether you can climb over it and get to the other side of divorce, you might ask yourself, Can I really do this alone? The answer: Yes!

Here's something to consider: The most famous paralegal in history was Abraham Lincoln. (Go ahead and snicker, but it's true.) Despite what you might think, Abe was not a lawyer. If you were to use today's criteria for being a lawyer, Abe wouldn't meet them. Instead, he'd fit the criteria for a paralegal. Lincoln never went to law school, never took a bar exam, and never joined a bar association. He apprenticed with a lawyer to learn his trade, just like a blacksmith (think of this book as your apprenticeship through your divorce). Much of the law back then was the preparation of legal documents, and there were many books available to show people how to prepare their own documents. Lawyers were used primarily for advocacy and specific legal advice. In fact, the idea of lawyers going to law schools and even taking bar exams did not take place until the early twentieth century. So there were many famous paralegals in history.

The courts are not something to fear. They are places where you go to get something done and be granted certain rights, such as the right to get a divorce. All you have to do is fill out the proper forms and submit the proper paperwork. In a divorce, unfortunately, that task often requires some participation and cooperation from your spouse, but how else do you expect to get unhooked from a partner to whom you've previously pledged marriage for the rest of your life? Take each step of your divorce piece by piece and you'll get to the other side soon—and, hopefully, hassle-free.

We still have a lot of issues left to confront in the upcoming chapters. How do you deal with taxes? How will your children keep their medical insurance? What happens to the pension and retirement benefits? We'll explore these topics in chapter 6.

Retirement Benefits, Health Care, and Your Children

When you think back to your wedding day and all the planning you did leading up to that day (unless you did it the easy and cheap way in the Chapel of the Bells or city hall), you can probably recall the dollar signs everywhere and the negotiating you had to do to get what you wanted done and have the wedding of your dreams. Planning a wedding is much like any other business deal—you reach agreements with caterers, entertainers, restaurants, stationery stores, and so on . . . and combined, your agreements execute one big event. You also have to negotiate with your future spouse and reach an agreement about what kind of wedding you want. Planning a divorce is similarly a business deal and you have to deal with money—in negotiations and agreements—every step of the way.

Despite the emotional toll that divorce brings, it's best to treat it as a business transaction that aims to divide your financial selves from one another fairly, and with children always in mind if you have them. Your first concern upon contemplating divorce may have been spousal support, custody, and child support, but somewhere down the line you probably began wondering about all the other financial ties that bound you and your spouse together—namely, retirement funds, investment accounts, pensions, and insurance (specifically, health care). These are the vehicles through which families build wealth and plan for their futures. But what about families that break apart and whose futures are no longer dependent on the nucleus of that original family? What happens to retirement benefits, Social Security, and other shared benefits? How does access to health insurance change?

These questions haunt a lot of divorcing spouses—especially the ones who came to rely completely on their spouse's benefits. Women who raised children for decades as stay-at-home moms and assumed they'd be able to count on their husbands' benefits indefinitely get to divorce and ask themselves, Now what? The thought of losing all those benefits and having no sense of security for the future is troubling. But you don't necessarily lose your privilege of benefits in divorce. You don't always sign away your rights to part of a pension when you reach your final agreement with your spouse.

This chapter takes you through some of the more complex financial dealings you must consider in your divorce. If you've always relied on your spouse when it comes to your family's financial plans, this part may seem daunting as you acquaint yourself with confusing

Did you know that of the more than 1 million marriages that will end in divorce this year, two-thirds to three-quarters of those divorces will be filed for by women? Some experts call this the "walkaway wife" syndrome. As women join the workforce and gain more access to information, they become more confident in themselves and in their ability to recover from divorce.

documents (example: brokerage account statements) and encounter financial lingo (example: stock options). We'll also give you information on how to recover from losing access to a health plan and how to ensure that your kids remain covered.

Taking Stock

Before you can begin dividing up the assets that are not front and center at the beginning of your divorce, such as stocks, bonds, and retirement accounts, you must have your inventory of these assets complete and ready for negotiation. If, during the inventory process you completed in chapter 3, you avoided counting up and looking at your balance sheets for many financial assets that are represented on paper, now is the time to sit down and deal with these issues. The longer you were married and the more financial assets you shared, the longer this process may take. You may also want to consult with your financial planner or tax specialist for advice and copies of important records or documents as you figure out how to divide everything. If you've had the same CPA or tax advisor for many years, that person will likely have a thorough file on your family's assets that you should have on hand when you divvy up your marital property.

Stock Options

Approximately 10 million workers now have option plans, according to the National Center for Employee Ownership (NCEO). Stock options are an example of intangible assets, meaning you cannot necessarily touch them but they represent a value—on paper. (You can touch the paper that shows the value, but the piece of paper itself has no significant value.) If you and/or your spouse own stock options, deciding how to divide them can be tricky—especially if you don't plan on buying or selling your stock now and don't know when you will. Precise values of options are not always available, so how does one divide them fairly?

If the stock options have already been exercised (stock has been purchased), one way to divide them is to have the spouse who owns the shares give the other spouse a percentage of the proceeds once they are sold. If the couple does not anticipate having the kind of postdivorce relationship that will allow for this method, then another way is to have the stock owner pay the other spouse now for the amount the shares are worth today. This second choice, however, is not always a good one—especially if the stock gains or loses considerable value over time. Both spouses can reach an agreement about how best to divide the shares and, for example, hold on to a weak stock until it gains value. Their agreement can spell out exactly how each person will deal with his or her marital portion of the shares. Many experts suggest that holding out until the options are sold is fairest. That way, both spouses share the investment risk and take away an equal share of profits or losses.

In valuing stocks, bonds, retirement benefits, and so on, everything gets valued as of the date of separation. A spouse's right to have a share of the other spouse's benefits or financial assets refer only to what was accrued during the marriage, from the date of marriage to the date of separation. The actual date of separation will depend on your state's rules.

The tax consequences must always be considered. If you own the stock and later sell it all, giving your ex-spouse a

The value of any stock ownership plan is equal to the number of shares owned multiplied by the current dollar value of a share. Example: You own 100 shares of Starbucks. At $54 a share, for example, the value of your account is $5,400. You can find current stock prices online, in the newspaper, or by asking your stockbroker or financial advisor. These values change daily. If the stock owned is not in a publicly traded company (that is, it does not trade on the stock market floors on Wall Street), ask the company to give you the value of its shares.

certain percentage, all of the proceeds may appear on just your tax form instead of both yours and your ex's. This means Mr. Taxman will come after you because the income from the sale is listed on your tax form. To avoid this situation, ask the company to issue your ex-spouse a separate form for the stock proceeds so you'll both share the tax burden.

If the stock options have not been exercised (you have the option to buy stock but you haven't done so yet), splitting up *unvested options* can be one of the biggest areas of contention. The spouse who owns the options might try saying that they are worthless, but let's say you own the option to buy stock in a very successful company such as Starbucks or Coca-Cola or Microsoft. If you told your spouse that your options are worthless, will he or she believe you? Probably not.

If you ask the court to decide on the division of your options, it will likely divide them on the basis of how long you were married and when those options became available. Here's an example: Your husband receives stock options at Company Y that vest (become available for purchase) in three years. One year from now, you file for divorce. The court will consider at least one-third of those options—for the year you were married after the shares were granted—as marital property. Your ex-spouse can keep half of those.

A judge, however, can force one spouse to surrender those options if they haven't been exercised and determine that that spouse's income should go toward spousal and/or child support.

Stocks and Investment Accounts

Besides the stock options you may have with a company, you'll have to figure out how best to divide any investment accounts that hold regular stocks or funds and that do have a value today. For example, if you and your spouse have a mutual fund account with a brokerage firm, such as Fidelity, plus a self-directed account with a trading company, such as Ameritrade, you need to decide how you're going to split up those accounts. This assumes, of course, that these accounts are marital property. If, however, some of these accounts were brought into the marriage as separate property but later accrued more value either through contributions to the account or increases as the result of market conditions, you'll have to figure out how much from those accounts is considered marital property and find a way to divide the sum fairly.

Your divorce agreement should spell out who gets which investment accounts and cash amounts. You may have to wait

When you transfer stocks, bonds, or mutual funds to your spouse, you will avoid paying a capital gains tax even if the value of those assets has appreciated (increased) since first purchased. But if the asset being transferred was not a marital asset (that is, it was separate), a separate asset of one spouse that is fully transferred to the other as part of the settlement may have tax consequences. For more information about this issue, or your particular circumstances, talk to an accountant.

for your divorce to be final before you can do the actual splitting. Once you have your decree, you'll prepare a stock letter of instruction that you can send out to all the bank and investment accounts that says how the money or investments are to be split. You may have to provide copies of your divorce decree and in particular the page that specifically deals with that account and the signature page. Some banks and companies will want your signature on the letter to be guaranteed, and some won't. Your financial institution may have other paperwork for you to complete, especially if you are transferring ownership of accounts.

Retirement Benefits

Almost every state, either by statute or case law, has decided that retirement assets earned during the marital period are marital property and subject to distribution at the time of a divorce. The problem is that not every retirement asset is created equal, so finding the right way to divide retirement assets when you're not an expert on, for example, how pensions work and what the law says you can and cannot do, presents a challenge.

If you've worked long and hard to accumulate retirement benefits, losing them in a divorce can be disheartening. But you must treat your retirement benefits like any other marital asset. Only those benefits you've accumulated during your marriage can be considered marital property—so if you came into your marriage with a lot of retirement benefits already, those will not be part of your divorce agreement. Most people don't stay with the same employer for their entire working lives, which means they gather several retirement benefit plans from each employer. When you recorded your assets on chapter 3's worksheets, you should have listed all of your retirement benefits and not just the one you currently have with your employer.

Pensions. Fewer and fewer people get offered (or have) an old-fashioned pension at work. A pension is a type of *defined-benefit plan* that typically becomes activated (that is, you can draw from the money that accumulated during your working years at the company) once you retire. Specifically, a private pension is a company retirement plan (that usually comes automatically as a job benefit) in which a retired employee receives a specific amount based on salary history and years of service, and in which the employer bears the investment risk. Contributions may be made by the employee, the employer, or both.

A defined-benefit plan promises you a specified monthly benefit at retirement. The plan may state this promised benefit as an exact dollar amount, such as $100 per month at retirement. Or, more commonly, it may calculate a benefit through a plan formula that considers such factors as salary and service—for example, 1 percent of your average salary for the last five years of employment for every year of service with your employer.

Pensions can be difficult to evaluate and divvy up if the member of the plan is not retiring anytime soon, or if the member is not vested in the plan (has no right to the money yet). If your spouse is a member of a pension plan, you may have to wait until he or she retires to receive your share of the

Pensions are more common among employees who work for long-established companies, such as General Motors, IBM, General Electric, and most older Fortune 500 companies. There are also union plans, military pensions, and federal, state, and local pensions. Generally, these plans provide monthly income for life commencing on a specific plan-defined retirement date based on a formula using final salary, years of service, and a multiplier.

Since pension plans are becoming less common, many professionals are unfamiliar with how to value them. When you sit down to plot out your divorce, you need to have an accurate idea of how much the plan is worth. For example, let's say your spouse (in his 40s) says that the current payout on his pension is $2,000 a month. Does this mean you are entitled to $1,000? Will you agree to accept that amount? Consider this: During the next 20 years, let's say the income of your working spouse doubles or triples. Since the value of his pension will be calculated largely on his compensation during his last five years on the job, the payout will be far more than $2,000.

pension. States have rules for dividing pension plans, and they are not necessarily the same throughout the country. Some states impose limits on how much the nonmember spouse can receive from a pension plan if the marriage was brief.

You may find it helpful to consult a tax advisor with experience in the division of pensions in your state. An actuary with expertise in pensions and other benefit plans may be particularly helpful in this endeavor. Your tax advisor may lead you to a company that specializes in valuing pensions. But you don't need to spend oodles of money on hiring such a company unless you know that the pension has considerable value and you want to trade it for some other marital asset.

If you do not know how much lies in your pension fund or what the rules are related to your particular pension fund, start by contacting the pension fund manager at your company (sometimes called a *benefits coordinator* or *plan administrator*) and request as much information as you can get. If the information and statements overwhelm or confuse you, hire an actuary. Another good reason to hire an actuary or attorney who is well versed in your state's laws regarding pensions (and divorce settlements) is that the value shown on your plan summary statement may not reflect the actual value of your plan. (This is when your advisor might seek the help of a company that evaluates pensions.)

Another good resource for information is the following:

- U.S. Department of Labor's Employee Benefits Security Administration (EBSA); go to www.dol.gov/ebsa to locate the office closest to you where you can phone or mail correspondence. Electronic inquiries can be sent to askebsa.dol.gov.

The Department of Labor maintains a very thorough and info-packed web site that we encourage you to visit for more information on any topics related to retirement plans and your rights as an employee with benefits. Start by going to www.dol.gov/ebsa for the gateway to a library of information. If you wish to speak with a person or receive mail correspondence, the site can locate a branch office that you can contact.

In addition to the Department of Labor, the Social Security Administration (SSA) also keeps a database of individuals who have been identified by the Internal Revenue Service as having qualified for pension benefits under private retirement plans. This database is maintained by the SSA under the 1974 Employee Retirement Income Security Act (ERISA), which was enacted to protect the pension benefit right of workers. Under the provisions of ERISA, the SSA notifies claimants applying for Social Security benefits of any information it has on file about their vested pension benefits or those of the deceased number holder.

Also under the provisions of ERISA, the SSA can provide, upon request, any information there is on file about a person's vested pension benefits. To request information on a private retirement plan, send a written request to:

Office of Earnings Operations

Attention: ERISA Correspondence Group

P.O. Box 33007

Baltimore, MD 21290-3007

In your request, you should include the following information about yourself or the person who qualified for benefits: Social Security number, name, date of birth, parents' names, and signature; name of pension plan and month and year that you or your spouse terminated employment covered by the plan; the Privacy Act penalty statement: "I certify that I am the person to whom the record pertains, or a person who is authorized to sign on behalf of that individual. I know that the knowing and willful request or acquisition of records under false pretenses is a criminal offense subject to a fine of up to $5,000"; and your name and the address where the information will be sent.

Other Types of Retirement Plans. If you don't have any pension plan, but you work for a company that offers retirement benefits, chances are you have some kind of *defined-contribution plan.* Examples of these plans are 401(k)s, ESOPs (employee stock ownership plans), retirement savings plans (such as IRAs and SEPs), federal thrift plans, 403(b) plans, and profit-sharing plans.

Unlike a pension plan, a defined-contribution plan does not promise you a specific amount of benefits at retirement. In these plans, an employee and his or her employer (or both) contribute to an individual account under the plan, sometimes at a set rate, such as 5 percent of earnings annually. These contributions generally are invested on the employee's behalf. The employee ultimately receives the balance in the account, which is based on contributions plus or minus investment gains or losses. The value of that account will fluctuate due to changes in the value of the employee's investments.

These types of plans are not as difficult to evaluate and divide as the traditional pension plans. It is usually easy to identify the marital component of a defined-contribution plan on the marital property cutoff date and use a so-called qualified domestic relations order (QDRO) to split the value of that asset (see later discussion of QDROs). If you or your spouse participated in a retirement plan that predated your marriage (as in the case of having a job long ago that you left but that gave you some retirement money), the funds in that account are

---

Notes about Vesting

- *Vesting* means the employee has earned the right to benefits funded by employer contributions. As an employee, you always have a right to your own contributions.

- Two basic vesting schedules that most companies use are these: (1) Under the three-year schedule, workers are 100 percent vested after five years of service under the plan; (2) under the six-year graduated schedule, workers become 20 percent vested after two years and vest at a rate of 20 percent each year thereafter until they are 100 percent vested after six years of service. Plans may have faster vesting schedules.

What is ERISA? The Employee Retirement Income Security Act of 1974, or ERISA, protects the assets of millions of Americans so that funds placed in retirement plans during their working lives will be there when they retire.

ERISA is a federal law that sets minimum standards for pension plans in private industry. For example, if your employer maintains a pension plan, ERISA specifies when you must be allowed to become a participant, how long you have to work before you have an interest in your pension, how long you can be away from your job before it might affect your benefit, and whether your spouse has a right to part of your pension in the event of your death. Most of the provisions of ERISA are effective for plan years beginning on or after January 1, 1975.

ERISA does not require any employer to establish a pension plan. It requires only that those who establish plans must meet certain minimum standards. The law generally does not specify how much money a participant must be paid as a benefit.

not marital property. Gather all of your retirement paperwork and go through the plan reports to determine which ones were part of your marriage and which ones were not. If it gets too confusing or difficult to determine, consult with an actuary or CPA who has experience in managing retirement plans.

Before you can worry about how to split up any retirement plan, you must find out which type of plan you have, its value, and any rules applicable to the plan. Check with your plan administrator or read your summary plan description. If you or your spouse are unable to get the summary plan description, the summary annual report, or the annual report from the plan administrator, you may be able to obtain a copy by writing to:

U.S. Department of Labor

EBSA Public Disclosure Room

200 Constitution Avenue, NW, Suite N-1513

Washington, DC 20210

Technically, you should receive a summary annual report that tells you (or your spouse if your spouse is the participant) the value of your plan and any relevant information. If you have to resort to inquiring at the Department of Labor, be sure to include your name, address, and telephone number, which will assist the EBSA in responding to your request. (There may be a nominal copying charge.) You can also contact your local EBSA office.

Qualified Domestic Relations Order (QDRO). If you and your spouse decide to share the retirement benefits (which one spouse may have accumulated during the marriage), you may need to get a QDRO (pronounced QUAD-row or CUE-dro) from the court that directs your share of the money from the retirement account to you when the benefits become available after your divorce and in accordance with the terms of the divorce agreement, the rules of the retirement fund, and a judge's approval. In some retirement plans, QDROs are mandatory. You may also find that your tax advisor will suggest using one even if you're not required to do so, since QDROs have some tax-saving advantages.

Once the spouse who is earning the retirement benefits is eligible to receive those benefits, each of you will get your fair share of regular income from the plan. As a general rule, you should always use a QDRO to facilitate the distribution of funds to the nonparticipant spouse (also called the *alternate payee*) from a defined-contribution plan. It is the only way the plan can pay the alternate payee his or her share.

A QDRO can assign rights to pension benefits under more than one plan of the same or different employers as long as each plan and the assignment of benefit rights under each plan are clearly specified. But if you have more than one plan to share, you may have to obtain a QDRO for each of them. (This will depend on the specific rules of the retirement plan, so see the plan administrator for more information.) A QDRO will distribute the plan in an immediate tax-free lump-sum rollover to the nonparticipant spouse with any gains or losses between the marital property cutoff date (the day your divorce is final) and the distribution date included in the portion being awarded.

QDROs must contain the following information:

- The name and last known mailing address of the participant (one spouse) and each alternate payee (the other spouse)
- The name of each plan to which the order applies
- The dollar amount or percentage (or the method of determining the amount or percentage) of the benefit to be paid to the alternate payee
- The number of payments or time period to which the order applies

> For divorcing couples with a lot of money held in retirement accounts, exploring your options and finding the best way to divide your retirement assets may entail hiring an actuary, CPA, or other tax advisor. You must take into consideration many things: the value of your benefits in relation to your other marital assets and separate property, how long you want to wait to receive retirement money, your age (when you plan to retire), and any tax implications.

Most plan administrators have sample QDROs to give out so you know what kind of document you must create to meet the plan's rules. Once you have created a QDRO, you will submit it to the plan administrator for approval, and once approved, you'll submit it to the court for the judge's signature. The approval process for QDROs between you and the plan administrator may take several rounds, and several months, to complete. You can always visit a We The People store for help in creating your QDRO and getting it approved.

Other Options. If you don't want to entangle yourself in settling with your spouse on retirement accounts that you may not access (or even have access to) for a long time, you may want to come to an agreement at your divorce about splitting the value of those accounts so no one has to wait to receive (and share!) any benefits at a later date. This is especially true for younger divorcing couples who cannot imagine dealing with a retirement plan's payout decades away (although younger couples are less likely to have much in retirement funds to worry about). Nevertheless, consider these other options for handling your retirement money:

→ Let the spouse who is a member or participant of a retirement plan keep all of the benefits in exchange for more marital assets or a cash "reward" (the spouse who forfeits the benefits gets a greater share of the marital assets or a cash payout).

→ Pay the spouse who is not a member of or participant in a retirement plan a lump sum at the time of the divorce and call it a day. The lump-sum payout should be based on the current value of the plan—not a projected future value.

Be very careful about any lump-sum payments because they can bear heavy tax liabilities. If you are the one paying your former spouse a lump sum, consider transferring that money in a way so the other spouse does not have to claim that money as taxable income. Speak with your CPA or tax advisor about any decision to make a lump-sum payment. Both ends of the deal—the spouse making the payment and the spouse receiving the payment—need to be aware of any tax consequences.

Social Security

Depending on your age, you may or may not be too worried about the government funds available to you at a later date—when you retire—especially when those funds seemingly hang in the balance of how our government decides to run the country. Social Security—the so-called third rail of American politics—is a hotly contested issue that for many young Americans doesn't mean much if it will be depleted by the time they retire. Younger couples may not have any sizeable nest egg to split at divorce. And if they have a nest egg, it's not Social Security.

Nevertheless, Social Security benefits should not be left out of the negotiations at divorce. These benefits may not amount to much now (and maybe not much in the future, either), but you cannot assume that they are definitely not worth discussing.

> Social Security is a system of social entitlement; it is neither welfare nor is it based on means. The Social Security system provides benefits not only during retirement, but also for survivors and dependents in case of death or disability.

Technically, Social Security benefits are not marital property, but because such benefits constitute income, they deserve consideration when a couple divorces. Eligibility for Social Security benefits, including retirement and survivor benefits, depends on how long a person has worked to earn the credit required on record. Everyone born in 1929 or later needs 40 Social Security credits to be eligible for retirement benefits. Credits are the building blocks the Social Security Administration uses to find out whether you have the minimum amount of covered work to qualify for each type of Social Security benefit. If you stop working before you have enough credits to qualify for benefits, your credits will stay on your record. If you return to work later, you can add more credits so that you can qualify. No benefits can be paid if you do not have enough credits.

During your lifetime, you will probably earn more credits than the minimum number you need to be eligible for benefits. These extra credits don't increase your benefit amount, however; it is your average earnings over your working years that determine how much your monthly payment will be.

Divorce and Social Security

A person who is divorced for at least 2 years after at least 10 years of marriage may qualify for benefits on the former spouse's Social Security record. To receive benefits as a divorced spouse, you must be at least age 62 and your former spouse must be entitled to retirement or disability benefits. To receive benefits as a *surviving* divorced spouse (your ex-spouse has died), you must be at least age 60, or at least age 50 and disabled.

Remarriage. You cannot apply for and receive benefits from your former spouse if you remarry, unless your new marriage ends in death, divorce, or annulment. Benefits for an entitled divorced spouse are terminated upon remarriage unless the marriage is to a person entitled to certain types of Social Security auxiliary or survivor's benefits. Benefits can be paid to you, applying as a surviving divorced spouse who has remarried, if

- You remarry at age 60 or later; or
- You remarry at age 50 and after becoming disabled.

One exception: If you are already entitled to benefits as an aged or disabled surviving divorced spouse and you remarry, you'll continue to receive benefits regardless of your age at the time of remarriage.

The provisions for a divorced spouse's or surviving divorced spouse's eligibility for Social Security benefits are set forth by Congress and contained in the Social Security Act and Regulations. For more information about Social Security benefits, go to www.ssa.gov or visit your local Social Security office.

A divorced spouse or surviving divorced spouse who is entitled to benefits other than those on his or her former spouse's record cannot receive both benefits in full. For example, if you are a divorced spouse who worked under (or paid into) Social Security and you are entitled to higher benefits based on your own earnings, you would receive benefits based on your record only.

If you would like to receive an estimate of benefits you may receive as a divorced spouse or surviving divorced spouse, contact a representative of the SSA at 800-772-1213. They may be able to provide you with this information over the telephone. If not, visit one of their offices. You can get the address and directions to your nearest office from the Social Security Office Locator that is available online at www.socialsecurity.gov/locator/. Offices are scattered throughout the country, and one should be near you. Your local representative can also explain all the eligibility rules and how you can apply for benefits. (When you receive Social Security benefits based on your former spouse's record, you do not affect your former spouse's eligibility to receive his or her own benefits. Your former spouse need not have even applied for benefits at the time you apply.)

How Much Can a Divorced Spouse Receive from Social Security? The maximum benefit is 50 percent of the benefit the worker would receive at full retirement age. If you are applying for benefits on your ex-spouse's record, you don't have to wait for your ex-spouse to apply for his or her portion of the benefits. But you do have to be at least 62 years old. If you draw the money before you reach full retirement age, those benefits are reduced based upon your age when you receive those benefits. For a chart showing the reduction in benefits based on the year of birth, go to www.socialsecurity.gov/retire2/agereduction.htm.

Children and Benefits. Social Security benefits may also be paid to children when at least one of the parents becomes disabled, retires, or dies. The child, who must be under age 18 or, if still in high school, under age 19 (unless the child is disabled), can be the contributing spouse's biological child, adopted child, stepchild, or even a dependent grandchild. (The *contributor* is the person who has paid into Social Security.)

Children must meet eligibility requirements, but they can potentially receive up to one-half of the contributor's retirement benefits or disability benefits, or 75 percent of the deceased parent's basic Social Security benefit (up to the family maximum). If a stepchild is receiving benefits and the contributing spouse becomes divorced from the child's parent (in July 1996 or later), the stepchild's benefits will end the month after the divorce becomes final.

(Note also that Social Security benefits can be used to meet alimony and child support obligations.)

Survivor Benefits

If your former spouse dies and you qualify for Social Security benefits, this may include survivor benefits (think of it as a prize for outliving your former spouse). Unlike Social Security retirement benefits, you can begin to collect survivor benefits as early as age 60, or full benefits at 65. However, if you are caring for a child under the age of 16 or who is disabled, you may be able to collect survivor benefits at age 50.

Survivor Benefits and Remarriage. If you remarry before turning 60, you are no longer eligible to collect survivor benefits under your former spouse's record; however, if you remarry after turning 60—and you've been divorced for at least two years—then your benefits are unaffected.

Final Words on Social Security. Social Security is a revolving debate on Capitol Hill, and the rules that determine eligibility and how much one can receive are likely to change in the future. If you or your spouse has paid a considerable amount into Social Security, you should obtain a copy of your most recent record and visit your Social Security Administration office for information about benefits available after divorce. If both you and your spouse paid into Social Security, you may have less to negotiate, as both of you can retain sole rights to your

What is *full retirement age,* at which point a person who paid into Social Security is entitled to the maximum amount of benefits?

Full-retirement age was 65 for many years. However, beginning with people born in 1938 and later, that age is gradually increasing until it reaches 67 for people born after 1959. The following chart shows the steps in which the age will increase.

Year of Birth	Full Retirement Age
1937 or earlier	65
1938	65 and 2 months
1939	65 and 4 months
1940	65 and 6 months
1941	65 and 8 months
1942	65 and 10 months
1943–1954	66
1955	66 and 2 months
1956	66 and 4 months
1957	66 and 6 months
1958	66 and 8 months
1959	66 and 10 months
1960 and later	67

No matter what your full retirement age is, you can still start your benefits at a reduced rate as early as age 62.

benefits. Your Social Security office can help you understand the rules for dividing SS benefits at divorce.

When dividing your assets, including your retirement accounts, don't forget that you can always trade off one item for another. Don't be afraid to take a serious inventory of both your and your spouse's assets to determine what's fair and equitable. Take frequent-flier miles, for example. Even though they may be worth only two cents each, some people will go to any length to keep them. In one recent divorce settlement, the woman received an extra $25,000 from her husband's pension—provided she agreed to leave the miles alone. The lesson: Everything is negotiable.

TIME OUT! *I Don't Understand What You Mean By . . .*

Stock options   An option (an invitation), usually given to employees of large companies, to purchase stock in the company at a future date. The price of the option is established, so if the company's stock price rises above the option price, the employee is able to take advantage of the stock increase (current stock price minus established stock price).

Vested   This means you can take any of the money that your company has contributed to your plan because you've worked a certain numbers of years for your employer. *Vested* is an adjective referring to having an absolute (fully and unconditionally guaranteed) right, title, benefit, or privilege. Example: After 35 years at Company X, Ms. Loyalty's pension rights are now vested. Typically, you have to work a certain number of years for your employer before you are vested in its retirement plan.

Capital gains   The difference between the sales price and the original cost (plus improvements) of property. Example: You buy a house in 1967 for $40,000 and you sell it in 2005 for $650,000. Your capital gain is $610,000, which is subject to the capital gains tax.

Actuary   A person who specializes in the mathematics of risk and insurance. Actuaries who specialize in retirement issues are great sources of information and advice for long-term financial planning, as they typically help design retirement plans for companies and individuals.

Qualified domestic relations order (QDRO)   A QDRO is a court order that creates or recognizes the existence of the nonemployee spouse's right to receive all or a portion of the retirement benefits payable with respect to a participant under a pension plan. Example: Your spouse participated in his company's 401(k) retirement plan, and now that you are getting divorced, you have a right to some of the money in that plan. You will use a QDRO to receive those funds when your husband retires and begins to withdraw from that fund.

Survivor   One who outlives—survives—another. If your spouse dies, you (and everyone else in your family) survived him or her. You are a surviving spouse. Even if you are divorced from that person, you are a survivor and may have survivor rights.

Medical or Health Insurance

Obtaining health insurance is trickier than buying a homeowners, renters, or auto insurance policy. You can't make one phone call or click your way online to a good health policy. With 42 to 44 million Americans having no health insurance, the task of getting affordable insurance might seem impossible. But it's easier than most people think. Among the reasons why so many millions go without health insurance:

- Parents lack knowledge of available health care coverage options in their states or don't understand the eligibility guidelines.

- There are cultural and language barriers in many of the most underserved populations.

- Obtaining health insurance can be a lower priority for families who have more pressing needs, such as employment and housing.

- The application process is too complicated for many families, especially those who have trouble reading or understanding English.

- Government rules and verification requirements can pose barriers.

- Employer-sponsored insurance premiums are often unaffordable for low-income working families.

If you're the spouse who does not have access to health insurance through work or another connection, such as a union or trade association, you face a serious dilemma: losing all coverage once the divorce is final. For those who need access to medical services frequently, the thought of losing all coverage in a divorce prevents couples from going as far as divorce; instead, they choose to legally and permanently separate so both can keep their insurance. This may be a good enough reason to avoid divorce, but in reality, it does not offer the true benefit of getting a divorce—freeing yourself from a person you no longer want to be with. Following are some tips for finding good health insurance and making sure your children remain covered.

Your Children's Health Care

Your divorce agreement should indicate how your children will remain covered by either you, your spouse, or a policy obtained just for them. The court will want to see that they will not lose their health coverage as a result of the divorce—no matter who gets primary custody.

Your children can be covered by either your or your ex-spouse's insurance provider, or both. Typically, they will remain covered by the parent who has access to a group policy in an employer-sponsored plan. Group policies are preferred over individual policies, which tend to be more expensive and less comprehensive in coverage.

Having your children enrolled in a health maintenance organization (HMO) may be the *least* optimal method of covering them. Why? HMOs are not national health care providers, so they are limited to regional service. This can complicate your children's insurance. Your children might still be insured by your spouse's policy, but if you and the children move outside the HMO's service area, coverage for your children will be limited to emergency care only. If you or your spouse only have access to an HMO, be sure to ask about its coverage limits and what happens if your children need medical attention outside the coverage area. If you and your former spouse live in different cities or states (or simply different regions in reference to the coverage area), for example, you may find that the children are covered only when they are with one of you. To avoid this situation, look into other forms of health coverage that

Avoid double coverage. If your children have good health care under your former spouse's plan, you do not need to seek more care for them in a plan under your name. If your spouse has the group plan and you have an individual plan, both of you don't need to name your children as dependents. It doesn't make sense to pay for two separate family coverages. Keep the kids under your spouse's group plan. Individual policies are so expensive that adding dependents to one when the other parent has a group policy is a costly decision.

are not so restrictive when it comes to location. You need your children to be covered at all times.

A few HMOs will cover your children wherever they travel. For example, Blue Cross has an HMO plan called Away From Home Care (AFHC) that offers coverage nationwide. If your child is enrolled in that HMO, the child is covered even if you and your ex-spouse live in different states. (Note: The Away From Home Care plan is not sold in every state.)

Preferred provider organizations (PPOs) may have regional restrictions similar to those of the HMOs. So if your children are part of a PPO, make sure the organization has a national network if they will be spending time with the other parent outside their own network.

When you and your spouse explore the options for your children, you must keep their best interests in mind. Work through your issues as amicably as you can; the two of you should decide which group plan offers the best benefits for your children and put your children on that plan. Consider any special needs or medical attention your children might have. Remember that notices about changes in benefits and rules will be mailed to the parent who holds that plan, even if the other parent has custody. If you and your spouse aren't communicating well, the courts will generally make sure the spouse with custody has all the necessary information to guarantee health care for the children.

Individual Plans for Children. Although these plans are sometimes difficult to find, you can buy individual health insurance specifically for your children, even if they are as young as six months old. Experts say these plans are especially attractive options if you are divorced or if your children spend lengthy summer vacations with relatives halfway across the country, where your health plan might not have a network of doctors.

Before you rush into buying your children their own health plans, there are several factors to consider so you don't end up with a policy that omits needed coverage. First, understand that a child health plan is perhaps most useful when you and your ex-spouse live in different states and your policy will not cover your children outside of its regional network. In this case, an individual indemnity policy for the children might be the best solution. An *indemnity policy* is a fee-for-service policy, in which the children can see virtually any provider, no matter who they are staying with at the time. Indemnity plans, however, are generally not cheap, and adding a child to a group health insurance policy at work is almost always the better way to go.

No matter which plan you choose, make sure you know what benefits the policy provides and compare them to the benefits the child would receive under a group health plan, if one is available to you. The cheapest plan will not always provide the child with the best value for your health insurance dollars. Individual plans often don't cover wellness or preventive care, so you'd have to buy that coverage for an additional monthly fee. Deductibles, copayments, lifetime dollar limits, and out-of-pocket contributions also must be weighed.

In many states, individual health plans can reject your child due to a medical condition such as asthma or a history of ear infections. If the health plan accepts your child despite health problems, the premiums will likely be expensive. Health plans can also accept your child but refuse to cover certain existing medical problems, which means you'd have to pay for such treatment.

Shop for an individual plan as you would shop for any other good or service: Compare prices, quality, affordability, and access. Large and well-established insurance companies have representatives standing by to take calls and tell you what types of plans fit your needs. You do have options and you should spend the time investigating policies to find the right one at the right price. You can also use a health insurance broker if you know a good one that you trust. Stick to insurance companies that you've heard of, and avoid any companies that advertise on the street corner with offers that are too good to be true.

State and Federal Programs. Your state, and every state in the nation, has a health insurance program for infants, children, and teens. The insurance is available to children in working families, including families that contain individuals with varying immigration statuses. If you meet income qualifications, your child also might be eligible for health insurance through a state or federal program.

The Children's Health Insurance Program (CHIP), initiated in 1997, is a federally funded program designed to help reach the 8.1 million low-income American children who currently go without health insurance. CHIP aims to provide for children whose parents make too much to qualify for Medicaid but too little to afford private health insurance. If you think you might be one of those parents, you can get more information about CHIP in your state by calling the nationwide toll-free hotline: 877-KIDS-NOW. You can also find out more on the Insure Kids Now web site (www.insurekidsnow.gov), which offers information about eligibility in your state and applying for coverage. CHIP programs operate in all 50 states, five territories, and the District of Columbia.

Additionally, if you live in Rhode Island or Wisconsin, as a parent of a CHIP-eligible child, you may also qualify for health insurance under the program. These two states won special permission to use money from CHIP to cover parents as well as children. Rhode Island is also allowed to cover pregnant women under CHIP.

> American children are significantly more likely to have health insurance today than in 1997, when the State Children's Health Insurance Program was enacted into law. Kids who do not currently have health insurance are likely to be eligible, even if the parents are working. The states have different eligibility rules, but in most states uninsured children 18 years old and younger whose families earn up to $34,100 a year (for a family of four) are eligible.

COBRA. A federal law known as COBRA (short for the Consolidated Omnibus Budget Reconciliation Act of 1985) provides a vital bridge between health insurance plans for qualified workers, their spouses, and their dependent children when their health insurance might otherwise be cut off. Because of that security, COBRA has become the safety net for families in the midst of crisis, such as unemployment, divorce, or death. Although COBRA may be a good route for you to take if you lose your health care coverage the day of your divorce, it's typically not the best way to extend coverage for your children. But COBRA can be used this way. If you and your children are on a group health plan through your spouse's job and you get divorced, you and your children might be eligible for COBRA coverage, allowing you to keep the exact same health benefits until you find other access to coverage (within certain time limits).

Premiums for COBRA are not cheap, so use COBRA if you have no other access to medical coverage. If you have no preexisting conditions and decide against COBRA, you can still consider buying individual insurance or even a short-term major medical policy to tide you over until you land a new job with health benefits. If the day you get divorced is the day you lose coverage under your former spouse's plan, opting to use COBRA for the time being may be a good idea until you can find coverage elsewhere. However, try to keep your children on your ex-spouse's plan.

For more information about COBRA and your particular situation, contact your health care plan provider (the company with which you have a health care policy) or the person in charge of that plan at the company that offers the plan to employees. Companies that buy group health plans for their employees are often referred to as the *subscribers* of the plan.

Health Insurance for You

Your health care plans may not be at the top of your list soon after your divorce. But do your best to get some coverage and at the least, so-called catastrophic coverage, which will protect you if you land in an emergency room following a very bad accident and subsequently rack up hundreds of thousands of dollars in medical bills. Once you get divorced, you will lose your access to health care if you were under your former spouse's plan. Remember: You can always elect to use COBRA while you hunt for a new health plan for yourself. Because COBRA premiums are so high, try to find other health care options right away. Don't let your health care coverage lapse. COBRA cannot go on indefinitely. At some point, if you lose COBRA, you may have few other options.

If you cannot afford an individual policy or join a health maintenance organization, you can look into organizations or associations you can join that offer policies (think alumni organizations, guilds, unions, etc.), think about changing jobs to one that offers health coverage, and look into state-run programs that may offer coverage for low-income individuals. Unfortunately, many government programs help children get the coverage they need, but single parents often find themselves out of luck. Unless they can find a job that offers health benefits, finding affordable coverage can be a challenge. Start by asking your friends and neighbors how they got their health coverage, and call any of the major health care providers for information on plans that may fit your lifestyle and budget. At the least, you can buy a policy that has a high deductible and minimal coverage for routine doctor visits, but will not wipe you out financially if you do happen to have a major accident.

Working your health insurance policy's premiums into your new, postdivorce budget is very important. You may not have prioritized health insurance costs before divorce, but as a single parent now trying to reestablish yourself, taking charge of your health care is a step in the right direction.

More on the Children

We cannot express the importance of listening to your children from beginning to end as you get divorced. The last part of this chapter focuses on some visitation guidelines that have been put forth by the South Dakota courts, which every parent in every state should heed. Taking into account all the information we've given you up to this point—and all the decisions you've had to consider thus far—it's time now to turn the spotlight back onto the children. Even though you may be separating yourself from your spouse, your children will not be separating themselves from either you or your spouse. So you have to learn to deal with the other parent (your ex-spouse) for the rest of your children's lives. This can be a challenge in contentious divorces and even more contentious subsequent ex-spousal relationships. If you generate a lot of animosity, anger, and resentment during your divorce, you will only worsen the situation for your children and take longer to attain true family stability.

South Dakota's family courts operate much the same way as other family courts across the country. They hope that parents can arrive at their own decisions with regard to visitation, but they understand the trouble that parents can get into when deciding on issues and seeing their decisions through once the divorce is final. According to the South Dakota Unified Judicial System:

> A powerful cause of stress, suffering, and maladjustment in children of divorce is not simply divorce itself, but continuing conflict between parents, before, during, and after divorce. Similar conflicts can occur between parents who were never married. To minimize harm to their children, parents should agree on a parenting arrangement that is most conducive to frequent and meaningful contact for the children with both parents, with as little conflict as possible. When parental maturity, personality, and communication skills are adequate, the ideal arrangement is reasonable time with the noncustodial parent on reasonable notice, since that provides the greatest flexibility. The next best arrangement is a detailed visitation agreement made by the parents to fit their particular needs and, more importantly, the needs of the children.

The South Dakota Judicial System sets some very useful guidelines for parents, which we've summed up in the next section. (These guidelines are published in the South Dakota Codified Laws at SDCL ch. 25-4A, Appendix.) Note that some of these guidelines may not apply in your particular state, and you may have reached a different agreement with your spouse over many of these issues. If you haven't come to an agreement yet, perhaps some of the following tips will give you and your spouse the direction you need to reach that agreement.

General Rules

You and your ex-spouse should avoid speaking negatively about one another and firmly discourage such conduct by relatives or friends. Speak in positive terms about the other parent in the presence of the children. Encourage the children to respect the other parent. Children should never be used by one parent to spy or report on the other. The basic rules of conduct and discipline established by the custodial parent should be the baseline standard for both parents and any stepparents, and consistently enforced by all, so that the children do not receive mixed messages about appropriate behavior.

Children will benefit from continued contact with all relatives and family friends on both sides of the family for whom they feel affection. Such relationships should be protected and encouraged. But relatives, like parents, need to avoid being critical of either parent in front of the children. Your children should maintain ties with both the maternal and the paternal relatives. If your children's grandparents have a legal right to reasonable visitation in your state, the children should visit with the paternal relatives during times the children are with their father and with the maternal relatives during times they are with their mother. It is recommended that the parents prepare an annual calendar of agreed-upon dates so that both the parents and the children know where the children will be during the coming year.

If you and your spouse reside in the same community at the time of separation, but then one of you leaves the area, thus changing the visitation pattern, you must reach a new agreement with your former spouse about how future visitations will happen. In the case of South Dakota, the court considers apportioning between both parents the children's travel costs necessary to facilitate visitation with the noncustodial parent. In apportioning these costs, the court considers such factors as the economic circumstances of the parents and the reasons prompting the move. These guidelines are in the best interests of the children.

Parental Communication. Neither parent should speak negatively about the other parent (no matter how hard that may be). Parents should always keep each other advised of their home and work addresses and telephone numbers. Whenever feasible, all communication concerning the children should be conducted between the parents themselves in person, or by telephone, at their residences, and not at their places of employment.

Grade Reports and Medical Information. The custodial parent should provide the noncustodial parent with grade reports and notices from school as they are received and should authorize the noncustodial parent to communicate about the child directly with the day care service, the school, and the children's doctors and other professionals outside the presence of the custodial parent. Unless there are abuse, neglect, criminal, or protection orders to the contrary, the noncustodial parent should also be listed as the children's parent and as an emergency contact with the day care service, the school, and all health professionals. Each parent should immediately notify the other of any medical emergencies or serious illnesses of the children. The custodial parent should, as soon as reasonably possible, notify the noncustodial parent of all school or other events (for example, church or sports) involving parental participation. If the child is taking medications, the custodial parent should provide a sufficient amount and appropriate instructions to the noncustodial parent.

Visitation Clothing. The custodial parent should send an appropriate supply of children's clothing with them, which should be returned clean (when reasonably possible), with the children, by the noncustodial parent. The noncustodial parent should advise, as far in advance as possible, of any special activities so that the appropriate clothing belonging to the children may be sent.

Withholding Support or Visitation. Neither visitation nor child support should be withheld because of either parent's failure to comply with a court order. Only the court may enter sanctions for noncompliance. Children have a right both to support and to visitation, neither of which is dependent upon the other. In other words, no support does not mean no visitation, and no visitation does not mean no support. If there is a violation of either a visitation or a support order, the exclusive remedy is to apply to the court for appropriate sanctions.

Adjustments in This Visitation Schedule. This schedule should be understood as imposing specific requirements and responsibilities; however, when family necessities, illnesses, or commitments reasonably so require, the parents are expected to modify visitation fairly. The parent requesting modification should act in good faith and give as much notice as circumstances permit.

Custodial Parent's Vacation. Unless otherwise specified in a court order or agreed on by the parents, the custodial parent is entitled to a vacation with the children for a reasonable period of time, usually equal to the vacation time the noncustodial parent takes with the children. The custodial parent should plan a vacation during the time when the noncustodial parent is not scheduled to spend time with the children.

Insurance Forms. The parent who has medical insurance coverage on the children should supply to the other parent an insurance card and, as applicable, insurance forms and a list of insurer-approved or HMO-qualified health care providers in the area where the other parent is residing. A parent who, except in an emergency, takes the children to a doctor, dentist, or other provider not so approved or qualified should pay the additional cost thus incurred. When there is a contemplated change in insurance that requires a change in medical care providers and a child has a chronic illness, thoughtful consideration should be given by the parents to what is more important—allowing the child to remain with the original provider or taking advantage of economic or medical benefits offered by the new carrier. When there is an obligation to pay medical expenses, the responsible parent should be promptly furnished with the bill by the other parent. The parents should cooperate in submitting bills to the appropriate insurance carrier. Thereafter, the parent responsible for paying the balance of the bill should make arrangements directly with the health care provider and should inform the other parent of such arrangements. Insurance refunds should be promptly turned over to the parent who paid the bill for which the refund was received.

Child Support Abatement. Unless a court order otherwise provides, support should not abate (decrease) during any period when the children are with the noncustodial parent.

Missed Visitation. When events beyond either parent's control, such as illness, prevent a scheduled visitation, a mutually agreeable substituted visitation date should be arranged, as quickly as is feasible. Each parent should advise the other in a timely fashion when a particular visitation cannot be exercised. Missed visitation should not be unreasonably accumulated.

Visitation—A Shared Experience. Except with infants and adolescents, it usually makes sense for all the children to share the same schedule. Having brothers and sisters along may provide important support for children. Infants have special needs that may well prevent a parent from being with both infants and older children at the same time. Adolescents have special needs for peer involvement and for some control in their own lives that may place them on different schedules from their younger brothers and sisters. Because it is intended that visitation be a shared experience among siblings and unless these guidelines, a court order, or circumstances, such as age, illness, or a particular event suggest otherwise, all the children should spend time together with the noncustodial parent.

Telephone Communication. Telephone calls between parent and children should be liberally permitted at reasonable hours and at the expense of the calling parent. The custodial parent may call the children at reasonable hours when the children are with the noncustodial parent. The children may, of course, call either parent, though at reasonable hours and frequencies, and at the cost of the parent called if it is a long-distance call. During long vacations, the parent with whom the child is on vacation should make the child available for telephone calls every three days. At all other times, the parent with whom the child is staying should not refuse to answer the phone or turn off the phone in order to deny the other parent telephone contact. If a parent uses an answering machine, messages left on the machine for the child should be returned. Parents should agree on a specified time for calls to the children so that the children will be made available. A parent may wish to provide a child with a telephone calling card to facilitate communication with that parent.

Mail and E-mail Contact. Parents have an unrestricted right to send cards, letters, packages, and audio- and videocassettes or CDs to their children. Children also have the same right to send items to their parents. Neither parent should interfere with this right. A parent may wish to provide a child with self-addressed stamped envelopes for the child's use in corresponding with that parent. If the child and the parent have Internet capability, communication through e-mail should be facilitated and encouraged.

Privacy of Residence. A parent may not enter the residence of the other parent except by express invitation of the resident parent, regardless of whether a parent retains a property interest in the residence of the other parent. Accordingly, the children should be picked up and returned to the front entrance of the appropriate residence. The parent dropping off the children should not leave the premises until the children are safely inside. A parent should refrain from surprise visits to the other parent's home. A parent's time with the children is his or her own, and the children's time with that parent is equally private.

Special Considerations for Adolescents. Generally, these guidelines apply to adolescents as well as younger children. Nonetheless, within reason, the parents should honestly and fairly consider the wishes of their teenagers concerning visitation. Neither parent should attempt to pressure their teenager to make a visitation decision adverse to the other parent. Teenagers should explain the reasons for their wishes directly to the affected parent, without intervention by the other parent.

Day Care Providers. When parents reside in the same community, they should use the same day care provider. To the extent feasible, the parents should rely on each other to care for the children when one parent is unavailable.

For more guidance on dealing with visitation when you have one abusive or distant parent, turn to chapter 7, which explores some of the more unusual situations.

Conclusion

At the beginning of this chapter we mentioned that women are more likely to file for divorce today than men. One can argue that part of the reason lies in greater access to the information a person needs to get a divorce as well as the access to services that facilitate divorce proceedings, such as mediation and family law centers. Because more women are likely to be part of the workforce today, the fears of losing health coverage and going broke after divorce have

In the state of Georgia, the family (chancery) court refers divorcing parents to free counseling classes. At one such class, seven children took turns at the easel to write their thoughts under two categories:

What We Want the Grown-Ups to Know:
I'm angry about the divorce.
I'm sad when I don't get to see my dad a lot.
I'm worried about your safety.
I'm glad that I get to see both of my parents.
I'm sad when you're upset.

What We Want the Grown-Ups to Do:
Stop arguing.
Be nice.
Stop cussing.
Take responsibility.
Work out your differences.
Do fun things with us.
Listen 2 us more!

less of an impact on them. It may take them time to get back on their feet and return to the kind of lifestyle they had grown accustomed to during their married life, but in time they will likely regain what divorce took away from them.

Once you free yourself from your former spouse, you'll have a busy life readjusting—whether you're a man or a woman. Don't forget to revisit your will (if you have one) and rethink how you want your possessions to be distributed at your death. In some states, a divorce automatically revokes a will or the parts that relate to your former spouse. If you and your former spouse had a living trust set up, you should revoke the trust and establish a new one for yourself. If you've never had a living trust, now may be the time to consider using this powerful vehicle through which you manage your assets and make sure they get to whomever you wish at your death without a lot of legal hassles. You can refer to *We The People's Guide to Estate Planning* (Wiley, 2005) for all the information you need to set up and understand your own will or living trust. We'll give you some brief information in chapter 7 when we review pre- and postnuptial arrangements and how they affect divorce.

Don't forget to access your state's main web site for forms and procedural instructions. Appendix A lists the links, or you can go to www.wethepeopleforms.com and link to your local courthouse through our web site. You should be able to download many forms that you'll need throughout your divorce.

Besides pre- and postnuptials, other topics we have yet to discuss fall under the category of less-common situations, and they include common-law marriages, palimony, the threat of deportation at divorce, and a situation in which your spouse becomes abusive to you and/or your children. We'll delve into these subjects in chapter 7, as well as give you more guidelines to consider when establishing rules for visitation.

Odds and Ends in (Marriage and) Divorce

B y now you may feel stunned by too much information and too many things to do—decisions to make. You may not even need to refer to the sidebar issues covered in this chapter. Take a deep breath and relax. Try to keep things in perspective by reminding yourself that it's okay to feel emotional and overwhelmed; it's okay to feel angry and sad; and it's okay to proceed through your divorce at your own pace and take decisions one step at a time. You don't have to speed your way to a finalized divorce agreement. When courts impose a separation requirement on a couple before they can get divorced, the intent is to allow the couple a cooling-off period. This is an important time to gather your thoughts so you can make good decisions.

One thing you do have in your favor—especially if you settle your divorce outside the courtroom—is your privacy relative to people in the spotlight. Imagine being famous and having your marital problems, separation, and divorce smeared all over the covers of the tabloids and gossipy magazines. Although your divorce does become public record, no one is going to announce your nitty-gritty details to the world and make money from your story. The likes of Trump and Turner endure divorces that get a lot of media attention because huge dollar signs accompany their high-profile relationships. When Ivana and Donald Trump divorced (after a 13-month legal battle), she used her divorce to reinvent herself as a role model for ex-wives around the world, publishing a guide to divorce titled *The Best Is Yet to Come* (Pocket Books, 1995). When Ted Turner divorced his wife, Jane Smith Turner, after 22 years of marriage, in 1988, he gave her $40 million—the largest divorce settlement in Georgia's history at the time.

Your custody negotiations can also remain under wraps; if you and your spouse can quietly come to an agreement about your children, you do more to protect your children and make them feel safe and secure than anything else can. About the nastiest custody battle in recent times was between Mia Farrow and Woody Allen once Woody hooked up with Mia's adopted daughter, Soon-Yi Previn, from a previous marriage.

Your story probably isn't as outrageous or scandalous as the ones that make for good tell-all books and magazine covers. In truth, your story is probably just like the experience of any other hardworking, normal American who simply is not happy in a failed marriage. When Brad

Pitt's and Jennifer Aniston's split made the cover of multiple magazines (and the television news) in early 2005, some wondered why people were so transfixed by reading about them and obsessed by their relationship. The magazines that covered the breakup raced to get the best story (with photos) in print. People's strong reaction to news of another failed marriage—especially among the famous and beautiful—is normal. We subconsciously like hearing about the troubles that celebrities have because it humanizes them. But more important, it validates our sense that everyone has faults (no matter how rich or poor, ugly or beautiful) and everyone has a right to make mistakes and correct them. In other words, learning about someone else's troubles somehow makes us feel better about ourselves.

Is My Marriage Even Valid?

Occasionally, people who live as a married couple later learn that their marriage is not legal. This can happen if, for example, one supposed spouse kept a prior marriage secret, or both thought incorrectly that an earlier marriage had ended in divorce. (A truly unusual situation would be if one person was presumed dead, thus ending the marriage legally, but later shows up alive to find his or her former spouse remarried.) A marriage may also become invalid if it took place between close relatives, underage individuals, or people incapable of entering into the marriage contract because of mental incompetence.

If a marriage was improper for reasons such as these, a court may grant an annulment instead of a divorce. (See chapter 2 for information about annulments.) When a court grants an annulment, the parties often are free to go their separate ways without any further obligations to each other. Many states, however, apply additional principles of law to protect a person who thought he or she was in a valid marriage but, in fact, was not.

Common-law marriage: A judicially recognized marriage in some states, usually based on cohabitation.

Common-law Marriages

A common misperception is that if you live together for a certain length of time (seven years is what many people believe), you are automatically in a common-law marriage. This is not true anywhere in the United States. Even in states where common-law marriages are possible, you must meet certain requirements that go beyond just physically living together for a number of years.

States That Recognize Common-law Marriage

Only a few states recognize common-law marriages:

Alabama	Ohio (if created before 10/10/91)
Colorado	Oklahoma
Georgia (if created before 1/1/97)	Rhode Island
Idaho (if created before 1/1/96)	South Carolina
Iowa	Texas
Kansas	Utah
Montana	Washington, D.C.
New Hampshire (for inheritance purposes only)	

Once upon a time, particularly during the pioneering days, it was common for states to consider a woman and man to be married if they lived together for a certain length of time, had sexual intercourse, and related to one another in public as husband and wife, even though they never went through a formal marriage ceremony or obtained a marriage license. In other words, if they acted married and lived together as if married, then they were said to be in a common-law marriage. Only a few states recognize common-law marriages anymore: Alabama, Colorado, Georgia (if created before 1/1/97), Idaho (if created before 1/1/96), Iowa, Kansas, Montana, New Hampshire (for inheritance purposes only), Ohio (if created before 10/10/91), Oklahoma, Rhode Island, South Carolina, Texas, Utah, and Washington, D.C. The majority of the states no longer recognize common-law marriages. (Note: Every state is constitutionally required to recognize as valid a common-law marriage that was recognized in another state.)

Common-law Marriage Rules. Even in the states that recognize common-law marriage, the couple faces certain restrictions, some of which are that they.

- Have the capacity to and intend to marry.
- Regard themselves as husband and wife.
- Live together for a significant period of time.
- Clearly represent themselves to others as being husband and wife. (Merely living together is not enough to create a marriage.) Some ways of doing this are by using the same last name, referring to one another as husband or wife, and filing a joint tax return.

If a common-law marriage is valid, the partners have the same rights and duties as if there had been a ceremonial marriage. Common-law marriages do not mean they can end in a common-law divorce. There is no such thing. If you have established yourself as married under common law in a state that recognizes common-law marriages, then you must get a formal divorce to end it. If you fear that your state will declare your partnership a valid marriage because you live in a state that allows common-law marriages and you act as if you are married, then you can create a document with your partner that states you have no intention of getting married, common-law or not, and sign and date the document. Otherwise, you have little to worry about because common-law marriages are not so common anymore.

For more information about common-law marriage and specific requirements in your state, go to www.unmarried.org.

If you get married in another country, your marriage is most likely valid in the United States. In general, marriages that are legally performed and valid abroad are also legally valid in the United States. If you wonder about your particular case, however, contact your state's attorney general's office for more information. You may also find information about marriages abroad on your state's main web site or by going to the U.S. Department of State's Bureau of Consular Affairs at www.travel.state/family (more on this site later).

Palimony

Another rare situation among splitting couples is palimony. *Palimony* is akin to alimony; however, it refers to couples who never legally married but lived together for a long period and then ended their relationship. Palimony cases are rare; you hear about them mainly when they involve famous or extremely wealthy people (example: Michelle Marvin versus Lee Marvin in 1976 or the more recent $9 million palimony lawsuit dropped on comedian Bill Maher by his former girlfriend). The earliest known case, *Sarah Althea Hill v. Senator William Sharon,* occurred in California in 1880, and Ms. Hill lost. But palimony cases were extremely unusual back then. Palimony cases have been more common in the last 20 years.

Palimony cases turn on whether or not there was an agreement that stated one partner would support the other in return for the second being a homemaker and performing domestic duties. Written palimony contracts are rare, but the courts have found implied contracts, especially when a woman has given up her career, managed the household, or assisted in the man's business for a long time. Like divorce cases, palimony cases must be treated individually on a case-by-case basis. But palimony cases often involve more gray areas, such as the line between a mutual relationship or affair and one that makes palimony a reasonable request. Palimony suits may be avoided by contracts written prior to or during the relationship.

Pre- and Postnuptial Contracts

Pre- and postnuptial contracts are no longer meant for only the rich and famous. They are powerful documents that can help settle issues more quickly in a divorce. If you and your spouse had one set up before your divorce, you should have an easier time reaching an agreement because a lot will have already been spelled out in your pre- or postnuptial. This saves you money, time, pain, and anguish.

There is not much of a difference between a pre- and a postnuptial agreement. Both are legally binding documents between two agreeing people who articulate exactly what each person's rights and responsibilities are should they get divorced or should one spouse die. The only difference between a prenuptial and a postnuptial is that one is signed and made effective before the marriage and the other is made official during your marriage. Prenuptials are a lot more common than postnuptials (you may never have heard of a postnuptial until now, but they do exist).

Creating a Pre- or Postnuptial Agreement

The greatest value in having a pre- or postnuptial agreement is that such an agreement puts you in control of what will happen to your assets if you get a divorce. *You* get to choose what happens—not your spouse, not other family members, and most important, not your state. People opt to create pre- or postnuptial agreements for a variety of reasons. Here are the most common:

- You've acquired some considerable wealth—perhaps your own business or enterprise—by the time you contemplate marriage and you want to protect what you've already accumulated in the event you get divorced.

- You have children from a previous marriage and you want to make sure they get some of your assets at your death without having to endure any contests or legal hassles. (Note: A prenuptial won't resolve all of your inheritance issues because it cannot substitute for a will, but it can be a great supplement to a valid will that spells out your wishes for when you die.)

- You've already experienced one awful divorce (or more) that cost you a bundle and you've wised up to how a prenuptial can help prevent the problems related to divorce.

Notes from an Attorney about Premarital Agreements

When you buy a house you don't plan on it burning down, yet you buy fire insurance. When you buy a car you don't plan to injure someone while driving, yet you buy liability insurance. Even though you don't expect bad things to happen to you, you take steps to protect yourself from potentially devastating events that can wipe you out financially—and emotionally. So why is it that when people get married they don't take the same precautions by preparing a prenuptial agreement? It is probably a result of the conflict between the romantic notion of "until death do us part," versus your statistical 1 in 2 chance of getting a divorce.

Premarital agreements are becoming ever more common and should be considered part of your routine financial planning. After all, you have only a 1 in 1,200 chance of having your home burn down, but a 1 in 2 chance of a divorce! Invest in a premarital agreement and think of it as divorce insurance.

What exactly is a prenuptial agreement, you might ask? It is a contractually binding agreement entered into prior to the marriage in which the parties agree how their assets and liabilities (that is, debts) will be divided in the event the marriage ends in divorce, separation, or even death. These agreements are governed by the laws of each individual state and can be enforced by the courts if needed. The validity of a prenuptial agreement depends on the state where you live.

A prenuptial agreement does not need to be viewed as something negative. It should be viewed as a normal financial planning tool that can save thousands in divorce attorney fees and countless months of aggregation arguing over assets. It is far easier to make these decisions during a time of bliss rather than a time of a troubled relationship.

—Derek Thiele, Attorney-at-Law

A less common reason to draft a prenuptial is to set out exactly what kind of marriage you want to have—how many kids, how they will be raised, what religion they will learn, what each spouse's responsibilities will be, and so on. Such lifestyle prenuptials are not very typical, and they certainly aren't easy for a court to enforce. But it's interesting to note that some churches, although not calling them prenuptials, do urge couples to create a similar document if they intend to get married in that particular church. Most important to churches is the agreement between the couple to have children and raise them in a certain religion.

Using a pre- or postnuptial agreement to supplement your estate planning is among the biggest reasons to consider these documents. Even though the laws in most states dictate that a surviving spouse has a legal right to at least one-third of a deceased spouse's assets no matter what a will says, you can use a prenuptial to write down your own inheritance rules. For blended families in which an older couple shares children from previous marriages, being able to write down their own wishes with regard to the distribution of their assets to children is important. And, although a will or living trust can accommodate such things, the addition of a pre- or postnuptial that reinforces those wishes makes the arrangement ever more clear and solid.

A pre- or postnuptial agreement can be a great addition to your estate planning by clearly indicating who gets what in lieu of what the law says a spouse must get. Usually used in combination with a will or living trust, a pre- or postnuptial agreement can help manage the disposition of your assets at your death because each spouse gets to make specific bequests, while agreeing to forgo certain rights of inheritance.

The Value of a Will or Living Trust

If you don't have a will or living trust already, you may want to consider creating these valuable documents so that you can leave your possessions to whomever you wish at your death. If you don't prepare for your death with a will or living trust, the state in which you reside will ultimately make decisions for you with regard to your personal belongings and assets. Being in control of what happens upon your death and helping your family avoid costly, unnecessary procedures involves having a will or living trust that clearly lays out your wishes and assists your family in making difficult decisions. These documents are as useful to divorced individuals as they are to married couples.

You and your spouse may also find it helpful to plan for your children's futures through other estate planning tools, such as certain trusts or accounts set aside for a college education or vocational school. Discuss your options with an estate planner or your trusted financial advisor (and pick up a copy of *We The People's Guide to Estate Planning* for all you need to know about financial family planning).

Reaching Agreements. To create a pre- or postnuptial agreement, you and your partner (or spouse) must agree to the terms you intend to set out. As in divorce, if you cannot reach an agreement on issues you want to include in your pre- or postnuptial, you can employ a mediator in the same way a divorcing couple would use one. A mediator can create the neutral forum in which the two of you can negotiate and resolve your differences.

You can make your agreement as detailed or as brief as you want. If, for example, your only concern is a business venture or large inheritance that you want to protect, you can create an agreement that reflects only that asset. But if you take the time to create and legalize a pre- or postnuptial, you may as well add as many provisions into the document as you can to avoid other thorny future problems. Some questions you may want to address are as follows:

- Will there be children? How many? When?
- Who will be the breadwinner? Who will sacrifice a career for taking care of the children?
- If one person gives up a career to support the other's career or be a stay-at-home parent, how will that parent be compensated—especially in the event of divorce?
- What kind of debt is acceptable?
- How will marital assets get divided at divorce?
- Who will keep the home or other major assets acquired during the marriage?
- How will debts be shared at divorce?
- How will you buy property together? Will you share titles?
- How much will each of you financially contribute to the marriage? How will you share each person's income?
- How will you share household responsibilities, including paying bills, managing money, and maintaining the home?
- How will you share future decision making, especially when it's serious?
- Where will you live, or where are you willing to move to—or not move to?
- How will you deal with issues related to children from previous marriages?

- How do you want to handle inheritance issues?

- How will you solve major debt problems that one—or both—of you have brought into the marriage?

- Are there any assets that you'd like to address specifically in an agreement, such as a business or a piece of separate property one person brings into the marriage?

These are just a few items to consider. You can even include provisions for how you will handle serious disputes in your marriage, if counseling will be mandatory before contemplating divorce, and how you will split major holidays between two families. Your age and your wealth will determine what kind of agreement you need to make. Older couples typically have more to protect, and those who are approaching retirement age may have a slew of other issues to deal with in a pre- or postnuptial agreement. Younger couples may not have weighty issues to discuss, but it doesn't hurt to lay out some expectations with regard to children, basic living issues, and how shared assets and debts will be managed.

State Rules. Your state will have certain rules for drafting and legalizing a pre- or postnuptial agreement. Because prenuptials are more common, the laws are less defined about postnuptials. When you write out how you and your partner will divide property and debts, you may want to look first at how your state typically deals with the division of assets and debts in the event of divorce. Remember, you can choose to divide your assets and debts however you wish in your nuptial agreement (assuming both parties can agree to that division), but you may find it helpful to reference your state's rules when trying to figure out your agreement.

States also have their own rules for making nuptial agreements legal and enforceable in court. Generally speaking, you must adhere to the following:

- ☑ Your agreement is in writing (hopefully typed and professionally presented).

- ☑ Neither party has been forced or threatened to create or sign this agreement.

- ☑ Neither party has hidden any assets or debts, or been dishonest about anything addressed in the agreement that could later lead to fraud.

- ☑ Both parties were involved in negotiating the terms to the agreement.

- ☑ Both parties sign the agreement.

If you violate any of these basic rules, and any rules that your state may impose, a court can change certain provisions made in the agreement or invalidate it entirely. Nuptial agreements are not meant to give one person a serious advantage over the other. If the agreement significantly favors one person over the other, any contest to the legality of the agreement in the future may be easier to make.

Also, if you are trying to draft a postnuptial agreement hastily because one or both of you thinks your marriage is heading for divorce, beware of the potential consequences. The court will view any postnuptial signed just before divorce as a crafty maneuver by one party to defraud the other. It's best to draft any postnuptial agreement while you and your spouse are enjoying a good marriage and you simply want to clarify a few issues because you failed to do so prior to your marriage.

Keeping Your Agreement Up-to-Date. As you would a will or living trust, you need to keep your nuptial agreement up-to-date. Revisit your agreement from time to time (once every five years or so) or at least when things change considerably in your marriage and you feel the need to review that agreement. Make sure that it reflects your wishes and needs, and that it's still a fair and mutually agreeable document. You can always make formal changes to it or revoke (cancel) it entirely and create a new one.

Getting Help. You'll have to do some research in your state before drafting your nuptial agreement and making it legal. In some states you have to get a notary public to sign your agreement. As part of our services, We The People can help you create and legalize a prenuptial agreement that meets your state requirements—that is, if we have a store in your state. Otherwise, you may find it helpful to consult an attorney in your area who is familiar with these documents and can guide you through the process. The person you need to help you create a pre- or postnuptial document may depend on the kind of issues you are trying to address. For example, if your main issues are about children from previous marriages and the laws of inheritance, you may want to seek the services of a family estate planner, or if your main concern is a family business (on just your side of the family), you may want to hire a business lawyer to help you.

You don't usually file your agreement with any court or legal entity. The agreement becomes a contract that you keep in a safe place, usually with your other important documents such as your will and titles to property. It's a good idea to make a copy to give to someone else, such as your accountant.

Marriage to an Alien

If one of the spouses of a divorcing couple was an alien (not a U.S. citizen) before the marriage and began the naturalization process of becoming a citizen soon after the wedding, a divorce presents special problems. U.S. citizens can marry whomever they want from other countries, but the process of granting their alien spouses rights to permanent residency, and later citizenship, is long and tedious. What happens when a couple decides to get divorced while one person's green card or citizenship papers are still pending? Does that spouse get deported?

What used to be called the Immigration and Naturalization Service (INS) is now part of the Department of Homeland Security (DHS) and is called the U.S. Citizenship and Immigration Services (USCIS). CIS has always been concerned that aliens seeking permanent resident status in the United States will marry solely to gain that status, thereby circumventing the immigration laws. This concern was addressed by Congress in the Marriage Fraud Act of 1986, and later amended by the Immigration Act of 1990.

An attempt to gain resident status without a legitimate marriage is marriage fraud. If the CIS discovers that a couple has married just to get one person's immigration papers, the consequence can be a denial of an immigrant visa, a refusal of admission as a conditional or permanent resident, the loss of resident status previously granted, and deportation from the United States.

If you marry a U.S. citizen (or a lawful permanent resident) and soon thereafter (within two years) apply for permanent residency, you will be granted a conditional resident status that is conditional for two years. If you marry a U.S. citizen but don't apply for any immigration papers within those first two years, you can be approved for lawful permanent status without waiting out the two-year conditional status. This procedure of skipping the conditional status,

> ## TIME OUT! *I Don't Understand What You Mean By . . .*
>
> **Alien**   Anyone who is not a U.S. citizen.
>
> **Immigrant**   An alien who intends to reside permanently in the United States.
>
> **Nonimmigrant**   An alien who intends to visit, live, or work temporarily in the United States.
>
> **Permanent resident alien**   An alien who is admitted by the Citizenship and Immigration Services to enter the United States in order to reside permanently.
>
> **Conditional resident alien**   An alien who receives resident status based on a marriage of less than two years to a U.S. citizen. In order to become a permanent resident alien, the alien and his or her spouse must file a joint petition with the CIS within 90 days of the second anniversary of the day the CIS granted conditional resident status.
>
> **Naturalization**   The process of acquiring citizenship for anyone who did not become a U.S. citizen by birth.
>
> **Green card**   A green card is actually an alien registration receipt card given to aliens after they have acquired resident status in the United States. It covers both conditional and permanent resident aliens. The card used to be green but is now rose-colored.
>
> **Immigrant visa**   A document package issued by a U.S. consul abroad that an alien presents at the U.S. border to be admitted as a conditional or permanent resident.

however, requires certain paperwork and meeting certain requirements. Once the conditional period is over (or if there is no conditional period), then both spouses must file a joint petition and await an interview by the CIS that allows the CIS to determine whether the marriage is legitimate. In other words, the CIS wants to know that you married for love and not for money or a ticket into the United States.

Couples who start divorce procedures during this critical time period when one's paperwork is pending with the CIS face serious challenges. Until an individual is granted permanent residency status, a divorce can complicate matters and jeopardize a person's ability to attain that green card, which is symbolic of the permanent residency status. You do not necessarily face deportation immediately, but the red tape you'll have to contend with—forms, filing, paperwork, interviews, waiting periods, and so on—can be frustrating. It may not be an endeavor you want to undertake alone, and hiring an immigration attorney to assist you might be a smart idea. Make sure your attorney has experience in juggling immigration laws and a divorce that complicates matters.

Citizenship and Immigration Services maintains several offices throughout the country. You can locate the nearest branch by going to www.uscis.gov and clicking your way to a directory. The web site contains a lot of useful information, but you may also find that the practical side to this information—the exact how-to for getting things done—is not so easy to find. Immigrating to America can be an overwhelmingly frustrating experience when you consider the level of paperwork and rules you must follow—down to the number of months you're allowed out of the country while paperwork is pending. Adding a divorce into the mix amplifies the complications. Most immigrants who eventually attain citizenship endure many years of encounters with the CIS. If you need to get something accomplished through this government agency, you learn to work diligently and practice patience every step of the way.

Spousal or Child Abuse

Throughout much of this book, we've assumed that you're going through a normal divorce in the sense that serious allegations of abuse or misconduct are not part of your experience. Most marriages end because couples grow apart and no longer feel emotionally tied to one another. But a few do end after one spouse endures years of abuse from the other spouse.

> According to researchers, there are more than 100 female victims of abuse per 1,000 couples every year. And abuse is not just physical— emotional abuse, whether on its own or in conjunction with violence, is also very common.

Spousal abuse refers to the deliberate attempt by a partner in an intimate relationship to control or intimidate the other partner. The couple may be married, unmarried, or the same sex. Sadly, too many individuals in abusive relationships remain in the relationship and never have the courage to leave their abuser. Men can be victims of abuse by their female counterparts (after all, David Gest did sue Liza Minnelli for domestic violence, accusing her of beating him five times in their 15-month marriage), but women are typically the victims. In fact, 90 to 95 percent of domestic violence victims are women. Abused women often think they don't deserve anything better. They may even fear their husband will hurt them if they try to leave. Many have been under the control of their husbands for so long—and are financially dependent on them—that they have no financial ability to leave. They may feel trapped and unable to find the means with which to escape from their situation.

If Your Spouse Becomes Violent

Spousal abuse is no laughing matter, but it can be difficult to get help in some situations. If your spouse becomes violent or threatening, you should call the police right away and request that they file a report. Unfortunately, some police officers do not like to get involved in domestic disputes and may act reluctant to respond quickly or do the proper paperwork. They may direct you to your local crisis shelter and say that they cannot do much else. Depending on where you live (state and county), you may have no trouble getting your local police to assist you and make you feel safe. In fact, some counties require an arrest to take place if a person calls and alleges that he or she has been a victim of serious abuse and the responding officers verify that is the case. But if you experience the opposite, do your best to get any incident recorded in writing so that when you ask the court for a protective order, you have proof. Record the names and badge numbers of the police who respond to your call.

What Is Spousal Abuse? Domestic violence is a pattern of abuse and violent behavior used for the purpose of gaining power and control over a spouse or intimate partner and can be any or all of the following:

- *Physical assault:* Includes pushing; punching; slapping; biting; burning; kicking; hair pulling; choking; being denied food, sleep, or medical treatment; not being allowed to leave; and the use of objects to cause injury

- *Psychological assault:* Includes isolation from family and friends, emotional and verbal abuse, name-calling, threats, intimidation, forced dependency, control over where you go and what you can do, being locked out of the house or abandoned in a dangerous place, and stalking or closely watching your whereabouts
- *Sexual assault:* Includes rape, unwanted touching, or being forced to engage in unwanted sexual acts
- *Property or economic abuse:* Includes destruction or stealing of personal belongings and property, abuse or threats to pets, hitting walls or throwing things, and refusing basic needs such as food, clothing, medical care, or transportation

The reality of domestic violence is that it does not go away on its own. It tends to worsen over time and become more frequent. The effects on your children can also be devastating. Part of the abuser's power comes from the secrecy and his or her ability to continue the violent behavior. Pregnancy can be a dangerous time. Approximately 25 to 45 percent of all women who are abused are abused during pregnancy.

Getting a Protective Order. Trust your instincts and seek help if you fear that your spouse will harm you and/or your children. Ask the court to issue a protective order, which prohibits your spouse from coming within a certain distance of your home, your workplace, or where your children are located when they are not with you (school, playground, day care center). If your spouse violates the order, he or she can be arrested.

If you need a court order on a day when the courts are closed, you can ask your local police to give you a temporary protective order that is effective for a few days—until you can get to the court. You may also want to file criminal charges with the police and have proof of those with you when you visit the court and ask for your protective order. Find out from your police which civil court you need to visit. It may or may not be the same place where family law cases are handled.

After you ask the court for a protective order, you might need to attend a hearing where a judge will listen to your story. Providing any proof of your story will help you get your order. Your spouse may not be at this first hearing, but he or she will have the opportunity to tell his or her side of the story at a second hearing. A judge will likely order the abusive spouse to enter an anger management program, attend a substance abuse program, or get some counseling.

Memorize or keep a list of important telephone numbers; leave a written set of important phone numbers with a friend or in a secure place that you will be able to access. The list might include numbers for a shelter, domestic violence counselors, your children's school, your friends and/or relatives, and people you can call and places you can go in an emergency.

Cycles of Violence

Domestic violence occurs in a repetitive three-phase pattern:

Phase 1: Increased tension, anger, blaming, and arguing

Phase 2: Battering—hitting, slapping, kicking, choking, use of objects or weapons, sexual abuse, and verbal threats and abuse

Phase 3: Calm state; the abuser may deny violence, say he was drunk and that he's sorry, and promises never to do it again

Keep important documents together in a safe place. A domestic violence hotline counselor or advocate can help you decide where. These documents and other necessities could include the following:

- ☑ Order of protection
- ☑ ATM card
- ☑ Money/cab fare/coins for phones/phone card
- ☑ Checkbook
- ☑ Credit card
- ☑ Passport
- ☑ Green card/work permit/visa
- ☑ Welfare ID
- ☑ Cell phone
- ☑ Driver's license and registration
- ☑ Social Security card
- ☑ Your partner's Social Security number
- ☑ Medical records
- ☑ Address book
- ☑ Insurance policies
- ☑ Important legal documents
- ☑ Police records
- ☑ Record of violence
- ☑ Baby's things (diapers, formula, medication)
- ☑ Children's school and immunization records
- ☑ Birth certificates
- ☑ Medications
- ☑ Clothing
- ☑ Eyeglasses
- ☑ Lease
- ☑ Pictures
- ☑ Anything of sentimental value
- ☑ Nonperishable snacks for children (e.g., juiceboxes and crackers)

The Crisis Shelter. If you fear for your life and do not want to remain in your home at the mercy of your abusive spouse, you should seek a crisis shelter as fast as possible. Take your children with you. Crisis shelters also maintain hotlines you can call if you don't feel ready to leave and want some advice on preparing to leave. If your situation is dire and you need immediate help, call 911.

The National Domestic Violence Hotline is a good number to have. If something about your relationship with your partner scares you and you need to talk, call the National Domestic Violence Hotline at 800-799-SAFE (7233) or 800-787-3224 (TTY); fax: 512-453-8541; address: P.O. Box 161810, Austin, Texas 78716. The web site at www.ndvh.org has a directory for getting help in your state and finding local support groups. Assistance can also be obtained by e-mailing ndvh@ndvh.org, though this is not an emergency e-mail contact. If you need immediate assistance, call the hotline. You can also refer to your phone book for local shelters and hotlines. Look under "Crisis Intervention." (Note: If your spouse is monitoring your every move, he or she may search your computer to find out where you've been on the Internet and whom you've e-mailed, so you may not want to visit the NDVH site or e-mail them directly. Computer use can be tracked and is impossible to completely clear. If you are afraid your Internet and/or computer usage might be monitored, use a safer computer, call your local hotline, and/or call the National Domestic Violence Hotline.)

Making the decision to leave your spouse and actually doing so are among the most difficult situations a person can face. It takes courage and a willingness to lose what you leave behind until a court can take action and respond to your requests for a divorce and a division of property. If you are not ready to leave but think you may be ready at some point in the future, do some preparatory work by saving up some money in your own bank account; keep an extra set of keys hidden, give them to a close friend, or put them in a safe place; and have that friend store some clothing and items for daily living that you may need if you decide to leave abruptly. (See the list in the preceding box.) Talk with people you trust and let them know what is going on. You may also want to speak with your children, alerting them to the danger they may face if they are present when you are being attacked or battered by your spouse. Give them a code word they should know that means "Go directly to the neighbor's house and call the police." When you say the code word, they will know what to do. Given the age of the children, they will most likely be fully aware of what's going on and want to hear you talk to them about the problem. You need to make them feel safe and secure, which can be hard in an abusive household. A support group or hotline can tell you exactly how to handle the children and what you can expect.

The Stalking Ex-Spouse. You don't have to endure a stalking ex-spouse who follows your every move, hides around your street corner to spy on you, and threatens to harm you or your children if you do something to anger him. Get a protective order from the court, and if the situation is serious, request a temporary restraining order while you await the court's ruling on the protective order. Record what you can about your ex-spouse's behavior to prove to the courts that you have a case against him or her. If you live in a state that has antistalking laws, you may also be able to file criminal charges against your ex-spouse for violating those laws. Call the Domestic Violence Hotline for more information (800-799-SAFE) and for some guidance on dealing with this matter.

The statistics are staggering:

• Nearly one in three adult women experiences at least one physical assault by a partner during adulthood. According to the U.S. Surgeon General, domestic violence is the single largest cause of injury to American women today.

• Twenty-eight percent of all annual violence against women is perpetrated by their partners. Overall, around 45 percent of all violent attacks against female victims 12 years old and older by multiple offenders also involve offenders they know.

• By the most conservative estimate, each year 1 million women suffer nonfatal violence by an intimate; by other estimates, 4 million American women experience a serious assault by an intimate partner during an average 12-month period.

Child Abuse

If your spouse is abusive toward you, he or she might also be abusive to the children. A person who loses control and acts impulsively with a spouse may be capable of doing so with children. Studies show that child abuse occurs in 30 to 60 percent of family violence cases that involve families with children. It's your job to protect your children as best you can, especially when violence is involved. The moment you know abuse has occurred—whether you are married or divorced—you need to file a criminal report with the police and prepare to take action.

If you're already divorced and you think your ex-spouse is abusing your children while they visit with him or her, you should act immediately. Start by calling the police and pressing charges against him or her. You must also request the court to intervene and issue an order that prevents your ex-spouse from seeing the children until an investigation into your allegations takes place. If you believe that your children have been physically abused, bring them to the doctor for a physical examination. Document the alleged abuse as much as you can by visiting a doctor; getting photos of unusual bruises, cuts, or marks; and filing a police report for every incident that occurs to your knowledge. Report your former spouse to your local child protective services agency. You also may call the toll-free child abuse hotline in your state, if one exists, or the National Child Abuse Hotline at 800-4-A-CHILD.

Don't try to take the law into your own hands. Wait until a court issues an order that either stops your former spouse from visiting with the children or creates conditions under which the former spouse can visit with them, such as restricting visitations and requiring adult supervision during those visits.

Witnessing spousal abuse has long-term, emotionally detrimental effects on children. Depending on the nature of the spousal abuse and the time and circumstances of its occurrence, the court may require that the abusive spouse successfully complete appropriate counseling before being permitted unsupervised time with the children. If one parent proves to the court that the other parent is abusing a substance, such as drugs or alcohol, the court will likely issue an order that ceases all visitation rights until that spouse gets proper treatment.

A good source of information about child abuse and how to handle a situation of child abuse in your home is the Office for Victims of Crime at www.ojp.usdoj.gov/ovc/help. You can reach this office by e-mail at AskOVC@ojp.usdoj.gov, or call 800-851-3420 (TTY 877-712-9279). By mail: Office for Victims of Crime Resource Center, National Criminal Justice Reference Service, P.O. Box 6000, Rockville, MD 20849-6000.

Neglect

Although neglecting a child may be considered child abuse, it's common for the noncustodial parent to lose touch with the children for a long time and for a variety of reasons. Example: The noncustodial parent has such a bad relationship with the other parent that he or she avoids contact entirely, which also means not seeing the children. If the parent later decides to continue a stronger relationship with the children, courts suggest that visitation begin with brief visits that gradually become routine and follow a normal visitation schedule.

Kidnapping

Any noncustodial parent who threatens to kidnap or hide the children should have supervised visits. Child abductions that make headlines and prompt the so-called Amber Alerts typically happen when one parent decides to take the children away from the other parent. Some parents

Child abductions by strangers fill parents' minds with worry, but the reality is that 75 percent of all child abductions are perpetrated by a family member or acquaintance. The U.S. Department of Justice reports that half of all abducted children are taken by a family member, 25 percent are taken by an acquaintance (such as a parent's boyfriend or girlfriend), and 25 percent are abducted by strangers. Almost all children kidnapped by strangers are taken by men, and about two-thirds of abductions by strangers involve female children. But in 43 percent of cases, family abductions involve a female parent.

who kidnap their own children do so because they fear losing their children in a custody battle (or perhaps they already have), or they seek revenge on the other parent. Parents who kidnap their own children because the other parent is abusive or harmful are taking the law into their own hands and may find themselves punished rather than rewarded. The federal government and all states have laws to prevent and deal with kidnapping. A parent convicted of kidnapping could face jail time.

If Your Spouse Runs Off with the Kids. The moment you realize that your spouse has taken your children with no intention of returning them is the moment you get on the phone and call the police. If the police will not respond quickly enough, visit the police station in person and bring the following:

- Custody papers and all other relevant court orders.
- A recent photo of your child and the abductor. (Find a recent photo where your child is pictured in a natural, full frontal pose. If you don't have a photo of the abductor, ask family and friends. Photos of the abductor with and without facial hair, with different hairstyles, or with and without glasses are most helpful. Be sure that you retain copies of every photo for your records and further submissions. Never surrender your last copy of any photo.)

Keep a notebook with all the information you collect in your search. Write down the police officer's name, badge number, telephone number, and police report number. Record all aspects of the investigation. Always note the date, the name of the agency, the person you spoke with, what they said, and their contact information.

Other important people to contact in addition to the police (even if the police place these calls) are the following:

- The Federal Bureau of Investigation
- The National Center for Missing & Exploited Children (NCMEC) at 800-THE-LOST
- The Missing Children Clearinghouse in your state and the states to which you believe your child might have been taken
- Child Find of America (800-I-AM-LOST)
- Nonprofit missing children's organizations

Each organization will ask you to fill out their paperwork and send them photographs. If you have access to a fax machine, request that they fax the application to you in order to save time. Additionally, call your children's school and advise them of the abduction. Ask them if there was a request for records and advise them that if there is a request for records to contact

According to the Federal Bureau of Investigation, 2,300 missing-children reports are filed each day—cases that might be solved more easily if parents were able to provide a few key pieces of information: their child's height, weight, and eye color, and a clear photo that's less than six months old. However, 22 percent of parents surveyed in one study did not know their child's height, weight, and eye color—and in households with two or more children, the percentage rose to 29 percent. Parents of children younger than six years old were less likely than parents of teens to be able to give an accurate physical description of their children.

you and/or the police. Also contact your children's physicians (pediatrician, eye doctor, dentist, etc.), and alert them to the abduction. Ask them if there was a request for records and advise them that if there is a request for records to contact you and/or the police. Finally, contact the Bureau of Vital Statistics and put a hold on your children's birth certificates.

Use the media as much as you can by telling your story to local television and radio stations, as well as reporters for newspapers and other publications.

Before the Abduction. If you fear that the other parent will take the children, you should take a few precautions. Some parents falsely think that if they steal the children away and move to another state or country, they will not have to pay child support or they can try to change the order for support in another state. This is not so.

Child Support Enforcement offices exist in every state (in California, for example, the office is called the California Department of Child Support Services), and they are supposed to help enforce child support collections. New laws have come into play since the Clinton administration that aim to enhance child support collections and prevent deadbeat parents from moving around a lot—changing where they live and where they work. A new high-tech computer network system is helping the Administration for Children and Families (ACF) in the Department of Health and Human Services (HHS) do the job. The states provide information to HHS regarding the amount of past-due child support owed by noncustodial parents. The ACF network system includes information that can help locate noncustodial parents, such as wage information from employers, account information from banks, certain tax information from the Internal Revenue Service (IRS), and benefit information from various other federal and state agencies. And once a delinquent noncustodial parent is found or the parent's income and assets are identified, state officials can take a number of actions to collect the overdue child support, up to arresting and bringing the parent to court as a last resort. Most of these new automated tools are the result of the Welfare Reform Law of 1996.

States submit child support cases with past-due amounts to the Office of Child Support Enforcement. If the past-due amount exceeds $5,000, the OCSE automatically forwards the case to the Department of State for passport denial.

To prevent the other parent from getting far with your children, start by notifying authorities and, in particular, your local Child Support Enforcement office. You may not be able to get your local police to actually do anything, since a crime has not been committed (yet), but inquire what they suggest you do. Also go to the federal Office of Child Support Enforcement's web site at www.acf.dhhs.gov/ and search under your own state to locate the office near you. That office should contact the Federal Parent Locator Service (FPLS) about your case.

If your ex-spouse owes you $5,000 or more in back child

If you are wrongly accused of child abuse by your vengeful ex-spouse, you have rights. You should seek an attorney who can help defend you against your ex-spouse and reverse any damage done to you as a result of the accusations. For additional information and added support, contact the National Association of State VOCAL Organizations (NASVO). NASVO was founded in 1987 out of VOCAL, or the Victims of Child Abuse Laws. NASVO is the national umbrella organization for approved chapters of VOCAL. Such victims include not only those who find themselves falsely or wrongly accused of child abuse and neglect but also foster children who find themselves abused by the system. As an organization, NASVO is dedicated to reform in the national and state policy on child protection as well as foster care. NASVO's national hotline is 800-745-8778.

support payments, he or she may find it difficult to leave the United States on a passport. States submit child support cases with past-due amounts to the Office of Child Support Enforcement. If the past-due amount exceeds $5,000, the OCSE automatically forwards the case to the Department of State for passport denial. You can further prevent your ex-spouse from taking your child out of the country by contacting the passport office and requesting that your child be denied a passport if the office receives an application for one. Regional passport agencies are located throughout the country.

For answers related to questions concerning international parental child abduction and denial of passports to minors in the case of an abduction, or if your former spouse succeeds in leaving the country with your children, contact the U.S. Department of State's Office of Children's Issues (your own state may have a similar office you can contact by going to your state's main web site). You can access the OCS's comprehensive site at http://travel.state.gov/family (the OCS web site is an excellent source of more information and links to other useful resources). Or you can call 888-407-4747 or 202-736-9090; fax: 202-736-9133. The OCS's national address is:

Department of State
Office of Children's Issues
SA-29, Fourth Floor
2201 C Street, NW
U.S. Department of State
Washington, DC 20520-2818
Child Abduction Prevention

More Visitation Guidelines for Every Situation Possible

Chapter 6 presented some visitation guidelines that are suggested by the South Dakota family courts. Every court will have its own guidelines that judges are supposed to take into consideration when listening to testimony in a divorce trial or granting parents their orders in a divorce agreement. We didn't give you all of the guidelines, as they can get lengthy in their attempt to cover every situation possible regarding divorce, but here, you'll find some interesting guidelines that may be helpful when you are negotiating visitation and trying to move forward in your postdivorce life.

The younger your children are at the time of divorce, the more you have to think about with regard to their developmental and emotional needs and how, for example, a father can fit into the picture when a baby needs to be breast-fed and cared for by its mother for a certain time period. Because parenting is often approached one day at a time (especially by first-time parents), planning parenting for the future at divorce can be extremely challenging. These guidelines do a good job of outlining how parents should share custody, given the children's ages and the location of the parents. Remember: Parents are not the only ones affected by divorce. What's more, parents are not the ones who have to experience the actual shift from one parent's care to that of the other. At every age of a child, the visitation schedule must reflect the specific needs, and sometimes the wishes, of the child—not those of the parent.

Children under Age Five

An infant presents a unique situation when the parents divorce. Forcibly weaning a child, whether breast-feeding or bottle-feeding, during the upheaval of parental separation is not appropriate for the physical health or emotional well-being of the child. Until weaning has occurred without forcing, a nursing infant should have visits of only a few hours with the father. However, a mother should not use breast-feeding beyond the normal weaning age as a means to deprive the father of visitation.

Infants (children under 18 months of age) and toddlers (18 months to three years) have a great need for continuous contact with the primary caretaker, who provides a sense of security, nurturing, and predictability. Generally, overnight visits for infants and toddlers are not recommended unless the noncustodial parent is very closely attached to the child and is personally able to provide primary care. Older preschool-age children (age three to five) are able to tolerate limited separations from the primary caretaker. South Dakota's guidelines for children under age five, like any family court's guidelines, are designed to take into account children's developmental milestones as a basis for time with the noncustodial parent. Since children mature at different rates, the guidelines may need to be adjusted to fit the child's individual circumstances. Parents who share the parenting responsibilities equally will not have to use their state's guidelines so long as they agree on how those responsibilities will be shared and their plan works out in the real world. The children should be attached equally to both parents in that situation.

Children over Age Five When Parents Live within 200 Miles

The physical distance between two divorced parents plays a big role in how they can share custody and, in particular, how easy it is for the noncustodial parent to visit with the children. In some communities, 200 miles may seem like a very long distance that prohibits parents from routinely sharing the children on alternate weekends unless transportation is easy. But for many parents, the distance isn't significant and both will go to any lengths to see their children as much as possible. At your divorce, you must make a realistic commitment to see your children if you are not the custodial parent. Following are days and special time periods to consider and carefully map out:

- Weekends
- Mother's Day and Father's Day
- Summer vacation
- Winter (Christmas) vacation

- Holidays (Easter, Memorial Day, 4th of July, Labor Day, and Thanksgiving)
- Birthdays (children's and parents')

Parents should plan for potential conflicts between regular and holiday weekends and visitation before and during long vacations. Provisions about visitation cancellations and the how-tos of picking up and returning the children should also be made. Additional visitation should always be an option. The children's time with the noncustodial parent should be liberal and flexible. No guidelines are meant to prevent you and your ex-spouse from agreeing to a better time-sharing plan that is in the best interests of your children at any given time.

Children over Age Five When Parents Live More Than 200 Miles Apart

Divorced parents who live more than 200 miles apart may have easier visitation schedules because they cannot share the children as frequently and routinely as parents who live closer together, but they must adhere to stricter schedules that ensure both parents get to spend ample time with their children. This kind of distance makes visitation rules less flexible because there are fewer visits to arrange and shuffle. However, each visit is longer, and children may adapt well to such a plan, enjoying the extended-stay experience they get from being with one parent for a chunk of time.

When mapping out a parenting/visitation plan with your ex-spouse who lives far away, you still must create some provisions for dealing with conflicts that interfere with the set schedule of visitation, cancellations of visitations, and the option to extend visitation. Again, the best interest of the child should always be your priority.

The New Relationship

Among the more difficult steps a child must take in your postdivorce life is accepting any new romantic relationships that bring a new person into the family. If your ex-spouse begins a new relationship, it will have an emotional impact on you no matter how much you disliked your spouse at your divorce. Children can experience even deeper troubling feelings when one parent finds a new love interest. They may feel threatened by this person, wondering whether he or she will steal the parent away from them or try to be a substitute mom or dad. Both parents need to be sensitive to the danger of exposing children too quickly to new relationships while they are still adjusting to the trauma of their parents' separation and divorce.

The most you can do to protect your children (and your own sanity) after divorce when you try to reenter the dating world and reestablish yourself as a single person is to keep the lines of communication open between you and your children. Don't ever assume they understand what's going on in your head or that you know what's going on in their heads. If your relationship with your children deteriorates, try counseling and spending more time with your

Rebound relationships get their stereotype for a reason: They don't typically last long. It's not uncommon for divorced men and women to quickly find love and jump into another committed relationship before they have finished working through their previous marriage's problems and understanding why and how it failed. Rebound marriages have a high failure rate. In fact, people who remarry after divorce have *less than a 50/50 chance* of staying married the second time!

children than with any new love interest. Now is not the time to act selfishly and forget your children's needs and emotions. Read books that help train newly divorced parents how to cope in their postdivorce life, how to guide children through the difficult time, and how to be a continual role model. If you exhibit your anger, unhappiness, and feelings of loss too much at and beyond your divorce, your children will pick up on these emotions and carry them with them long into adulthood. You don't want to jeopardize their ability to find love, happiness, and a stable family life in their future, so keep them confident in the institution of marriage.

Conclusion

The institution of marriage and the reality of divorce today are two competing but intertwining subjects that may always define the human condition. We have a primal need to be connected to someone else for support, safety, and the production of children, but we also have a primal need to be independent, autonomous, and in control of our own destiny. Whether you're in a marriage or going through divorce, your life is about compromise, negotiation, and the push and pull that naturally accompany the experience of relationships.

We hope we've given you the groundwork in this book for understanding divorce and how you can best work your own way through divorce without the expensive aid of attorneys, who can quickly turn an amicable divorce into an exhausting tennis match that costs you bundles of money, time, and anguish.

Taking care of your emotional self will help ensure that your children survive your divorce and recover quickly. They will always be affected by your divorce to an extent that is largely dependent on how you and your ex-spouse behave now and in the future. Don't underestimate the power of good counseling while you deal with your emotions and try to keep things in perspective. Your children can also benefit from counseling. The proper attitude can do more than you probably realize, and if you don't know what your attitude exactly is at this time, ask someone. Ask a friend, or even your children, how they think you are acting. The answers might surprise you. You may find yourself relying on others to keep you in tune with yourself. Because divorce can alienate your emotions *from yourself,* having a good network of support will ultimately allow you to evolve emotionally and prepare for welcoming your next new stage in life.

Take good care of yourself and your children. You (and they) deserve it. By now, you've probably come a long way (at least mentally, if not literally) since first thinking about divorce. You've learned a lot of useful information that will help you accomplish the goal and reach many more goals in the future.

CHAPTER 8

Frequently Asked Questions

This chapter is dedicated entirely to answering the most frequently asked questions about divorce. We've organized the chapter according to topic, so you can easily locate a set of questions that pertains to one part of the process.

Customers who enter our stores are full of questions when they first contemplate divorce. The process initially seems daunting, and people sometimes feel embarrassed that they have to ask about how to get a divorce. Feelings of defeat naturally come with filing for divorce (or even thinking about it), but there's nothing to be embarrassed about. Divorce is not a topic you want to learn about unless you have to go through the process. Keep your head up high and accept your emotions, for the best you can do is gather as much information as you can and proceed thoughtfully.

Please note: Generally speaking, there are many exceptions to the various rules. Divorce is a state-run legal procedure. Many questions can be hard to answer in any particular way because options may exist depending on state law. Always check your local family court's rules and don't ever hesitate to call your local court's clerk and ask specific questions. You can always come into one of our stores and leave the heavy lifting to us (check appendix B for a store near you). Log on to the Web and visit www.wethepeopleforms.com or www.wiley.com/go/wethepeopleforms to click your way to your state's main court site. From there, you should be able to locate your local court online for information, forms, and specific Q&A that relates to your jurisdiction. Remember: Self-knowledge and competent advice are the two key ingredients to a successful future.

Thinking about Divorce

Q. Do we have to go to court to get a divorce?

A. If you and your spouse can reach an agreement, you may not have to go to court. Your papers will go to court, where a judge will sign them, but you may not have to be physically present. However, some courts do require one or both spouses to appear in court—especially if there are minor children and no lawyers involved. If you've already reached an agreement with your spouse and you must appear in court, that appearance is likely to be brief.

Q. How long does it take to get a divorce?

A. States have different laws that govern how long you must wait before you can be legally divorced. For example, California law requires a minimum of six months before you can legally be an unmarried person. The paperwork can take less time, but it can also take much longer. Many states also have separation requirements (see chapter 2 about separation), as well as residency requirements in your state and county.

Q. Do I have to have a reason to get a divorce?

A. Grounds are the legal reasons for your divorce. Each state has different sets of grounds for divorce. Most have fault and no-fault options. For example, you can claim irreconcilable differences in a no-fault divorce. Or you can claim adultery in a fault divorce. Fault divorces must be proven in court. Saying you no longer want to be married is reason enough to call for a divorce based on irreconcilable differences. (See chapter 2 for specific information.)

Q. What is a covenant marriage?

A. A growing trend in the marriage industry is the so-called covenant marriage, whereby the couple getting married sign an agreement that says, in the event they want to end their marriage, they will not get a no-fault divorce and must have actual grounds, such as abuse or infidelity, to get divorced. More states are proposing covenant marriage laws in an attempt to combat the high divorce rate.

Q. How much does a divorce cost?

A. The total cost will depend on what kind of services you pay for to get through your divorce. Costs to include in your calculations are filing fees, the cost of serving the other spouse copies of the paperwork, mediation fees, document preparation fees (paying someone to help type your forms), and any legal fees. The paid or unpaid time you have to take off from work to deal with your divorce also affects your overall costs. It's impossible to put an exact figure on your overall divorce costs. The key is to minimize your costs by avoiding runaway legal fees and engaging in long disputes with your spouse over the issues. The longer it takes to reach an agreement and settle, the more it will cost.

Q. Do I need an attorney?

A. Not all legal matters require an attorney. By avoiding attorneys, you avoid extra costs and potentially avoid additional anguish and frustration. Attorneys can make an amicable divorce turn sour very quickly. Although attorneys can be useful for some complicated and contested divorces, you do not need an attorney to help you complete and file the paperwork, nor do you need one to help you work out issues. The more you can resolve issues directly with your spouse, the better off you'll be. If your issues are very difficult to resolve, try mediation first, before welcoming attorneys into the mix.

Q. What do my spouse and I have to decide if we get divorced?

A. The three most important items to consider are assets, debt, and kids (ADK). You and your spouse must reach an agreement on how you will divide marital property (the property you acquired while you were married) as well as debt (what you jointly owe); whether one spouse will pay alimony to the other, and if so, how much and for how long; and how your children, if any, will be shared, including financial and caring responsibilities.

Q. My spouse and I are going to separate until we decide whether we're going to get divorced. I need spousal and child support, however, so what do I do?

A. You ask the court to order temporary spousal and child support. Try to discuss with your spouse how much support you think you need and reach an agreement. You may also want temporary orders that indicate who will have primary custody of the children and how visitation will work out during your separation. If you think you will be separated for quite some time, you may want to create a more formal separation agreement that you submit to the court and that lays out the same groundwork that a divorce agreement would with regard to spousal and child support, the division of assets and debts, and child custody and visitation. This agreement can later become the framework for a divorce agreement.

Q. Do I have to formally separate from my spouse before filing for divorce? If so, for how long?

A. Not all states require a formal separation before you file for divorce; you may be able to start divorce proceedings right away. Check with your local family court's rules.

Initiating Divorce

Q. I don't know where my spouse is; can I still get a divorce?

A. Yes. The law makes provisions for those who cannot locate their spouses. You can still file for divorce, but you will need to prove to the court that you've done your best to track down your spouse. If your spouse does not respond within a certain time period, your case will proceed and you will be granted a divorce. (See chapter 5 about how to serve your spouse copies of your divorce papers when you cannot locate him or her.)

Q. My spouse refuses to give me a divorce; what are my options?

A. You do not need to have a cooperating spouse to obtain a divorce in most states. If one spouse does not want to remain married, that is enough reason for the courts to grant a divorce. However, the divorce process can take longer in this situation. A spouse can attempt to block the divorce by contesting the impaired status of the marriage, but such an attempt is rarely successful.

Q. My spouse wants a divorce, but I don't. What do I do?

A. There is nothing you can do legally to prevent or stop a divorce if your spouse files. You may want to suggest to your spouse that both of you seek counseling before filing for divorce. But if your spouse is uncooperative and has initiated the process by hiring a lawyer, you may want to find your own lawyer to help you out. You should not try to avoid the divorce case.

Q. What is the difference between a divorce and a legal separation?

A. Both legal separation and divorce are legal procedures that have similar characteristics: They require court filings (and fees), they take time, and they deal with the issues of custody, support, and property division. The main difference is that in a legal separation, the spouses remain married and they may resume the marital relationship at any time.

Q. What are the legal grounds for obtaining a divorce?

A. The grounds (reasons) for divorce depend on the state and may be based on no-fault or fault. A no-fault divorce is available in some form in all 50 states; many states also have fault-based grounds as an additional option (example: adultery, cruelty, abuse, desertion, insanity). A no-fault divorce is one in which neither the husband nor the wife officially blames the other for the breakdown of the marriage. Common bases for no-fault divorce are irreconcilable differences, irretrievable breakdown, and incompatibility. Another common basis for no-fault divorce is that the couple has lived separately for a certain period of time (this also varies from state to state) with the intent that the separation be permanent. (See chapter 2 for more information.)

Q. What is the date of separation?

A. The answer depends on your state. In some states, the date of separation is the day you and your spouse decided you didn't want to be husband and wife anymore—even if you are still living together. In other states, the date of separation is the day one spouse moves out, or it can be determined by the court.

Q. If I am separated from my spouse, am I permitted to have intimate relationships with other people?

A. If you live in a no-fault divorce state, it will not be an issue if you establish intimate relationships with individuals who are not your spouse. However, if child custody or primary residence of the child is an issue, your other relationship may have an impact on a court's decision regarding the child.

Q. I am separated and have bought a new house. Will this be considered a marital asset in a divorce?

A. Generally, any property obtained before the divorce is final will be considered marital, especially if marital assets were used to buy the property. Some states treat property purchased by a spouse or debts effective after the separation of the parties as separate property if marital assets were not used to purchase the property or secure the debt.

Q. Do I have to file in the state where I got married?

A. No. You file in the state where you currently reside. For residency requirements, see chapter 1.

Q. What is a default divorce?

A. If you and your spouse have resolved your issues and can proceed in an uncontested, no-fault manner to court, you can expect a quicker judgment and court proceeding if your divorce is a default divorce. This happens when one spouse files the paperwork and the other spouse does not file an answer to the court upon receipt of the paperwork copies. The other spouse is said to be in default. This means the case will go forward as an uncontested matter, which allows the divorce to move toward the judgment phase.

Q. What is a declaration of disclosure?

A. A declaration of disclosure lists full and accurate information about your assets, debts, income, and expenses to your spouse. Spouses must always be completely open and honest in their dealings with each other. Your court may require that you give your spouse a preliminary declaration of disclosure within a certain time period following the filing of your initial paperwork, and then a final declaration of disclosure at or before the time you enter into any final agreement for support or the division of property. In other words, you are telling the court that you have complied with the disclosure law. In some courts, you and your spouse can waive the final declaration of disclosure in your marital settlement agreement.

Q. What is the procedure for getting a divorce?

A. If your case is uncontested and you and your spouse can come to agreement on all the issues you need to decide on, then your case should go as follows (again, this will depend on your specific state's court procedure; this is an example):

1. You file a petition (or complaint), which contains general information, and a summons at the courthouse.
2. Copies are given to your spouse.
3. No sooner than X number of days (depending on your state) after your spouse receives those copies, you can file the final papers that contain your specific information.
4. About X number of weeks (depending on your local court) after the final papers are filed at the courthouse, the judge will sign your papers to finalize your divorce, and both parties will receive copies directly from the court.

Q. How do I find my local family court, where I can get forms to fill out and file my paperwork?

A. Courts that deal with family law are sprinkled throughout the United States, and depending on where you live—both your state and your county, the name of the court that deals with divorces may be a circuit court, a state superior court, or a district court (in other words, it may not be labeled "family court"). You can find links to court sites at www.wethepeople forms.com or in appendix B of this book. Alternatively, you can call the court nearest you and ask which court deals with divorce filings in your area. Look in the government pages of your phone book for numbers.

Q. Will there be anyone at the court to help me fill out and file my forms?

A. Many family law courts have information centers open to the public that provide family law information, referrals, and general assistance. These centers provide the legal forms you need and procedural guidance in many areas of family law, including divorce, legal separation, annulments, summary dissolutions, paternity, and domestic violence prevention cases. The office staff may consist of attorneys, paralegals, and support personnel, but none of them can give legal advice or represent you.

Q. How do I serve my spouse the divorce papers?

A. You can serve your spouse in a variety of ways, but your state will dictate which options you have. For couples doing their own divorce (without attorneys) and who can cooperate with one another (that is, the spouse who does not file will voluntarily accept being served), typically the spouse who files hires a neutral third party to deliver copies of the papers to the other spouse at an appropriate time. This person can be a friend, relative, professional process server, officer from the sheriff's office, or constable. If you do not know where your spouse is located or you believe your spouse has moved to another state, you may have to ask the court's permission to hire a professional server in that state or publish a notice in the paper where you believe your spouse is currently residing. (See chapter 5 for more details on service options.)

Q. I've received a summons and a copy of the divorce papers that my spouse filed in court. Should I respond to the court even though I am in agreement with my spouse?

A. If you do not respond, you will be in default and your case will proceed in an uncontested manner. But you may wish to respond to the court so you have a voice in the case and you show the court that you want to be included in the divorce proceeding. Your case will then proceed in a contested manner, but you will reach an agreement with your spouse and get it approved (signed) by a judge.

Reaching Agreements

Q. What if my spouse and I can't agree on all the issues? Do we have to go to court?

A. If you and your spouse cannot reach an agreement—and you've tried everything possible, from hiring a mediator to arbitration—then you will have to go to court and ask the judge to rule. The vast majority of divorces, however, do not require litigation (a judge to rule in lieu of an agreement). About 95 percent of all divorces get settled without going to trial. If you force a judge to make decisions for you, you are least likely to get what you want.

Q. How can I come to an agreement with my spouse?

A. You can decide on your issues and reach an agreement in a variety of ways: (1) informal discussions—you and your spouse reach an agreement through informal discussions; (2) mediation—you and your spouse resolve the issues with the help of a mediator; (3) collaborative law—each of you hires a lawyer trained in collaborative law, and all of you commit to resolving the case without going to court; (4) attorney negotiation—each of you hires a lawyer, and negotiations between the lawyers result in an agreement; or (5) court— if discussion, mediation, and negotiation do not settle all divorce issues between you and your spouse, a judge will make the decisions. You can use a combination of these methods to arrive at your agreement in full. Couples often find they can negotiate between themselves for the majority of issues and use mediation for some of the harder issues. This is the best way to reach an agreement because it limits the costs associated with divorce and keeps the couple in control of their own divorce. Moreover, mediation best preserves and/or improves the working relationship between the couple and results in better compliance with the agreement.

Q. What is mediation?

A. Mediation is a process by which two disagreeing sides meet with a neutral third party— called a *mediator*—to review the issues and try to come to an agreement using an environment that's cooperative and aimed at problem solving. Mediators help you and your spouse get over the emotional barriers to negotiation and help you devise a sensible divorce agreement that meets the needs of both of you. Unlike lawyers, mediators work with both spouses at the same time. They don't represent the individual spouses' interests the way a lawyer does.

Instead, mediators facilitate an ongoing negotiation between the spouses, which, in well over 80 percent of cases, results in an agreement satisfactory to both sides.

Q. What education and training do mediators have?

A. Anyone can be trained to be a mediator. Some mediators are laypeople, and they can be trained to mediate more than just divorce (they can mediate other types of disputes, such as business disputes). Professional mediators can also be lawyers and mental health professionals, who have hours of mediation training in addition to their graduate education and years of experience in law or therapy. Certified marital mediators have at least 48 hours of mediation training and have gone through an internship program.

Q. What if my spouse won't come to mediation?

A. If your spouse refuses to try mediation and has already hired an attorney, you should probably seek your own attorney and get ready for a contentious journey. But most spouses are open to mediation because of the costs (and mental anguish) mediation can save both of you. Be open to choosing a mediator with your spouse and don't rush out to find one who you think fits your needs. Encourage your spouse to mediate by explaining the true cost of inviting attorneys in and leaving issues to the courts. It may take time to find a mediator whom you both like, but the benefits of using mediation as opposed to having a judge make decisions for you are enormous.

Q. Do my spouse and I have to be in agreement to come to mediation?

A. No, you just have to be willing to try mediation to resolve your issues. Mediation works in most cases. You can be at odds with your spouse over a variety of issues and use mediation to reach agreements that prevent you from having to go to court and ask a judge to decide.

Q. What exactly happens when you meet with a mediator? How long does it take?

A. Every mediator works differently, but typically what happens is you and your spouse will meet with the mediator in a series of sessions, each one usually one to two hours long. Under the direction of the mediator, you'll gather and exchange financial and other information. Each of you gets to explain your feelings and thinking about each issue. The mediator will not take sides but can help each of you clarify what you say and offer possible solutions for reaching an agreement. How long mediation takes will depend on the number and nature of your disputed issues and how well you work together with the mediator. Some couples are able to resolve their issues in one or two sessions. For most couples, three to five sessions are needed. Complicated cases may require more sessions.

Q. What is co-mediation?

A. Co-mediation is when a pair of mediators, usually from different backgrounds, meets with you. One might be a lawyer and the other a mental health professional. Because of their respective professional backgrounds and experience, this approach offers unique support in making both custody and financial decisions.

Q. Who determines how assets and debts get divided in a divorce?

A. In an amicable divorce, where a couple reaches a so-called marital settlement agreement together, they are free to divide their assets and debts as they see fit. In deciding how to divide assets, you may want to refer to your state's guidelines if you're having trouble arriving at a fair and equitable division. If the court must decide how to divide your assets, it will refer to state laws about property and then rule. Whether you live in a community-property state or a non-community-property state may affect the outcome of your division when presented before a judge. Other variables include how much in debts each person is accepting, how much nonmarital property each spouse has, each spouse's earning power, the duration of the marriage, the contribution to the marriage, and the age and health of both spouses. (See chapters 4 and 5.)

Q. What is a marital settlement agreement?

A. A marital settlement agreement (MSA) is a mutually agreeable contract between you and your spouse that divides your assets and debts and resolves other issues in your divorce. An MSA becomes your divorce agreement (your judgment), and you will be ordered to comply with its terms. It must be signed by both you and your spouse. By having an MSA, you and your spouse get to decide everything and have total control over the outcome. If you have children, a parenting plan may be included in your MSA. In many states, by having an MSA, you may not have to appear in court. Your MSA will go to court with the rest of your final papers for the judge to sign.

Q. How do we determine what is separate property?

A. Separate property is property that either party brings into the marriage, is acquired during the marriage with separate funds, or is received by inheritance or particular donation (such as a gift). Marital property is anything acquired during your marriage. If you live in a community-property state, each spouse owns an undivided one-half interest in any property acquired during the marriage. In non-community-property states, each spouse is entitled to an "equitable distribution" of marital property. Under equitable distribution, the split is made based on "what is fair."

Q. What is a parenting plan?

A. The parenting plan is part of your divorce agreement if you have children, and it may be the most important matter you deal with. The parenting plan establishes how you and your soon-to-be ex-spouse will continue to care for and raise your children. The plan refers to all of the arrangements for the children and how you and your spouse will share parental responsibility. If you cannot agree about the parenting plan, the matter will be decided in court by a judge. In most courts, a judge will suggest counseling or mediation before having to make decisions for parents. You may, for example, be required to meet with a court counselor, who will attempt to mediate.

The Courts

Q. What do I wear to court?

A. Dress appropriately. You should appear well-groomed, prepared, and serious about dealing with your divorce. You do not need to don a three-piece suit, but avoid being overly casual, with threadbare jeans, a T-shirt, and open-toed shoes. Dress like you're going on a job interview.

Q. Do I take my children with me to court?

A. Do not take children into the courtroom unless the judge requests it. This is your divorce—not your children's—and they should not hear what goes on in that room.

Q. What if the judge asks me a question I cannot understand or cannot answer?

A. You can always ask the judge for clarification if you don't understand something that was said. You may have a very kind and patient judge, or you may have a grouchy judge who doesn't have a lot of extra patience. No matter your experience, don't ever be afraid to speak up and ask for more explanation. Always remember to address the judge as "Your Honor."

Q. Can I change my divorce agreement at a later date?

A. Yes, you can modify your agreement, but your circumstances must have changed for a judge to approve any major amendments. For example, if you want more child support, you will have to ask the court to order more child support because your circumstances have changed. You can always make informal changes to your agreement with your ex-spouse, but if you don't have a court order signed by the judge, they cannot be enforced. (See chapter 5.)

Q. My spouse and I could not agree on anything during our divorce, so we had a judge make most of the decisions for us. I don't like the outcome; can I appeal his decision?

A. Divorces that are settled by judges (*litigated* divorces) are very difficult to appeal. If a judge decides your divorce settlement and you are not happy with it, you face another round of obstacles that means more time, money, frustration, and another trial. You cannot file an appeal anytime you like, as each state has the appeal window open for only a certain time period following the decision. You must have a legal reason to file an appeal, and the process is not something you can do yourself (you will need an attorney).

Custody, Support, and Visitation Issues

Q. How do courts determine who gets custody of children in a divorce?

A. Courts do not like to make decisions for parents with regard to their children. A court will do whatever it can to try and get two warring parents to reach a reasonable agreement about custody issues, including sending the parents to a session of parenting classes or referring them to (more) mediation. If the parents cannot agree on custody of their child, the courts decide custody based on what's in the best interest of the child. Determining the child's best interest involves many factors, no one of which is most important. (See chapter 4.)

Q. What is joint custody?

A. Joint custody has two parts: joint *legal* custody and joint *physical* custody. A joint custody order can have one or both parts. Generally, it's best for both parents to share joint legal custody and for one to have primary physical custody.

Legal custody refers to both parents sharing the major decisions affecting the child, such as those concerning education, health care, and religion. It can also refer to other parenting decisions, such as at what age the child can start to date, which extracurricular activities will be allowed (and paid for), methods of discipline, and what the child does during summer breaks.

Physical custody refers to the time spent with each parent. The amount of time is flexible and can range from a moderate period of time for one parent, such as every other weekend, to a child dividing the time equally between the two parents' homes. In situations where the time spent with both parents will be divided equally, it helps if the parents live close to one another. (See chapter 4.)

Q. How is child support determined in a divorce or paternity case?

A. Every state has adopted child support guidelines. (Your local family court can tell you what the guidelines are in your state.) Some states use tables that indicate a support amount for different ranges of income, similar to tax tables. Although some states base support on the payor's income, many states take both parents' income into consideration when calculating child support. Usually, the parent without the child the majority of the time will pay support, but if both parents share time with the child equally, the parent with the greater income usually pays support. The support may be reduced based upon the amount of time the payor spends with the child. Some states also cap support at a certain income level. If a parent is intentionally not working or is working at less than he or she is capable of earning, the court can *impute income,* which means setting support based upon what the parent is capable of earning rather than actual earnings. States vary on what expenses are included in child support. For example, some states include medical expenses and day care, while other states add those costs on top of the child support. (See chapter 4.)

Q. What happens if a parent does not pay court-ordered child support?

A. Millions of children don't get their deserved child support in full each year. Several methods of enforcement are in place to help single parents collect their child support. A payor's obligation, for example, can be taken right out of his or her paycheck upon a court order. This is called *automatic withholding.* Many states have criminal penalties for failing to pay child support, and all states operate their own Child Support Enforcement offices to facilitate the collection of child support payments. Congress has enacted many new enforcement mechanisms, facilitating greater collaboration between federal and state governments. These include suspension of driver's licenses and professional licenses, seizure of tax refunds, seizure of bank accounts and investment accounts, and even publishing the name and picture of the deadbeat parent on posters and in newspapers. The law also improves interstate enforcement by bolstering federal services to locate parents across state lines and by requiring all states to have common paternity procedures in interstate cases. (See chapters 4 and 7 for more.)

Q. Can we deviate from the child support guidelines and make our own decision about how much child support will be paid?

A. The child support guidelines reflect what's in the best interest of the child—not the parents. A court will want the order for child support to be in the best interest of the child, so parents are urged to follow it. A deviation can be made, however, if both parents are in agreement, but it must be approved by the court.

Q. What factors affect child support?

A. In most states, child support is a computer-generated number based on the gross income of one or both parents, expenses for the child such as health care and day care, and the amount of time spent with each parent.

Q. Do grandparents have visitation rights to their grandchildren?

A. Yes. Grandparents can ask the court (file a petition) to get visitation rights. Their rights do not come automatically, but all states have enacted legislation enabling grandparents to petition the courts for visitation rights with grandchildren. Some states have extended this right to other relatives, such as great-grandparents, aunts, uncles, siblings, stepparents, and even nonrelatives with whom the child has a close relationship.

Q. I receive overtime in my work. Is this included in the calculation of my income for purposes of child support?

A. It depends on the nature of the overtime and your state's laws. If you voluntarily perform overtime in certain months, it might not be a part of the calculation for child support income. If the overtime is required by your employer, however, it might be included in your income.

Q. I am self-employed, in commission sales, or have irregular income. How do I calculate my income for child support?

A. To arrive at an estimate for your monthly income, take your total income over the past year or three years and divide by 12 or 36, respectively. This will give you an approximation if you cannot calculate an average income based on inconsistent monthly amounts.

Q. Can children give their opinion on which parent they want to primarily reside with?

A. Courts will listen to children over a certain age, and that age depends on the state. In some states, for example, a child over the age of 12 years may give his or her opinion, especially if there is a dispute.

Q. How do courts decide all issues involving a child if the parents cannot agree on terms?

A. The court will use the "best interest of the child" standard in almost every issue involving the child. Although the courts believe that the needs of the parents are important, they will generally not permit any action that would not be in the child's best interest.

Q. Am I required to pay for my child's college education as a part of my child support obligation?

A. This will vary from state to state. All states will permit parents to come to an agreement on this issue as a part of their divorce, but only a few states require parents to assist their children with college expenses as a part of a divorce settlement.

Property Issues

Q. My husband and I bought a house a year ago, but now we are divorcing. How can I keep the house?

A. The laws of your state will dictate your options. But more important is how you negotiate with your spouse and what kind of agreement you can reach with regard to the home. You can agree to buy out your spouse's share of the house, trade the home for another asset, or accept more of the marital debt in return for keeping the house. You can also sell the home and split the profit or loss, or agree to sell the home at a future date. If you're the primary caretaker of your children (and they live with you under primary custody), the court is likely to rule in your favor because judges don't want children to be uprooted. The important thing to remember is that whichever decision you make for keeping the home, you're able to continue maintaining the home and paying the mortgage. (See chapter 3 for more.)

Q. Can a judge award my retirement funds to my former spouse to pay for back spousal support?

A. Your state's laws will determine what a judge can and cannot do to force you to pay for back alimony. If a debt is owed and is not paid, a judge can order that assets be seized or liquidated to pay the outstanding debt. Typically, judges are not this aggressive unless the payment is for child support or there are other extenuating circumstances. Alimony payments can be harder to enforce than child support payments, which can come directly from your paycheck by court order.

Q. How is property divided at divorce?

A. Most couples can figure out through discussion and negotiation how to divide their assets and debts fairly—without leaving it all to a judge. But if a couple cannot agree, they can submit their dispute to the court, which will use state law to divide the property. Division of property does not necessarily mean a physical division. Rather, the court will give each spouse a percentage of the total value of the property. Each spouse gets items whose worth adds up to his or her percentage.

Q. How do courts divide property?

A. Courts divide property under one of two schemes: equitable distribution or community property. In non-community-property states, courts use equitable distribution, in which assets and earnings accumulated during the marriage are divided equitably (fairly). This may mean, for example that two-thirds of the assets go to the lower wage earner and one-third to the higher wage earner. Many factors go into determining equitable distribution, such as fault in the divorce, age and health of the spouses, and potential earning power. In community-property states (Arizona, California, Idaho, Louisiana, Nevada, New Mexico, Texas, Washington, Wisconsin, and Alaska by agreement), all property of a married person is classified as either community property, owned equally by both spouses, or the separate property of one spouse. At divorce, community property is generally divided equally between the spouses, while each spouse keeps his or her separate property.

Q. How do we distinguish between community and non-community property?

A. Community property in general includes all earnings during marriage and everything acquired with those earnings. All debts incurred during marriage, unless the creditor was specifically looking to the separate property of one spouse for payment, are community-property debts. Separate property of one spouse includes gifts and inheritances given just to that spouse, personal injury awards received by that spouse, and the proceeds of a pension that vested (that is, the pensioner became legally entitled to receive it) *before* marriage. Property purchased with the separate funds of a spouse remain that spouse's separate property. A business owned by one spouse before the marriage remains his or her separate property during the marriage, although a portion of it may be considered community property if the business increased in value during the marriage or both spouses worked at it.

Property purchased with a combination of separate and community funds is part community and part separate property, so long as a spouse is able to show that some separate funds were used. Separate property mixed together with community property generally becomes community property.

Q. Once we decide who gets what, how do we transfer assets?

A. You don't need to do any formal paperwork for small assets for which no title, deed, or other document is attached. For assets that do have titles or deeds, you will have to reregister those documents to reflect the change in ownership. For brokerage or bank accounts, contact the institutions that hold those assets and ask about how you change the names on those accounts to reflect the division. For retirement accounts, you may have to use a QDRO, or qualified domestic relations order (see chapter 6).

Q. What do we do about our retirement accounts?

A. You and your spouse must decide how you want to divide the marital portion of any retirement account, which can be a pension plan, 401(k), IRA, or other such account. Contact your plan administrator for guidance on splitting these types of assets. You may have to use a QDRO, or qualified domestic relations order, approved by the court, which orders the plan to direct funds to the nonemployee spouse. (See chapter 6.)

Other Issues Related to Divorce

Q. What if we reconcile and want to cancel our divorce?

A. You can dismiss your divorce proceeding at any time, but how you do so will depend on where in the process you stand when you decide to stop. If you have filed your paperwork but no response has been filed by the other spouse, and a judge has not entered a ruling, you can file a dismissal form. If, however, you and your spouse have proceeded further and the court is awaiting your agreement for a judge to sign and finalize, both of you will have to fill out and sign the dismissal form. This must happen before your divorce is final, which indicates that your marriage is legally over.

Q. What if I want to file for bankruptcy?

A. If one spouse is considering bankruptcy with large amounts of marital debt, the other spouse will be affected. Therefore, your spouse should be notified and given the opportunity to join in the bankruptcy proceeding.

Q. What is collaborative divorce?

A. Collaborative divorce is a new kind of divorce procedure whereby a couple agrees to avoid litigation (the courtroom battle) and approach their negotiations in a cooperative manner using attorneys. Each spouse must retain his or her own attorney (an attorney who specializes in collaborative law), and as a team, both sides work together to reach a fair settlement of all the issues. Collaborative divorce is similar to mediation in that it takes place outside the court process, but it is different from mediation in that each party has his or her own attorney, who can advise them separately and meet with them individually. Collaborative law does typically cost more than reaching agreements on your own and using mediation.

Q. What is a document preparation service?

A. We The People is a great example of a document preparation service. We help you obtain the forms you need and understand any local rules you need to follow, and we type your forms so they appear professional and meet requirements. We can also file the paperwork for you. Legal document companies generally work well with mediators, too, so having the combination of a good mediator and a good document preparer by your side is an excellent plan.

Q. Does my divorce have to be completed within a certain time?

A. For most couples, this is not a concern. Your state will say when you must complete your divorce, and it will give you lots of time (years). If your divorce is not final within that time frame, the court will close your case.

Q. What is the difference between an uncontested and a contested divorce?

A. An *uncontested* divorce is one where the spouses agree on all the issues—the reasons (grounds) for divorce, custodial arrangements, support and alimony, and property/debt division. In a *contested* divorce, one or more of these issues are disputed. Typically, you may not know at the time of your initial filing whether your divorce is contested or not. Once you begin to negotiate with your spouse over the issues, you'll know. But the vast majority of couples can come to an agreement and eventually get an uncontested divorced. They may have to hire a mediator to help resolve contested issues, but in the end their divorce is uncontested.

Q. If I am separated from my spouse, is there a certain length of time after which we are automatically granted a divorce?

A. No. If you want a divorce, you must go through the legal procedure in the state where you reside.

Q. I am not a U.S. citizen, nor am I a permanent resident. My wife is a citizen, and I am currently awaiting my green card. Can I file for divorce?

A. Your divorce proceeding may affect your greed card status, depending on where you are in the process. You may want to seek the advice of an immigration attorney to help your case. Or consult with your local Citizenship and Immigration Services office to understand your options.

Q. I am on my husband's health policy from his workplace. Will I lose my health insurance after my divorce? Will my children, if I have custody?

A. Your children will be able to remain on your husband's health policy, but you will not. You can, however, apply for COBRA, which will allow you to keep your health insurance for a specified period of time or until you find other coverage. (See chapter 7 for more details.)

Q. If my church annuls my marriage, does that mean I am legally annulled in the eyes of the state?

A. No. Religious annulments and legal annulments are two separate processes. You must meet specific criteria in either type of annulment, and you may qualify for one but not the other. Many people wrongly assume that getting an annulment is easier than getting a divorce. That is not always the case. An alternative to a regular divorce in some states, however, may offer a simplified version for ending your marriage. Different states may have a different name for this type of simplified divorce, such as *summary divorce*. Check with your state for more information.

Q. My spouse is physically abusive and I fear for myself and my children. What can I do?

A. Seek help immediately. Call the National Domestic Violence Hotline at 800-799-SAFE (7233), or refer to your phone book for local shelters and hotlines. Look under "Crisis Intervention." These organizations will guide you through what you need to do. You may also need to get a protective order from the court, which will prohibit your spouse from coming within a certain distance of your home, your work, or where you children are located when they are not with you (school, playground, day care center).

Q. What does paternity mean?

A. Paternity means fatherhood. By taking steps to establish legal paternity, a mother gives her child a right to the same benefits as children of married parents, such as inheritance rights, access to the father's medical history, and financial support by the father. Due to the number of out-of-wedlock births, paternity cases outnumber divorce cases in many courts. They establish many of the same issues that divorce cases do—namely, custody, visitation, and child support. (See chapter 2 for more details.)

CHAPTER 9

Definition of Terms

The following is an alphabetical list of terms you're likely to encounter during your divorce process. When filling out your forms and negotiating with your spouse, you may find reference to this list useful. Most of these terms have already been defined and described throughout the book.

Abandonment. The act of leaving someone, such as a child or spouse, without any intention of returning.

Absolute Divorce. The final ending of a marriage. Both parties are legally free to remarry.

Actuary. A person who specializes in the mathematics of risk and insurance. Actuaries who specialize in retirement issues are great sources of information and advice for long-term financial planning, as they typically help design retirement plans for companies and individuals.

Adultery. Voluntary sexual intercourse between a married person and someone who is not the married person's spouse.

Affidavit. "I promise the info on this page is true." A piece of paper (a document) that you sign saying that all the information on the document in question is true. An affidavit is a sworn statement in writing. You typically sign an affidavit to say that you have done something, such as filed paperwork or delivered paperwork to someone else.

Alien. Anyone who is not a U.S. citizen.

Alimony. Payment of support (not child support) from one spouse to another so that the spouse receiving the payment can maintain the lifestyle that he or she was accustomed to during the marriage. Also called *spousal support* or *maintenance.* Types of alimony include the following:

Rehabilitative: This type of alimony is the most commonly awarded alimony. It is awarded in a situation where the recipient is younger or able to eventually enter or return to the workforce and become financially self-supporting. Rehabilitative alimony may include payments for the education necessary to enable the recipient to become self-supporting.

Lump sum: This type of alimony is one payment of alimony instead of periodic (usually weekly or monthly) payments.

Permanent: This type of alimony is to be paid until either the death of the payor or the remarriage of the recipient. Some agreements may include a "cohabitation" clause stating that alimony ends when the recipient cohabits with another person in the avoidance of marriage. Permanent alimony settlements are, generally speaking, a thing of the past.

Temporary: This type of alimony lasts for a specific period of time, usually one to two years. It may be awarded when the persons involved are on almost equal ground but due to certain circumstances one person may need financial assistance in order to get back on his or her feet.

Annuity. A type of policy that pays an amount of money (also called an annuity) yearly, or at other regular intervals. Annuities are sometimes referred to as upside-down life insurance policies because they insure against the risk of living too long. Payments are made periodically during one's lifetime (or for a defined period of time).

Annulment. A declaration that a marriage is void and null, as though it never existed. One can obtain a legal annulment, a religious annulment, or both.

Answer. The formal response to the court once divorce papers have been served. In contested divorces, the spouse who is served divorce papers must respond to the court within a set time period, usually 20 to 60 days.

Arrearages. Unpaid payments. If a spouse has not made the payments owed to the other spouse, those overdue payments are called arrearages and the person is said to be in arrears (behind) on payments.

Assets. Your "stuff." Specifically, any real property (your house), personal property (your car), or intellectual property (your patent rights to an invention) that you own an interest in (a legal share in). Money owed to you and portions of property (such as half of a house you share with your wife) are also examples of assets.

Automatic Wage Reduction. The automatic deduction from a parent's paycheck for child support payments. Those payments go directly to the custodial parent. Employers receive the court order and must comply with the deduction.

Bankruptcy. A legal procedure for dealing with debt problems of an individual or company whereby you request a discharge or adjustment of certain debts.

Capital Gains. The difference between the sales price and the original cost (plus improvements) of property. Example: You buy a house in 1967 for $40,000 and you sell it in 2005 for $650,000. Your capital gain is $610,000, which is subject to the capital gains tax.

Child Support Guidelines. The amount of child support to be paid, under normal circumstances, according to a schedule established by the state, based upon income. It is federally mandated that all states establish guidelines for child support.

Clerk. A county employee who does the intake and review of the documents before they are sent to a judge. An official or employee who handles the business of a court or a system of courts, maintains files of each case, and issues routine documents. Almost every county has a clerk of the courts or county clerk who fulfills those functions, and most courtrooms have a clerk to keep records and assist the judge in the management of the court.

COBRA. Consolidated Omnibus Budget Reconciliation Act. An act passed by Congress that requires certain employers to offer health insurance to departing employees. Employees pay the full premium plus a reasonable administrative fee. COBRA typically lasts 18 months from the date of termination. When a spouse loses access to heath care upon divorce, he or she can apply for COBRA coverage until other coverage is found or the eligibility for COBRA expires.

Collaborative Law. A new type of divorce procedure available in some states and counties whereby both couples obtain their own attorneys, but agree to approach the divorce process as a team effort—each attorney assisting the couple in resolving conflicts or legal issues (as opposed to fighting and disagreeing with one another). Usually, all parties sign a contract in which they agree not to go to court. Under the collaborative law process, both spouses attend informal discussions and conferences with their attorneys.

Collateral. An asset used as security (a pledge or promise) for repayment of a loan. Many people use large assets like homes, cars, and home furniture as collateral for loans. Example: Your car is collateral on the car loan. Your house is collateral you've used to secure a business loan from a bank.

Collusion. An agreement between two or more persons in which one party brings false charges against the other. In a divorce case, spouses who agree to use adultery as grounds to obtain a divorce more quickly (in a fault system), when that, in fact, did not happen, are said to be colluding. Collusion is illegal.

Common-Law Marriage. A state recognition of marriage if a couple has lived together for a certain period of time and intends to marry officially. Only a few states recognize common-law marriages.

Community Property. A form of property ownership solely between a husband and a wife recognized in only a few states. Those states are Arizona, California, Idaho, Louisiana, Nevada, New Mexico, Texas, Washington, and Wisconsin and the commonwealth of Puerto Rico (couples in Alaska can sign an agreement that identifies certain property as community). Specific community-property laws differ greatly among the states, but they all share a defining feature: All assets acquired during the marriage by either spouse are automatically split, so that each spouse owns a separate, undivided one-half interest.

Complaint. The legal paperwork that initiates a case. Sometimes called a *petition.* One who files a complaint is called a *complainant.* One who files a petition is called a *petitioner.*

Conditional Resident Alien. An alien who receives resident status based on a marriage of less than two years to a U.S. citizen. In order to become a permanent resident alien, the alien and his or her spouse must file a joint petition with the U.S. Citizen and Immigration Services within 90 days of the second anniversary of the day the CIS granted conditional resident status.

Contested Divorce. A divorce in which disagreements exist between the two spouses and for which mediation, arbitration, or litigation is necessary to reach a final divorce agreement.

Creditor. The person to whom money is owed. During a separation and/or divorce, you and your spouse should have a clear understanding of how you will deal with the debts you owe and the creditors to which those debts are tied.

Custodial Parent. The parent with whom the child(ren) live most of the time. The noncustodial parent is the parent with whom the child(ren) do not live most of the time.

Custody. The legal right and responsibility awarded by the court for the care of a child. The common types of custody arrangements are

Joint physical custody: Each parent has significant periods of physical custody to assure the child of frequent and continuing contact with both parents. It does not have to be 50/50; even 70/30 would be okay.

Sole or primary physical custody: The child lives with and is under the supervision of one parent most of the time.

Joint legal custody: Both parents share the right and responsibility for making decisions relating to the child's health, education, and welfare. (The noncustodial parent does not have to locate the custodial parent to obtain medical attention for the child.)

Sole or primary legal custody: One parent has the right and responsibility to make decisions relating to the child's health, education, and welfare.

Joint custody: Both parents have joint physical and joint legal custody.

Debt. Something owed, an obligation to pay.

Debtor. The person who owes a debt. A person who has filed a petition for relief under the bankruptcy laws.

Declaration. A document you write and sign that tells the court your story in addition to asking the court for something, such as spousal support, custody, or child support.

Declaration of Disclosure. A written document that lists for the other party (your spouse) full and accurate information about your assets, debts, income, and expenses.

Decree. A declaration of a court announcing the legal consequences of the facts. A divorce decree is the final written order for divorce.

Deed of Trust. A document that pledges real property to secure a loan. The property is deeded by the titleholder (trustor) to a trustee (often a title or escrow company), which holds the title in trust for the beneficiary (the lender of the money).

Default. A person's failure to answer a complaint, motion, or petition.

Default Divorce. A divorce whereby the filing spouse submits the paperwork and the other spouse fails to respond formally with the court (he or she defaults) by filing a written response within a given time period or appearing in court. The divorce then proceeds in an uncontested manner, and judgment is made based on the filing spouse's information.

Defendant. The person (the spouse) who is served divorce papers once the other spouse has filed. Also called the *respondent.*

Disability Insurance. A type of insurance that protects some of your income should you become unable to work due to illness or injury. If you become disabled, the policy will pay you a certain percentage of your income, which will help you maintain daily living and continue to care for your children. A court can require a self-employed parent, for example, to obtain some disability insurance.

Discovery. A process by which information regarding a case is obtained, particularly with regard to the opposing side. Various ways to complete this process include written questioning or deposing (interviewing) witnesses or experts for the record.

Dissolution. Another word for divorce, officially used in California since 1970 and symbolic of the no-fault, nonconfrontational approach to dissolving a marriage.

Divorce. The termination of a marriage by legal action, requiring a petition or complaint for divorce by one spouse. Some states still require at least a minimal showing of fault, but no-fault divorce is now the rule, in which incompatibility is sufficient to grant a divorce. The main issues in divorces are division of marital assets, child custody and support, alimony (spousal support), and child visitation. Only state courts have jurisdiction over divorces, so the petitioning or complaining spouse can only file in the state in which he or she is and has been a resident for a certain period of time.

Divorce Agreement. A written agreement that spells out the terms of the divorce and the relationship between the two spouses after the divorce. These agreements usually cover asset and debt division, child custody and child plans, spousal support, and any other relevant issues related to the divorce.

Emancipated Minor. A young individual who has not reached the legal age of adulthood (18 or 12, depending on the state) but wishes to be considered a legal adult in the eyes of the law. If he or she meets specific legal requirements and successfully goes through a court process, he or she may be considered emancipated.

Equitable Distribution. The rule of property division in most states, which divides assets and property between the husband and wife based on grounds of fairness. What is fair and reasonable is determined by a study of many factors, such as the income-producing power of both spouses, how much each retains as separate property, and their age and health.

Equity. The money value of your property, such as a home, that does not include the lender's portion of the value. Example: Your home is worth $250,000. You owe the bank $220,000. Your equity is $30,000. Another example: Your car has a value of $4,000, but there is a $3,500 lien on it (you owe someone money because you've used your car as collateral for a loan), so your car now has an equity value of only $500.

Ex Parte. Latin meaning "for one party," referring to motions, hearings, or orders granted on the request of and for the benefit of one party (that is, one spouse) only.

Expenses. What you spend, or the money that you need to pay for monthly expenses, such as food and rent.

Fault Divorce. A divorce in which one spouse alleges fault or marital misconduct against the other spouse. Grounds for fault divorces include adultery, cruelty, and abandonment.

Foreclosure. The forced sale of real estate to pay off a loan on which the owner of the property has defaulted.

Green Card. A green card is actually an alien registration receipt card given to aliens after they have acquired resident status in the United States. It covers both conditional and permanent resident aliens. The card used to be green but is now rose-colored.

Grounds. The legal reasons for a divorce.

Hearing. Any proceeding before a judge or other magistrate (such as a hearing officer or court commissioner) without a jury in which evidence and/or an argument is presented (sometimes with testifying witnesses) to determine the facts and issues of a case. In divorce cases, hearings are usually conducted with a family law judge listening to your and your spouse's cases in order to grant any motions or requests for custody, visitation, support, and so on.

Immigrant. An alien who intends to reside permanently in the United States.

Immigrant Visa. A document package issued by a U.S. consul abroad that an alien presents at the U.S. border to be admitted as a conditional or permanent resident.

Income. How much you make from all sources, or the amount that appears on your pay stubs.

Injunction. A court order that tells someone to do something or prohibits some act after a court hearing. For example, upon filing for divorce, both spouses receive an injunction that prevents either person from stealing, selling, or vandalizing marital property.

Intangible Property. Assets that do have value but that you cannot necessarily touch, such as stock in a company, retirement benefits, a pension, or bonds.

Interest. Your financial right to, title to, or legal share in something, such as a piece of land or a business. Example: You and your wife own a home in a community-property state. You have 50 percent interest in your house.

Joint Tenancy. A term that relates to the ownership of real property, which provides that each party owns an undivided interest in the entire parcel, with both having the right to use all of it and usually the right of survivorship. This means that upon the death of one joint tenant, the other has title to it all. Example: You and your wife share joint tenancy in your home.

Jurisdiction. The authority of the court to hear a case.

Liability. Legal responsibility for one's acts or failure to act. If you fail to meet your responsibility, you become open to lawsuits or court-ordered actions that force you to accept responsibility. For example, a financial liability is a responsibility to pay, such as a tax liability that refers to what you owe in taxes.

Limited Divorce. A type of divorce that is not absolute—that is, the two parties have separated under certain legal responsibilities, but their marriage is not officially over and they cannot remarry.

Liquid Asset. Any asset that can be quickly and easily converted to cash. Paper money and coins are the most liquid forms of cash. Other examples of liquid assets include bank accounts, stocks, Treasury bills, certificates of deposit, and money market accounts.

Living Trust. A document that distributes your estate after death and avoids the probate process. A living trust is set up while you are alive and remains under your control until your death. Also called an *inter vivos* trust. Creators of living trusts are called the *settlors, grantors,* and *trustors.* They are also lifetime beneficiaries of their living trusts.

Living Will. A document that formally expresses your wishes to forgo or receive extraordinary medical treatment when you become terminally ill.

Maintenance. Another word for spousal support or alimony. Maintenance is often used in reference to separation agreements.

Marital Property. Assets earned or acquired by either spouse during the marriage that are not separate property. This includes debts incurred by either spouse up to the time of separation.

Marital Settlement Agreement. A contract between the husband and the wife that divides property and debts and resolves other issues of the divorce.

Master. A court official who hears cases like a judge. A master's decision is reviewed by a judge before becoming final.

Mediation. A process by which you and your spouse work with a neutral third party (a mediator) to settle major issues and prepare your divorce agreement. This process is voluntary and nonbinding. Mediators do not provide legal advice, nor do they take sides; they simply create the neutral environment through which couples can discuss their contested issues and reach an agreement.

Motion. A formal request made to a judge for an order or judgment. Motions are made in court all the time for many purposes: to continue (postpone) a trial to a later date, to get a modification of an order, for temporary child support, for a judgment, for dismissal of the opposing party's case, for a rehearing, or for dozens of other purposes.

Naturalization. The process of acquiring citizenship for anyone who did not become a U.S. citizen by birth.

No-Fault Divorce. A divorce in which neither spouse is required to prove fault or marital misconduct on the part of the other. To obtain a divorce, a spouse must merely assert incompatibility or irreconcilable differences, meaning the marriage has irretrievably broken down.

Nonimmigrant. An alien who intends to visit, live, or work temporarily in the United States.

Order. A court ruling that tells (orders) someone to do or not do something. Orders can also establish certain rights and responsibilities of a person under the order.

Order to Show Cause Hearing. A court hearing at your family court where you have filed temporary orders and need a family law judge to rule on your request(s). The document that declares this hearing is called the *Order to Show Cause* document, and it officially tells your spouse to come to court at a specific date and time and explain (show cause) why the court should not grant the request listed on the document.

Palimony. Similar to alimony, it applies to couples who never legally married but who lived together for a long period and then ended their relationship.

Parenting Plan. A written pact with your spouse that lays out exactly your intentions and plans for your children—from custody arrangements and precise visitation schedules to how their medical and dental care will be covered and who can make important decisions about invasive treatment, for example. Parenting plans almost always accompany or are part of a separation agreement or marital settlement agreement.

Paternity. Fatherhood. It's a court case that establishes who is the father of a child. In addition to the desire to give the child a known natural father, proof of paternity leads to the right to child support, birthing expenses, and the child's inheritance from his or her father.

Pendente Lite. Latin for "pending litigation." You may see this term in reference to alimony in your divorce agreement or separate maintenance in your separation agreement. Both alimony *pendente lite* and separate maintenance refer to spousal support. When spousal support payments get figured out for the purpose of a separation agreement, the court can use this figure later on during a divorce proceeding. Thus, the spousal support determined at separation is pending the litigation that happens at a later date during the actual divorce.

Permanent Resident Alien. An alien who is permitted by the Citizen and Immigration Services to enter the United States in order to reside permanently.

Personal Property. All personal assets that do not include real property (home). Examples: cars, furniture, clothing, books, jewelry, money, bank accounts, and paintings.

Petition. A formal written request (asking the court for something). Your divorce petition is your formal request for a divorce to the court. In your petition, which is also called a *complaint,* you establish the facts and present some of the issues of your divorce. This is one of the first papers you'll file to begin your case.

Plaintiff. The person (the spouse) who initially files the divorce papers with the court. Also called the *petitioner.*

Pre- or Postnuptial. A written contract between two people who are about to marry (pre) or who have already married (post) that sets out the terms of possession of assets, treatment of future earnings, control of the property of each, and potential division if the marriage is later dissolved.

Pro Se/Pro Per. To represent yourself in court without an attorney.

Proof of Service. A document that someone signs telling the court that he or she delivered copies of all the court-filed papers. It can also be called a *certificate of service.*

Property. Everything you own, both real (such as a home) and personal (such as your car). Also called *assets.* Assets you acquire during your marriage are called *marital assets.*

Qualified Domestic Relations Order (QDRO). A qualified domestic relations order is a court order that creates or recognizes the existence of the nonemployee spouse's right to receive all or a portion of the retirement benefits payable with respect to a participant under a pension plan. Example: Your spouse participated in his company's 401(k) retirement plan, and now that you are getting divorced, you have a right to some of the money in that plan. You will use a QDRO to receive those funds when your husband retires and begins to withdraw from that fund.

Real Property/Real Estate. Land and things permanently attached to the land.

Restraining Order. A court ruling that tells (orders) someone to hold back (restrain) from doing something, such as contacting and/or coming within a certain distance of another person, or selling assets, or draining a bank account.

Secured Debt. Debts secured by assets that can be repossessed or foreclosed on, such as your home mortgage, car loan, or rented furniture. A secured creditor is one who holds an item of yours as security for the debt. The bank that loaned you the money to buy your house holds a mortgage or trust deed lien on your house as security for the loan; therefore, the mortgage company is a secured creditor.

Security Interest. A generic term for the property rights of a lender or creditor whose right to collect a debt is secured by property or asset. Example: Your mortgage company has a security interest in your home.

Separate Property. Assets that belong just to one spouse and not to both. Separate property is (a) property that was acquired before the marriage or (b) property that at any time was given specifically to one spouse by gift or inheritance.

Separation. Married persons living apart, either informally by one leaving the home or agreeing to separate while sharing a residence without sexual relations, or formally by obtaining a legal separation or negotiating a separation agreement that sets out the terms of separate living.

Service. The act of providing a copy of the papers being filed to the other party.

Stock Options. An option (an invitation), usually given to employees of large companies, to purchase stock in the company at a future date. The price of the option is established, so if the company's stock price rises above the option price, the employee is able to take advantage of the stock increase (current stock price minus established stock price).

Summons. A call to court. A document issued by the court at the time a lawsuit (example: divorce) is filed, stating the name of both plaintiff (example: filing spouse) and defendant (example: other spouse), the title and file number of the case, the court and its address, the name and address of the plaintiff's attorney (if any), and instructions about the need to file a response to the complaint within a certain time (such as 30 days after service), usually with a form on the back on which information of service of summons and complaint is to be filled out and signed by the process server (the person who delivers the summons).

Surviving Spouse. The person who outlives his or her spouse. The second spouse to die.

Survivor. One who outlives—survives—another. If your spouse dies, you (and everyone else in your family) survived him or her. You are a surviving spouse. Even if you are divorced from that person, you are a survivor and may have survivor rights.

Tangible Property. Tangible assets are things that are literally tangible—things that you can touch. They are physical articles (things) as distinguished from things you can't necessarily touch such as rights, patents, copyrights, and franchises. Examples of tangible property include homes, cars, furniture, electronics, jewelry, and household goods. These items have value in and of themselves.

Temporary Order. A court ruling that tells (orders) someone to do something or not do something for a specified (temporary) period of time, such as pay child support or spousal support until the divorce agreement is finalized.

Uncontested Divorce. A divorce in which both spouses are in full agreement with all the issues.

Unsecured Debt. A debt that is not tied to any asset. Credit card debts are classic unsecured debts. Others include personal loans or medical bills. An *unsecured creditor* is one who holds no security or collateral for its loan. In other words, your credit card company cannot reclaim the things you've purchased on the card to help pay for the money it is owed. Unsecured debts generally are characterized as those debts for which credit was extended based solely on the creditor's assessment of your future ability to pay.

Vested. This means you can take any of the money that your company has contributed to your plan because you've worked a certain numbers of years for your employer. *Vested* is an adjective referring to having an absolute (fully and unconditionally guaranteed) right, title, benefit, or privilege. Example: After 35 years at Company X, Ms. Loyalty's pension rights are now vested. Typically, you have to work a certain number of years for your employer before you are vested in its retirement plan.

Visitation. A legal right that a noncustodial parent has to spend time with his or her children.

Will. A statement that spells out your wishes at your death, specifically your desires about the distribution of your assets. Also called a *last will and testament*. To be valid, the will must be signed by the person who made it (testator), dated, and possibly witnessed. There are many types of wills: *Holographic wills* are handwritten, *noncupative wills* are spoken (oral) wills, and so on.

Links to State Divorce Courts

STATE	COURT WEB SITES
Alabama	www.alacourt.gov
Alaska	www.state.ak.us/courts
Arizona	www.supreme.state.az.us
Arkansas	www.courts.state.ar.us
California	www.courtinfo.ca.gov
Colorado	www.courts.state.co.us
Connecticut	www.jud2.state.ct.us/webforms
Delaware	www.courts.state.de.us
Florida	www.flcourts.org
Georgia	www.georgiacourts.org
Hawaii	www.courts.state.hi.us
Idaho	www.isc.idaho.gov/judicial.htm
Illinois	www.illinoissecondcircuit.info/
Indiana	www.in.gov/judiciary/selfservice
Iowa	www.judicial.state.ia.us/families
Kansas	www.kscourts.org
Kentucky	www.kycourts.net/forms
Louisiana	www.state.la.us/
Maine	www.courts.state.me.us
Maryland	www.courts.state.md.us/courtforms
Massachusetts	http://mass.gov/courts/selfhelp
Michigan	www.courts.michigan.gov
Minnesota	www.courts.state.mn.us
Mississippi	Refer to your local court for information
Missouri	www.osca.state.mo.us
Montana	www.lawlibrary.state.mt.us
Nebraska	http://court.neb.org/courts.htm

Nevada	http://nvsupremecourt.us
New Hampshire	www.courts.state.nh.us
New Jersey	www.judiciary.state.nj.us
New Mexico	http://nmcourts.com
New York	www.courts.state.ny.us
North Carolina	www.nccourts.org
North Dakota	www.courts.state.nd.us
Ohio	www.sconet.state.oh.us
Oklahomo	www.oscn.net/static/forms/districtforms.asp
Oregon	www.ojd.state.or.us
Pennsylvania	www.courts.state.pa.us
Rhode Island	www.courts.state.ri.us
South Carolina	www.sccourts.org
South Dakota	www.sdjudicial.com
Tennessee	www.tsc.state.tn.us
Texas	www.co.travis.tx.us/records_communication/law_library/forms.asp
Utah	www.utcourts.gov
Vermont	www.vermontjudiciary.org
Virginia	www.courts.state.va.us
Washington	www.courts.wa.gov/forms
West Virginia	www.state.wv.us/wvsca
Wisconsin	www.courts.state.wi.us
Wyoming	http://courts.state.wy.us

We The People Store
Addresses

ALASKA

545 E Northern Lights Blvd.
Anchorage, **Alaska** 99503
(907) 276-3006, (907) 260-8007 fax

ARIZONA

15224 No. 59th Ave.
Glendale, **AZ** 95306
(602) 942-6777, (602) 942-1670 fax

2815 So. Alma School Rd.
Mesa, **AZ** 85210
(480) 456-1412, (480) 456-1896 fax

2524 Indian School Road
Phoenix, **AZ** 85016
(602) 340-0290, (602) 956-6080 fax

3329 E. Bell Rd. Suite 18
Phoenix, **AZ** 85032
(602) 953-4063, (602) 953-4065 fax

2545 E. Speedway Blvd.
Tucson, **AZ** 85716
(520) 318-4987, (520) 318-9987 fax

CALIFORNIA

918 San Pablo Ave.
Albany, **CA** 94705
(510) 559-3456, (510) 559-8186 fax

27064 South La Paz Road
Aliso Viejo, **CA** 92656
(949) 425-0630, (949) 425-0634 fax

1137 W. Valley Blvd.
Alhambra, **CA** 91803
(626) 300-8011, (626) 300-8015 fax

1665 W. Katella Ave.
Anaheim, **CA** 92802-3021
(714) 772-0449, (714) 772-0745 fax

6332 Beach Blvd.
Buena Park, **CA** 90621
(714) 523-5000, (714) 523-5002 fax

649 W. Imperial Hwy
Brea, **CA** 92821
(714) 255-9110, (714) 255-9105 fax

356 E. Olive, #101
Burbank, **CA** 91502
(818) 848-4421, (818) 848-4289 fax

528 Myrtlewood Dr.
Calimesa, **CA** 92320-1505
(909) 446-1778, (909) 446-1700 fax

21722 Devonshire Street
Chatsworth, **CA** 91311
(818) 882-7622, (818) 882-7623 fax

4474 Treat Blvd.
Concord, **CA** 94521
(925) 246-0370, (925) 246-0373 fax

1909 Harbor Blvd.
Costa Mesa, **CA** 92627-2666
(949) 574-8880, (949) 574-8881 fax

7603A Amador Valley Road
Dublin, **CA** 94568-2301
(925) 479-9600, (925) 479-9700 fax

345 No. 2nd Street
El Cajon, **CA** 92021
(619) 442-4599, (619) 442-3994 fax

18044 Ventura Blvd.
Encino, CA 91316
(818) 774-1966, (818) 774-1576 fax

1107 4TH St.
Eureka, **CA** 95501
(707) 442-0162, (707) 442-3386 fax

1600 Travis Blvd. Ste. B
Fairfield, **CA** 94533
(707) 428-9871, (707) 428-9873

12752 Valley View St.
Garden Grove, **CA** 92845
(714) 934-8382, (714) 934-8304 fax

1415 E. Colorado Blvd.
Glendale, **CA** 91205
(818) 546-1787, (818) 546-1791 fax

17818 Chatsworth St.
Granada Hills, **CA** 91344
(818) 363-5837, (818) 363-5637 fax

22551 Foothill Blvd.
Hayward, **CA** 94541
(510) 728-7600, (510) 728-7647 fax

4479 Hollywood Blvd.
Hollywood, **CA** 90027
(323) 666-8200, (323) 666-6558 fax

1435 University Avenue
(Hillcrest)
San Diego, **CA** 92103-3404
(619) 295-2688, (619) 295-2691 fax

17131 Beach Blvd.
Huntington Beach, **CA** 92648
(714) 843-6229, (714) 843-0106 fax

698 S. Vermont Ave. #105
(Koreatown)
Los Angeles, CA 90005
(213) 389-2200, (213) 389-2212

1826 W. Avenue J
Lancaster, **CA** 93534
(661) 726-7646, (661) 726-9190 fax

2115 Bellflower Blvd.
Long Beach, **CA** 90815
(562) 985-1101, (562) 985-0103 fax

729 W. 7th St.
Los Angeles, **CA** 90017
(213) 489-1980, (213) 489-2600 fax

5324 Wilshire Blvd.
Los Angeles, **CA** 90036
(323) 937-2311, (323) 937-2317 fax

2496 Lincoln Blvd.
Marina Del Rey, **CA** 90291-5041
(310) 577-8333, (310) 577-8330 fax

2400 Alicia Parkway #1A
Mission Viejo, **CA** 92691
(949) 951-4411, (949) 951-4571 fax

1347 McHenry Ave.
Modesto, **CA** 95350
(209) 523-8227, (209) 523-2830 fax

39440 Murrieta Hot Springs Rd. #2
Murrieta, **CA** 92563
(951) 600-9870,

11369 Riverside Drive
North Hollywood, **CA** 91602
(818) 762-8647, (818) 762-8541 fax

11755 Imperial Hwy. Ste. 200
Norwalk , **CA** 90652
(562) 863-1991, (562) 863-1992 fax

3753 Mission Ave.
Oceanside, **CA** 92054
(760) 754-9059, (760) 754-8059 fax

244 Grand Ave.
Oakland, **CA** 94610
(510) 452-2320, (510) 452-2324fax

595 The City Drive #200
Orange, **CA** 92868
(714) 634-4885, (714) 363-0469 fax

2400 Saviers Road
Oxnard, **CA** 93033
(805) 487-1210, (805) 486-1548 fax

73121 Country Club Dr.
Palm Desert, **CA** 92260
(760) 346-7074, (760) 346-7544 fax

2127 El Camino Real
Palo Alto, **CA** 94306
(650) 324-3800, (650) 324-3801 fax

762 E. Colorado Blvd.
Pasadena, **CA** 91101
(626) 535-0100, (626) 535-0175 fax

135 Keller St, Ste. C
Petaluma, **CA** 94952
(707) 769-1639, (707) 763-4204 fax

9030 Foothill Blvd., Ste. 112
Rancho Cucamonga, **CA** 91730
(909) 466-4500, (909) 466-4502 fax

2968 Churn Creek Rd.
Redding, **CA** 96002
(530) 222-8747, (530) 222-9777 fax

6519 Magnolia Ave.
Riverside, **CA** 92506
(951) 369-3591, (951) 369-3749 fax

4211 B Arden Way
Sacramento, **CA** 95864
(916) 679-6780, (916) 485-2469 fax

517 S. Main St. Ste. #101
Salinas, **CA** 93901

209 North Maclay
San Fernando, **CA** 91340-2908
(818) 838-3900, (818) 838-3907fax

411 Divisadero Street
San Francisco, **CA** 94117
(415) 701-9800, (415) 701-9801 fax

441A Marsh St.
San Luis Obispo, CA 93401
(805) 596-0100, (805) 596-0200 fax

903B Irwin St.
San Rafael, **CA** 94901-3317
(415) 453-1700, (415) 453-1711 fax

1501 State Street
Santa Barbara, **CA** 93101
(805) 962-4100, (805) 962-9602 fax

500 Soquel Ave. Suite B
Santa Cruz, **CA** 95062
(831) 458-5155, (831) 458-5156 fax

920 South Broadway
Santa Maria, **CA** 93454
(805) 928-9700 (805) 928-8815

2922 Wilshire Blvd.
Santa Monica, **CA** 90403
(310) 264-0517, (310) 264-0597 fax

22933 Soledad Canyon Road
Saugus, **CA** 91350
(661) 255-8488, (661) 255-9459 fax

13565 Ventura Blvd.
Sherman Oaks, **CA** 91423
(818) 906-0086, (818) 906-8096 fax

4360 Cochran St.
Simi Valley, **CA** 93065
(805) 526-7351, (805) 526-7799 fax

800 E. Thousand Oaks Blvd.
Thousand Oaks, **CA** 91360
(805) 371-7575, (805) 371-7577 fax

4727 Torrance Blvd.
Torrance, **CA** 90503
(310) 370-8399, (310) 370-6399 fax

13732 Newport Ave. Suite 1
Tustin, **CA** 92780
(714) 730-5196, (714) 730-5584 fax

7219 Balboa Blvd.
Van Nuys, **CA** 91406
(818) 989-7431, (818) 989-7433 fax

2827 E. Thompson Blvd.
Ventura, **CA** 93003
(805) 641-2010, (805) 641-3767 fax

1830 Hacienda Dr. #5
Vista, **CA** 92081
(760) 941-1604, (760) 941-2610 fax

2061 MT. Diablo Blvd.
Walnut Creek, **CA** 94596
(925) 407-1010, (925) 472-0102 fax

21904 Ventura Blvd.
Woodland Hills, **CA** 91367
(818) 704-9394, (818) 704-9396 fax

1648 Westwood Blvd.
W. Los Angeles, **CA** 90024
(310) 441-5400, (310) 441-1119 fax

COLORADO

3125 28TH St.
Boulder, **CO** 80304
(303) 544-1066, (303) 544-1067 fax

14 N. Main St.
Brighton, CO 80601
(303) 654-9983, (303) 654-9984 fax

1806 A Dominion Way
Colorado Springs, **CO** 80918
(719) 590-7779, (720) 229-0186 fax

62 E. Arapahoe Rd.
(Arapahoe)
Centennial, **CO** 80122
(303) 991-3651, (303) 991-3654 fax

7115 E. Hampden Ave.
Denver, **CO** 80224
(303) 302-1000, (303) 302-1001 fax

2454 Hwy 6 & 50
Grand Junction, **CO** 81505
(970) 263-9191, (970) 243-4949 fax

3489 W. 10th St. #C
Greeley, **CO** 80634
(970) 352-5444, (970) 352-2024 fax

3355 So. Wadsworth Blvd.
Lakewood, **CO** 80227
(303) 984-2101, (303) 984-2135 fax

7330 W. 88th Ave., Ste. E
Westminster, **CO** 80021
(303) 421-0367, (303) 421-3425 fax

CONNECTICUT

1100 Main St.
Newington, **CT** 06111-2910
(860) 665-0540, (860) 665-0391 fax

165 Bank Street
New London, CT 06320
(860) 447-9984, (860) 447-9116

281 Connecticut Ave.
Norwalk, **CT** 06854
(203) 852-7006, (203) 852-1452 fax

163 Post Rd.
Orange, **CT** 06477
(203)795-9978, (203)795-9791

FLORIDA

1701 No. Federal Hwy
Boca Raton, **FL** 33432
(561) 347-5340, (561) 347-5341 fax

1722 Del Prado Blvd.
Cape Coral, **FL** 33990
(239) 573-7311, (239) 573-6001 fax

1820 Harrison Street
Hollywood, **FL** 33020

101 E. Commercial Blvd.
Fort Lauderdale, **FL** 33334
(954) 491-2990, (954) 491-2662 fax

16050 S. Tamiani Trail #104
Fort Myers, **FL** 33908
(239) 267-9955, (239) 267-9977 fax

320 Osceola Ave.
Jacksonville Beach, **FL** 32250
(904) 241-2533, (904) 241-1604 fax

3003 So. Tamiami Trail
Sarasota, **FL** 34239
(941) 366-8896, (941) 373-9875 fax

GEORGIA

1524 Church
Decatur, **GA** 30030
(404) 270-9199, (404) 270-9255 fax

561 Forest Parkway Ste. 3
Forest Park, **GA** 30297
(404) 608-0566, (404) 608-0776 fax

HAWAII

564 South Street
Honolulu, **HI** 96813
(808) 548-0379, (808) 548-0389 fax

IDAHO

7974 Fairview Ave.
Boise, **ID** 83704
(208) 658-1745, (208) 658-1746 fax

1587 E. 17th
Idaho Falls, **ID** 93404
(208) 522-5176, (208) 522-5186 fax

ILLINOIS

6218 W. Cermak
Berwyn, **IL**
(708) 484-9200, (708) 484-9700 fax

2411 Ashland
Chicago, **IL** 60614
(773) 529-9900, (773) 529-9697 fax

3210 W. 95th
Evergreen Park, **IL** 60805
(708) 422-2000, (708) 422-3549 fax

801 E. Ogden Ave.
Naperville, **IL** 60563
(630) 778-9770, (630) 778-9833 fax

INDIANA

4614 F Coldwater Road
Fort Wayne, **IN** 46825
(260) 471-4710, (260) 471-4710 fax

KANSAS

11600 Metcalf Ave.
Overland Park, **KS** 66210
(913) 383-0505, (913) 383-3737 fax

2243 North Tyler, Suite 107
(West Wichita)
Wichita, **KS** 67220
(316) 773-2400, (316) 773-2444 fax

410 North Hillside, Suite 900
(College Hill)
Wichita, **KS** 67214
(316) 685-5759, (316) 618-0827 fax

KENTUCKY

3126 Dixie Highway
Erlanger, **KY** 41018
(859) 727-6900, (859) 727-6900 fax

MARYLAND

511-C Eastern Blvd.
Essex, **MD** 21221
(410) 780-7084, (410) 780-7086 fax

507 Reisterstown Road
Pikesville, **MD** 21208-5303
(410) 580-2036, (410) 580-2039 fax

MICHIGAN

2841 Breton Road
Grand Rapids, **MI** 49512
(616) 245-7008, (616) 245-7009 fax

29961 Gratiot Ave.
(Detroit)
Roseville, **MI** 48066
(586) 774-5188, (586) 774-3425 fax

MINNESOTA

2002 Lyndale Ave. So.
Minneapolis, **MN** 55404
(612) 333-3777, (612) 874-9577 fax

MISSISSIPPI

1553 East County Line Rd. Ste. 200
Jackson, **MS** 39211
(601) 206-9980, (601) 206-9978 fax

MISSOURI

2722 S. Brentwood Blvd.
Brentwood, **MO** 63144
(314) 963-0600, (314) 963-0587 fax

NEBRASKA

9207 Maple St.
Omaha, **NE** 68134
(402) 502-9898, (402) 502-9897 fax

709 North 48 Street
Lincoln, **NE** 68504
(402) 464-2200, (402) 464-2201 fax

NEVADA

2300 South Carson St. Suite 4
Carson City, **NV** 89701
(775) 888-6830, (775) 841-0788 fax

6405-2 So. Virginia St.
Reno, **NV** 89511
(775) 853-4400, (775) 853-4448 fax

4850 W. Flamingo Road
Las Vegas, **NV** 89103
(702) 222-0414, (702) 252-0164 fax

NEW JERSEY

107 Broadway
Elmwood Park, **NJ** 07407
(201) 794-6491, (201) 794-6492 fax

534 Bloomfield Ave.
Verona, **NJ** 07044
(973) 857-0057, (973) 857-0097fax

NEW MEXICO

2828 Carlisle Blvd. NE Ste. B
Albuquerque, **NM** 87110
(505) 889-8900, (505) 889-2962 fax

NEW YORK

42-38 Bell Blvd.
Bayside, **NY** 11361
(718) 224-8704, (718) 224-8710 fax

1508 86TH ST STREET
Bay Ridge, **NY** 11228
(718) 259-8181, (718) 259-8355 fax

2349 Arthur Ave.
(Belmont)
Bronx, **NY** 10458
(718) 295-5700, (718) 295-5887 fax

133 Wolf Road
(Colonie)
Albany, **NY** 12205
(518) 435-9110, (518) 435-9273 fax

2091 Bartow Avenue
(Co-Op)
Bronx, **NY** 10475
(718) 671-6500, (718) 379-3900 fax

92 Willoughby Street
(Downtown Brooklyn)
Brooklyn, **NY** 11201
(718) 855-8585, (718) 855-8334 fax

116-28 Queens Blvd.
Forest Hills, **NY** 11375
(718) 793-4400, (718) 793-2977 fax

1986 Ralph Ave.
Georgetown Brooklyn, **NY** *11234*
(718) 968-0022, (718) 968-2034 fax

423B 2ND Ave.
Grammercy Park, **NY** 10010
(212) 213-2700

788 A. Manhatten Ave.
(Greenpoint)
Brooklyn, **NY** 11222
(718) 609-0900, (718) 349-2121 fax

3658 Broadway
Hamilton Heights, **NY** 10031
(212) 281-4800, (212) 281-3772 fax

377 West 125th St.
Harlem, **NY** 10027
(212) 280-3100, (212) 222-2596 fax

2175 Hylan Blvd.
(Hylan)
Staten Island, **NY** 10306
(718) 351-1200, (718) 351-1537 fax

519B 207th Street
(Inwood)
New York, **NY** 10034
(212) 942-1600, (212) 942-1604 fax

5661 Broadway
(Kingsbridge)
Bronx, **NY** 10463
(718) 543-5800, (718) 543-5661 fax

796 Ulster Ave.
Kingston, **NY** 12401
(845) 331-5833, (845) 331-1873

470 Hawkins Ave.
Lake Ronkonkoma, **NY** 11779
(631) 467-2667, (631) 467-4666 fax

45-01A Northern Blvd.
Long Island City, **NY** 11101
(718) 392-4300, (718) 392-4333 fax

250 East Houston St.
(Lower East Side)
New York, **NY** 10002
(212) 979-6100, (212) 979-6123 fax

447 Mamaroneck Ave.
Mamaroneck, **NY** 10543
(914) 835-7800, (914) 835-7806 fax

239 W. 72nd St.
New York, **NY** 10023
(212) 501-7700, (212) 501-0316 fax

3478 Jerome Ave.
(Norwood)
Bronx, **NY** 10463
(718) 994-6400, (718) 994-6579 fax

105-28 Cross Bay Blvd.
Ozone Park, **NY** 11417
(718) 845-8300, (718) 322-1542 fax

514 5th Ave.
(Park Slope)
Brooklyn, **NY** 11215
(718) 965-2228, (718) 965-2327 fax

1959 Westchester Ave.
(Parkchester)
Bronx, NY 10462
(718) 239-7600, (718) 239-8961 fax

211-36 Hillside Ave.
Queens Village, **NY** 11427
(718) 217-1500, (718) 217-1416 fax

3715 Nostrand
Sheepshead Bay, **NY** 11235
(718) 332-5600, (718) 332-0886 fax

861 Montauk Highway #3
Shirley, **NY** 11967
(631) 281-2212, (631) 281-2259 fax

46-14 Queens Blvd.
Sunnyside, **NY** 11104
(718) 472-3800, (718) 472-3810 fax

3427 East Tremont Ave.
(Throgs Neck)
Bronx, NY 10465
(718) 863-2200, (718) 863-2435 fax

554 West 181st Street
(Washington Heights)
New York, **NY** 10033
(212) 928-8000, (212) 928-8006 fax

127 Post Avenue
Westbury, **NY** 11590
(516) 333-3306, (516) 333-3308 fax

49 Westchester Sq.
(Westchester Square)
Bronx, NY 10461-3526
(718) 931-7500, (718) 931-7540 fax

148 Mamaroneck Ave.
White Plains, **NY** 10601
(914) 683-5105, (914) 683-0345 fax

NORTH CAROLINA

624 Tyvola Rd. Suite 101
Charlotte, **NC** 28217
(704) 665-6353, (704) 665-3695 fax

4940-C Capital Blvd.
Raleigh, **NC** 27616
(919) 713-0339, (919) 873-0273 fax

OHIO

794 Main St.
Milford, **OH** 45150
(513) 831-3380, (513) 831-3860 fax

OKLAHOMA

3747-B South Harvard
Tulsa, **OK** 74135
(918) 794-0305, (918) 794-0307 fax

OREGON

547 NE Bellevue, Suite 108
Bend, OR 97701
(541) 317-1287, (541) 317-1286 fax

400 NW Walnut Blvd. #200
Corvallis, **OR** 97330
(541) 738-9872, (541) 738-9873 fax

377 Coburg Rd. Suite C
Eugene, **OR** 97401
(541) 345-1128, (541) 485-9178 fax

520 S.E. 10TH Ave.
Hillsboro, **OR** 97123
(503) 693-8885, (503) 648-8001 fax

PENNSYLVANIA

301 W. Baltimore Pike
Springfield, **PA** 19018
(610) 626-4141, (610) 626-0848 fax

34 West Lancaster Ave.
Shilllington, **PA** 19607
(610) 796-1250, (610) 796-1068 fax

718 Market Street
(Center City)
Philadelphia, **PA** 19106
(215) 238-8809, (215) 238-8813 fax

2836 Cottman Avenue
Philadelphia, **PA** 19149
(215) 333-8281, (215) 333-8287 fax

RHODE ISLAND

298 Atwells Ave.
Providence, **RI** 02903
(401) 521-4700, (401) 521-4242 fax

TENNESSEE

86 Thompson Lane
Nashville, TN 37211
(615) 445-3611, (615) 445-7704 fax

8161 Kingston Pike
Knoxville, **TN** 37919
(865) 560-2221, (856) 560-2721 fax

TEXAS

13729 Research Blvd. Ste. 850
Austin, **TX** 78759
(512)996-8558, (512) 996-8445 fax

7726 Forest Lane
Dallas, **TX** 75230
(214) 265-8800, (214) 987-0287 fax

1500 N. 10th Street
McAllen, **TX** 78501
(956) 631-0551, (956) 631-0552 fax

2672 No. Belt Line Rd.
Irving, **TX** 75062
(972) 570-4800, (972) 570-5539 fax

WISCONSIN

4210 E. Washington Ave.
Madison, WI 53704
(608) 245-5003, (608) 249-2994 fax

Worksheets

TAKING INVENTORY OF YOUR FINANCES

CATEGORY 1: Monthly Expenses

EXPENSE	MONTHLY PAYMENT
Rent	$
Mortgage	
Electric	
Gas	
Phone	
Water/sewer	
Home maintenance	
Cable TV/internet access	
Phone/cell	
Food	
Clothing	
Car payments	
Gasoline/transportation costs	
Entertainment/newspapers	
Incidentals-gifts, laundry	
Medical and dental	
Taxes not deducted from paycheck	
Miscellaneous	

Installment payments
        Car
        Furniture
Other _____
	_____
	_____
	_____

TOTAL	$

CATEGORY 2: Credit Card Balances

CREDIT CARD	BALANCE
	$
TOTAL	$

CATEGORY 3: Other debts

DEBT	BALANCE
	$
TOTAL	$

CATEGORY 4: Property/Assets (What You Own)

ASSET	QUICK SALE VALUE*
Home(s)**	
Cash	
Checking, savings, CDs	
Security deposits held by utilities or landlord	
Household goods/furniture/electronics/appliances	
Books/pictures/art objects	
Clothing	
Furs/Jewelry	
Sports/hobby equipment/firearms/gadgets	
Cash value in insurance policies	
Annuities	
Interest in pension or profit sharing plans	
Stocks and interests in incorporated business	
Interest in partnerships/joint ventures	
Bonds	
Accounts receivable	
Alimony or family support to which you are entitled	
Tax refunds	
Equitable or future interests or life estates	
Interest in estate of descendent or life ins plan	
Other liquidated debts owed to you (claims, funds due you, benefits)	
Patents, copyrights	
Licenses and franchises	
Car(s) ***	

Boats/motors & accessories	
Aircraft and accessories	
Office equipment & supplies	
Machinery/fixtures	
Inventory (business)	
Stocks and interests in incorporated/unincorporated business	
Interest in partnerships/joint ventures	
Animals, crop, farm supplies etc (for farmers)	
TOTAL	

* A quick sale value is what you think your assets would sell for if sold quickly. Consider how much your assets would sell for in a pawnshop or at a garage or yard sale.

** If you have a mortgage on your home, list any home equity loans and liens you have here:

> Total liens and mortgages = _____
> Total ownership equity
> (Home value less total liens/mortgages) = _____

*** Use the current value of your car today if you tried to sell it quickly.

TOTAL-GROSS WAGES RECV'D LAST 12 MO.	$	
YOUR **MONTHLY** INCOME & list your average monthly income (divide total income by 12)	**Last month**	**Average** (divide your total inc. & taxes by 12)
Gross **MONTHLY INCOME** (BEFORE taxes)	$	$
Overtime - gross		
Commissions or bonuses		
Public assistance (TANF, SSI, GA/GR)		
Spousal support ☐ from this marriage/ ☐ from different marriage		
Pension/retirement payments		
Social Security retirement payments (not SSI)		
☐ Disability ☐ Social Security ☐ SDI ☐ private		
Unemployment compensation		
Workers compensation		
Other		
INVESTMENT INCOME		
Dividends/interest		
Rental property income		
Trust income		
Other (specify)		
SELF EMPLOYMENT INCOME - after business expenses		
I am the ☐ owner/sole owner ☐ partner ☐ other		
# of years in this business_____ Name of business _____		
Type of business _____		
ADDITIONAL INCOME		
other money you received in the last 12 months describe_____		
DEDUCTIONS	LAST MONTH	
Mandatory Union Dues (monthly)	$	
Mandatory retirement/pension fund contributions	$	
Court ordered child support (NOT this relationship)	$	
ASSETS	VALUE	
Cash/checking/savings/credit union/money market etc	$	
stocks/bonds/other assets you can sell	$	
all other property ☐ real or ☐ personal (less loans)	$	
	$	
	$	

List all persons living in your home whose **expenses you pay and are included below** (include their income)

NAME	AGE	RELATIONSHIP	INCOME

Other people living in your home

NAME	AGE	RELATIONSHIP	INCOME

MONTHLY EXPENSES

EXPENSE	AMOUNT	EXPENSE	AMOUNT
RENT { } MORTGAGE { } If mortgage average principle average interest real prop. taxes home insurance Maintenance and repair	$_____ $_____ $_____ $_____ $_____	EDUCATION - (specify)	$
HEALTH CARE not paid by insurance	$	ENTERTAINMENT, GIFTS, VACATION	$
CHILD CARE	$	AUTO TRANSPORTATION EXP. (gas, repairs etc)	$
GROCERIES AND household supplies	$	LIFE/ACCIDENT INS.	$
FOOD - EATING OUT		SAVINGS AND INVESTMENTS	$
UTILITIES	$	CHARITABLE CONTRIB.	$
TELEPHONE/Cell/Email	$	MONTHLY PAYMENTS listed below - ENTER TOTAL HERE	$
LAUNDRY AND CLEANING		OTHER - (specify)	$
CLOTHING	$		$
	$		$

MONTHLY INSTALLMENT PAYMENTS

CREDITOR	PAYMENT FOR	MONTHLY PAYMENT	BALANCE	DATE LAST PAID
		$	$	
		$	$	
		$	$	
		$	$	
		$	$	
		$	$	
		$	$	

COMPLETE THIS PAGE **IF CHILD SUPPORT** IS AN ISSUE

HEALTH INS. FOR MY CHILDREN { } IS   { } IS NOT AVAILABLE THRU MY EMPLOYER
       MONTHLY COST PAID BY ME $_____
       NAME OF CARRIER _____
       ADDRESS   _____
                                  _____
       POLICY #   _____

% OF TIME EACH PARENT HAS PRIMARY PHYSICAL RESPONSIBILITY FOR THE CHILDREN
       MOTHER _____%   FATHER _____%

ADDITIONAL CHILD SUPPORT TO BE REQUESTED

{ } Child care costs related to employment (also state amount currently paid and by who)

{ } Uninsured health care costs for children (state monthly amount and paid by who)

{ } Special educational needs of the children - describe

{ } Travel expense for visitation (amount and who pays now)

{ } Hardship deductions - (expenses that are extreme hardships)

Extraordinary health care   Amount paid: $ _____ need to pay until _____
Uninsured catastrophic losses $_____ need to pay until _____
Living expenses of <u>dependent</u>
 minor children who live with you $_____ need to pay until _____
(list names and ages)

INDEX